HISTORY
OF RUSSIA

Sergei Mikhailovich Soloviev

The
Academic International Press
Edition
of
Sergei M. Soloviev

History of Russia From Earliest Times

G. EDWARD ORCHARD
General Editor

Contributing Editors
HUGH F. GRAHAM
JOHN D. WINDHAUSEN
ALEXANDER V. MULLER
K.A. PAPMEHL
RICHARD HANTULA
WALTER J. GLEASON, JR.
WILLIAM H. HILL
G. EDWARD ORCHARD
LINDSEY A.J. HUGHES
NICKOLAS LUPININ
GEORGE E. MUNRO
DANIEL L. SCHLAFLY, JR.

SERGEI M. SOLOVIEV

History of Russia

Volume 46

The Rule of Catherine the Great

Turkey and Poland, 1768–1770

Edited, Translated and With an
Introduction by

Daniel L. Schlafly, Jr.

Academic International Press

1994

The Academic International Press Edition of S.M. Soloviev's
History of Russia From Earliest Times in fifty volumes.

Volume 46. *The Rule of Catherine the Great. Poland and
Turkey, 1768–1770.*
Unabridged translation of the text of Chapters I and II of Volume
28 of S.M. Soloviev's *Istoriia Rossii s drevneishikh vremen* as
found in Volume XIV of this work published in Moscow in 1965,
with added annotation by Daniel L. Schlafly, Jr.

ISBN: 0-87569-128-5

Composition by Peggy Pope

Printed in the United States of America

A list of Academic International Press publications is found at
the end of this volume.

ACADEMIC INTERNATIONAL PRESS
Box 1111 • Gulf Breeze FL 32562-1111 • USA

CONTENTS

Vaccination of the Empress and Heir—Outbreak of War with
Turkey—Establishment of the Council—Preparations for
War—Orlov Proposes a Mediterranean Expedition—Golitsyn
and Rumiantsev Placed in Command—Envoys to the Balkan
Christians—Military Conscription—Bank of State
Assignats—The Order of St. George—Attack by the Crimean
Tatars—The Siege of Khotin—Golitsyn Replaced by
Rumiantsev—Prince Peter Ivanovich Panin—Capture of
Khotin and the Danubian Principalities—Naval Prepara-
tions—Victories in the Principalities—Operations at Azov—
Mulim Peoples Enter Russia—Turks Incite Russia's Muslim
Subjects—The Porte Woos the Zaporozhian Cossacks—Plan
to Win the Tatars Away from the Porte—Naval Expedition to
Greece—Orlov Leads the Christian Revolt—Relations with
the Balkan Christians—Relations with Montenegro—The
Stepan Maly Affair—Relations with Venice—Prince Yury
Dolgoruky's Visit to Montenegro—Relations with Paoli—
Catherine's Situation in 1769—Correspondence with Bielcke
and Voltaire—Relations with Poland—Panin's Foreign Policy
Questioned—Russian Pressure on Poland—Kamieniec and
Other Polish Issues—Repnin and Stanislaw Augustus—
Catherine and Stanislaw Augustus—Volkonsky Replaces
Repnin—Volkonsky Plays a Strong Role—Plans for a Confed-
eration—Stanislaw Augustus Seeks Independence—Relations
with Prussia—Russia, Prussia, Austria and the Polish Question—
Relations with France—Relations with Denmark—Swedish
Affairs—Relations with England

II FOREIGN RELATIONS, 1770

Campaigns Against the Turks in the Danubian Principalities—
Rumiantsev's Victory on the Lagra—Victories at Akerman,
Brailov and Bender—Policy Towards the Tatars—The Fleet
Arrives in the Mediterranean—Operations in Greece—The
Battle of Chesme—Consequences of the Victory at Chesme—
Operations in the Caucasus—The Choglokov Affair—Prepa-
rations for Peace Negotiations—Prussia and the Prospect of
Polish Partition—Previous Plans to Partition Poland—Atti-
tudes Toward Partition—Partition is Considered—Maria
Theresa and the Partition of Poland—Frederick II, Joseph II
and Kaunitz Meet in Neustadt—Consequences of Neustadt for
Russia—Visit of Prince Henry to Russia—Frederick,
Catherine and the Peace Negotiations—Frederick's Reaction—
Frederick Opposes Russian Proposals—Austria Seizes Polish
Territory—The Polish Confederates—Catherine and
Poniatowski—Volkonsky and Poniatowski—Russia, Prussia
and Poland—Ostermann in Sweden—Prince Henry in Swe-
den—Danish Affairs—Cathcart Promotes an English Alli-
ance—Turkey and the Proposed English Alliance—Cathcart's
View of Russia

WEIGHTS AND MEASURES

Linear Measure

Verst: 500 sazhen, 1166 yards and 2 feet, .663 miles, 1.0668 km.
Sazhen: 3 arshins, 7 feet, 2.133 m
Arshin: 16 vershoks, 28in. (diuims) 72.12 cm
Chetvert: 1/4 arshin
Fut: 12 diuims, 1 foot, 30.48 cm
Vershok: 1.75 in., 4.445 cm, 1/16 arshin
Diuim: 1 inch, 2.54 cm
Desiatina: 2400 square sazhens, 2.7 acres, 1.0925 hectare
Chetvert (quarter): 1/2 desiatine, 1.35 acre (sometimes 1.5 desiatinas or ca. 4.1 acres)

Liquid Measure

Stof: Kruzhka (cup), 1/10 vedro, ca. 1.3 quarts, 1.23 liters
Kufa: 30 stofy
Vedro (paid): 3.25 gallons, 12.3 liters, 10 stofy
Bochka (barrel): 40 vedros, 121 gallons, 492 liters
Chetvert (quarter): 1.4 bochka, 32.5 gallons

Weights

Berkovets: 361 olbs., 10 puds
Pud: 40 funts, 36,113 lbs. (US), 40 lbs. (Russian), 16.38 kg
Funt: 96 zolotniks, .903 lb., 14.4 ozs., 408.24 grams
Grivenka: 205 grams
Korob (basket): 7 puds, 252 lbs.
Rad: 14 puds, 505.58 lbs
Chetvert (grain measure): 1/4 rad, 3.5 puds, 126.39 lbs., ca. 8 bushels
Chetverik (grain measure dating from 16th century): 1/8 chetvert, 15.8 lbs.
Zolotnik: 1/96 lb., 4.26 grams

Money

Chervonets (chervonny): A gold coin minted in the first half of the 18th century worth
    about 3 rubles
Muscovite Denga: 200 equals 1 ruble
Novgorod Denga: 100 equals 1 ruble
Ruble: 100 copecks, 200 dengas
Altyn: 6 Muscovite dengas, 3 copecks
Grivna: 20 Muscovite dengas, 100 grivnas equals 1 ruble, 10 copecks
Poltina (Poltinnik): 50 copecks, 100 dengas
Polupoltina (-nik): 25 copecks, 50 dengas
Poltora: 1 1/2 rubles
Peniaz: 10 equals one grosh (Lithuania)
Kopa grosh: 60 groshas, one Muscovite poltina
Chetvertak: silver coin equal to 25 copecks or 1/4 rubles (18-19th centuries)
Copeck: two Muscovite dengas
Foreign Denominations: 1 efimok or 1 thaler (Joachimsthaler)-about 1 ruble, 1 chervonets
    or chervonnyi—a ducat, about 3 rubles
Levok—Dutch silver lion dollar

Note: Weights and measures often changed values over time and sometimes held more than
    one value at the same time. For details consult Sergei G. Pushkarev, *Dictionary of
    Russian Historical Terms from the Eleventh Century to 1917* (Yale, 1970).

Russia in Europe

Turkey in Europe

PREFACE

This book is an unabridged translation of Volume 28, Chapters 1-2, which are pp. 277-441 in Volume XIV of the multi-volume edition of Soloviev's *Istoriia Rossii s drevneishikh vremen* (History of Russia From Earliest Times), 29 vols., St. Petersburg, 1851-1879, published from 1962 through 1966 in Moscow.

The present translation endeavors to render the text and Soloviev's thought as accurately as possible. No attempt has been made to reproduce his style and text word for word for this would have yielded a bizarre Russianized text. The main consideration has been to make his history as readable as possible consistent with accuracy, while retaining at least something of the flavor of the language of the era. An effort has been made to find English-language equivalents for all technical terms Soloviev employs (ranks, offices, titles, legal, administrative and so forth) in the belief that English is no less rich in such terms than other languages. This is intended to smooth the flow of the narrative for the reader and to avoid marring the pages with annoying untranslated words. The exception involves Russian words which have become common in English—boyar, tsar, cossack. In all of this the translator remains painfully aware of the inevitable shortcomings that may remain.

Soloviev's pages are featureless and interminable, one long and complex sentence marching after the last. To make the text easier to follow for today's readers, long paragraphs and sentences have been broken into shorter ones. Most of the subtitles are based on the descriptive topic headings clustered at the beginnings of the chapters in the Russian edition. These headings have been moved into the body of the text as subtitles to mark and ease for the reader the transition from one subject to another. In some cases, to even the frequency of breaks in the text or to show topics not listed by Soloviev at the beginning of chapters, new subtitles have been added. Soloviev's arrangement of the material has been followed strictly.

Brief explanatory or interpretive materials have been inserted into the text enclosed in brackets, or added as footnotes to each chapter at the end of the book. All material enclosed in brackets has been added by the present editor and all material in parentheses is the author's. Emphasized words or phrases in italics are the author's.

The general policy followed in annotating has been to identify prominent personalities at first mention, and to give explanation and elucidations of less common or obscure terms and passages, assuming the typical reader to have relatively little familiarity with Russian history. If brief, these have been included in the text in brackets; otherwise they appear as numbered footnotes at the back of the book by chapters. Most of the author's own notes are not included because their highly specialized archival, documentary and bibliographic nature is of value solely to specialists who, in any case, will prefer to consult the original Russian text. In addition, most of the notes added by the editors of the edition published in the Soviet Union which also are technical in nature—fuller bibliographic citations than those in Soloviev's notes—have not been included. When the author's notes and those of the Soviet editors are included, they are so designated. All other notes are those of the present editor.

Russian personal names are preserved in their Russian form except for Alexander, Alexis, Michael, Nicholas, Catherine and Peter, which English usage has made familiar with respect to Russian historical figures, and for important ecclesiastics whose names have been recast into Latin or Greek equivalents, especially for the earlier period of Russian history. This applies to prominent individuals; Russian forms usually are used for the less prominent. Certain other names and terms have been anglicized for the sake of clarity and because they are used widely—Casimir, Sophia, Danzig, boyar, rubles, versts, Dnieper river, and others.

The editors of the edition published in the USSR frequently have added patronymics and other names, and these have been retained without brackets; patronymics appearing in the original edition have been included also. Plural forms for names and terms which might be confusing have been anglicized—Vologdians rather than Vologzhane, Voguls and not Vogulichi, the Dolgorukys not Dolgorukie, and so forth. Even so, in a few cases the Russian plural form is used when this form is common. Most Slavic surnames show gender, and this has been preserved. Since an "a" at the word end usually signifies a female, Golovkin would have a wife or daughter Golovkina. The final "iia" in feminine personal names has been shortened to "ia"—"Maria" and "Evdokia" instead of "Mariia" and "Evdokiia."

Non-Russian names, locations, terms, ranks and so on are spelled according to the language native to the person or particular to the city, region or culture when this can be determined. Confusion arises at times because the text is not clear about nationalities. An excruciating example is Lithuania where at least three languages intermingle. In such cases the context is the guide used and as a last resort the Russian spelling in the text is accepted. Individuals whose names were once non-Russian but had been in Russian service for generations are named by the original spelling of the family name. Turkish, Tatar, Persian and other names and terms are spelled in the original according to accepted forms in scholarly books. In some instances, if not otherwise ascertainable they are translated from the Russian as given by Soloviev. The names of geographical locations conform to commonly accepted English usage—Podolia, Moscow, Copenhagen, Saxony and so forth.

Finally, with respect to transliteration, this translation follows a modified Library of Congress system omitting diacritical marks and ligatures, and rendering the initial "Z" and "/" as "ya" and "yu" ("Yasnaia" and "Yury"), the suffixes "bq," "crbq," "crfz" and "crjt" as "Dmitry Poliansky," "Polianskaia," "Polianskoe," and the form "jq" has been replaced by "oy" ("Donskoy" not "Donskoi") for certain family names familiar in this form in English. In some cases "i" has been inserted in place of hard and soft signs, or apostrophes indicating these signs. Hence Soloviev, not Solov'ev. The soft sign is not indicated by an apostrophe, as in some transliteration systems, but is dropped completely.

All dates, as in the original, except where otherwise specified, are according to the Julian calendar ("Old Style"); that is, for the seventeenth century ten days, and for the eighteenth century eleven days, behind the Gregorian used in the West. A table of weights and measures is included at the front of this volume for the convenience of the reader.

I would like to thank those who helped make this volume possible. Edward Kasinec and Benjamin Goldsmith of the Slavonic Division of the New York Public Library located a wide range of possible illustrations from their superb collection. The maps are from the University of Illinois at Urbana-Champaign where I was able also to find much of the material for the notes. Peggy Ramsdell conscientiously converted dictation and handwritten additions to a finished typescript. Dr. G. Edward Orchard has been a helpful and professional editor, while Peter von Wahlde saw the manuscript through to publication. Any mistakes or shortcomings are mine. I would like to dedicate this volume to my daughters, Maria and Theresa, who have had Soloviev as a family member for far too long and, above all, to my wife, Shannon, without whom it never would have been possible.

Daniel L. Schlafly, Jr.

INTRODUCTION

The present volume originally appeared in 1878 as Chapters I and II of Volume 28 of Soloviev's *Istoriia Rossii s drevneishikh vremen* (History of Russia From Earliest Times). This was the last volume but one of his *magnum opus*, appearing the year before he died. Soloviev was now at the end of a brilliant career of teaching, scholarship and public positions and was unquestionably the leading Russian historian of his generation. Born in 1820, the son of an Orthodox priest, Soloviev received an excellent education at home, at Moscow schools and at Moscow University, where he earned the *kandidat* degree in 1842. There and in travels in Western Europe from 1842 to 1844 he supplemented his studies of Russian history with wide reading in Western European history and thought. Back in Moscow, Soloviev completed his master's and doctor's degrees by 1848 and began a series of teaching and administrative positions which culminated in his tenure as rector of Moscow University from 1871 to 1877. He also tutored two sons and successive heirs to the throne of Alexander II, participated in various professional societies and directed the Kremlin Armory.

It was above all his scholarship which had won him national and international acclaim. Since 1850 the volumes of his *History of Russia From Earliest Times* had appeared at the rate of one a year, and by 1878 the breadth of his vision, the rigor of his methodology and the contours of his overall interpretation were well recognized. In addition Soloviev had published a number of specialized pieces and historiographical studies. Soloviev's love of Russia and its history is apparent on every page of his writings, and it was not surprising that this and his personal religiosity gave him a natural affinity for the Slavophiles. He was, however, above all a scholar, and he did not hesitate to follow his sources if necessary rather than romantic Slavophile views of Russian history and religion. For a

fuller analysis of Soloviev's life and work with a helpful biblio-
graphy, see Carl W. Reddel, "Soloviev, Sergei Mikhailovich (1820-
1879)," *The Modern Encyclopedia of Russian and Soviet History*,
Vol. 36, pp. 145-51 and his essay on Soloviev's *History* in Volume
1 of this edition.

These two chapters cover a relatively short period in the reign
of Catherine the Great, from late 1768 to the end of 1770. They are
almost exclusively devoted to foreign affairs, above all to the war
with Turkey which began in September 1768 and continued until
Russian military victories found political confirmation in the Treaty
of Kuchuk-Kainardji in 1774. The continuing agony of Poland, not
to reach its brutal resolution until the Third Partition which ended
its existence in 1795, receives almost as much attention. In this
framework there are also extensive treatments of Prussian and
Austrian policy and, to a lesser degree, that of France and England.
To round out the picture of Russia's international concerns at the
time, Soloviev provides comprehensive descriptions of Swedish and
Danish affairs.

Domestic issues play at best an insignificant role. A few pages
are devoted at the outset to the successful vaccination of Catherine
and the future Emperor Paul I against smallpox. There is a passing
reference to the Legislative Commission which continued to meet
until January 1769. The first issuance of assignats, or paper
currency, and military conscription are discussed briefly, but only
in the context of wartime needs. Otherwise there is no treatment
of social, economic or cultural questions. Statesmen and state
institutions appear only in relation to the conduct of the war and
of foreign relations.

At first sight these chapters seem to confirm charges that
Soloviev merely continued Karamzin's "statist" approach, lending
credence to Aksakov's assertion that he was writing a "history of
the Russian state" rather than a "history of the Russian people." Yet
the author saw the story of Russia as an organic and continuous
evolution and the centralized monarchy as the natural culmination
of the historical process.

Soloviev once wrote that the historian "ought to study the actions
of those in authority because these contain the richest material for

the study of national life." His treatment initially strikes the modern reader as incomplete, since even in the areas of military and diplomatic history we have become accustomed to a more comprehensive exposition of the interplay of broader forces in the formulation and execution of policy, as in Marc Raeff's "The Style of Russia's Imperial Policy and Prince G. A. Potemkin" in *Statesmen and Statecraft of the Modern West. Essays in Honor of Dwight E. Lee and H. Donaldson Jordan,* ed. G. N. Grob (1967).

Not only are Soloviev's methodology and interpretation here consistent with those in other parts of his work, but it can be argued they are particularly effective in dealing with the topic at hand. By 1768 Catherine's Russia was a nation with extensive interests and even broader ambitions. The conquests of the Great Northern War (1700-1721) had given it a strong position in the Baltic which Catherine was anxious to maintain and extend, leading to continual involvement in Danish and especially Swedish affairs. By this time Russia, in accord with N. I. Panin's "Northern System," was making a major effort to counter French influence in the area, coordinating its policy as much as possible with Prussia and England. The weakness of the Northern System soon became apparent. Russia initially had strong support in Denmark, thanks in large part to its pro-Russian foreign minister, Count Bernstorff, and could count on Denmark to help oppose French interests in Sweden. Then Bernstorff fell from power in 1770 as a result of intrigues in the court of King Christian VII, and with his fall the dominant Russian role also came to an end.

Soloviev described the failure of Russian policy in this period in Sweden as well. For decades France and Russia had supported rival aristocratic factions in Sweden, the pro-French Hats and the pro-Russian Caps. He gives a vivid account of Russia's strenuous and ultimately unsuccessful efforts to undermine the French party, including the use of threats and bribery. Although Russia was able to gain England's co-operation and use the good offices of Prince Henry of Prussia, another member of the Northern System, when he visited his sister who was queen of Sweden, pro-French sentiments among the nobility and, above all, on the part of the crown prince were too strong to overcome.

The picture Soloviev drew of Russia's relations with England on the whole is one of disappointment. Although there was co-operation in Danish and Swedish affairs, and England provided harbors for the Russian fleet which sailed to Mediterranean ports, lengthy negotiations for a formal treaty of alliance came to nought in 1770, despite the strenuous efforts of the English ambassador to Russia, Lord Cathcart. By this time Russia, flushed with its successes against the Turks, was reluctant to support English interests around the world, now believing it needed no help in the Mediterranean. No wonder, then, that Soloviev gives a lengthy summary of Cathcart's negative report about Catherine, her court, and her realm at the end of his second chapter.

Recent surveys of Catherine's reign which include useful summaries, with extensive bibliographies, of the same matters covered by Soloviev include Isabel de Madariaga, *Russia in the Age of Catherine the Great* (1981) and John T. Alexander, *Catherine the Great. Life and Legend* (1989). An excellent analysis of the Northern System as it operated in the Baltic and elsewhere is David M. Griffiths, "The Rise and Fall of the Northern System. Court Politics and Foreign Policy in the First Half of Catherine's Reign," *Canadian Slavic Studies*, 4, No. 3 (Fall, 1970), 547-69. See also David L. Ransel, *The Politics of Catherinian Russia. The Panin Party* (1975).

Farther south, the Prussian connection was even more important. While Russia had played a role in domestic Polish affairs since the days of Peter the Great, it had acquired the dominant position there upon the election of Stanislaw Poniatowski as king of Poland in 1764. In 1768 Petersburg's preference was still to keep Poland as a Russian protectorate and its king a Russian puppet. But other international considerations and, above all, increasing opposition and instability inside Poland made it more receptive to Prussian overtures for partition. Meanwhile, the French actively supported the anti-Russian Confederation of Bar in Poland, and the Austrians also had their eye on Polish territory. If the few months Soloviev covers in this section are not marked by events as decisive as those which preceded or followed them, he succeeds in presenting a vivid picture of Poland's complex and tragic situation. We see the

Commonwealth and its king at the mercy of domestic factions and, particularly, the ambitions of its powerful neighbors. Poniatowski had been placed on the throne by Russia, but now he strove to maintain some degree of personal and national independence.

Soloviev described these efforts in detail, particularly the king's relations with the two Russian ambassadors of this period and with Catherine herself. The latter were determined to maintain Russia's dominant role through personal pressure on Poniatowski, encouraging pro-Russian elements, presenting themselves as the protectors of the Orthodox minority in the Commonwealth and, finally, using force against the Confederation of Bar. Russian efforts to maintain control in Poland took on a special urgency upon the beginning of the Turkish war in September 1768. Soloviev showed how this raised Polish hopes while impelling the Russians to take stronger measures to assure political and military control, particularly along the long and unstable frontiers Russia, Turkey and Poland shared in the south.

In these chapters Soloviev demonstrates how Russia succeeded in maintaining its dominant position in Poland while simultaneously winning decisive victories over the Turks. He recognizes the limits of Russia's successes, particularly its inability alone to pacify Poland. This forced Petersburg to give more consideration to Prussian and Austrian plans for partition. Soloviev includes a lengthy discussion of various related proposals from the time of Peter the Great to the 1768-1770 period. The result was the First Partition in 1773.

It is not surprising that Polish affairs occupy a central place in Soloviev's account, and that they are a major subject of his lengthy recountings of Prussian-Russian and Prussian-Austrian negotiations. Some years before, in 1863, Soloviev had published *Istoriia padeniia Polshi* (History of the Fall of Poland), which covered the same ground he does here. For a modern treatment see Herbert Kaplan, *The First Partition of Poland* (1962). Also see Norman Davies, *God's Playground. A History of Poland* (2 vols., 1984), for an account much less favorable to Russia than Soloviev's.

Yet the dominant concern both of Catherine and of Soloviev remained the war with Turkey. Earlier clashes in the eighteenth century had been inconclusive, in contrast to Russia's successes in other areas. Hence Catherine eagerly accepted the challenge when the Turks, understandably viewing her aggressive policy in Poland as a threat to their domains, reacted to a cossack violation of its borders by imprisoning A. M. Obreskov, the Russian *chargé d'affaires* in Istanbul, in September 1768, an act which Russia regarded as a *casus belli*. Soloviev included full descriptions of the Russian preparations for war, debates over strategy, the unsuccessful efforts to incite the Orthodox Christians of the Balkans and the Caucasus to revolt against the Turks, Russian efforts to detach the Tatars of the Crimea and the northern Caucasus from the Porte, the campaigns of the Russian First and Second armies in the Balkans and the dramatic expedition of a Russian fleet to confront the Turks on their home territory in the Mediterranean which culminated in the great Russian naval victory at Chesme.

As with Russia's undertakings in the Baltic and Poland, this necessarily involved other European powers, and Soloviev described the role played by England, France, Austria, Prussia and Venice in the war and in the preparation for peace negotiations whereas France encouraged the Turks to resist Russia just as it had supported anti-Russian forces in Poland. Austria was concerned that Russia had abandoned their old alliance and feared a unilateral extension of Russian power close to its own borders. Faced with this possibility, Maria Theresa bowed to the urgings of Crown Prince Joseph and Court Kaunitz and allowed them to seek a rapprochement with her old nemesis, Frederick II. Prussia, although theoretically an ally of Russia, took advantage of Russian involvement with Turkey and in Poland to press the case for Polish partition and for mediation between Russia and Turkey, since Berlin wished no great gain in Russian power. The Venetian republic in Soloviev's depiction was but a remnant of its former power, "a rotting corpse," capable only of feeble reaction to the initiatives of others.

At the time this volume was being researched and written Russia was engaged in a war with Turkey which bore striking parallels to the conflict Soloviev describes. Once more there were revolts by Orthodox Christians against Turkish rule and Russian claims of a special protectorate over them. Initial Russian reverses were followed by eventual Russian victories and, as in the previous century, these caused concern among other European powers that Russia was gaining too strong a position in the Balkans and the Mediterranean. In both wars Russia took it for granted that it had an historic mission to extend its own dominion and drive Turkish power back. See George E. Munro, "Russian-Turkish War of 1768-1774," *Modern Encyclopedia of Russian and Soviet History*, Volume 32, pp. 186-89 and Volume 48 of this edition of the *History of Russia*.

Catherine II dominates these pages. As presented by Soloviev, she is determined, energetic, and decisive, effectively controlling not just the course of Russian events, but forcing the rest of the world to acknowledge her own and Russia's power and position as well. Soloviev was clearly as pleased as Catherine that the Russian naval expedition to the Mediterranean earned the respect of Europe, even of the French. She took the leading role in the formulation and execution of policy down to the smallest details, even ordering corrected maps for the Caucasian campaigns. Soloviev clearly endorsed Catherine's assiduously cultivated self-image as the tireless and dynamic servant of her state and people, as in his opening vignette of her deciding to have herself and Grand Duke Paul vaccinated against smallpox as an example to the nation and quoting her description of herself as the good shepherd who lays down his life for his sheep.

Soloviev also approved her general policy line, with some exceptions. He agreed with the picture of Russia as the innocent party in the conflict with Turkey and sympathized with Catherine's impatience at the slow progress of P. A. Rumiantsev's campaign in the Balkans and Admiral Spiridov's tardiness in sailing the Russian fleet to the Mediterranean. Neither did he question Russia's right to dominate Poland, even dictating domestic policy to Poniatowski, intriguing with opposition forces or using Russian forces within the country. We are supposed to sympathize, for example, with A. V. Suvorov's complaints about the difficulties of campaigning in Poland. He did say that the replacement of N. V. Repnin by M. N. Volkonsky as ambassador to Warsaw was a mistake, since the latter found himself following the same policies which had caused the recall of the former.

Soloviev also believed that Russia, as directed by Catherine, had
the historic mission of pushing Turkish power back by all means
at its disposal, whether by direct military action, weaning various
Tatar tribes away from Ottoman rule or inciting the Christian
peoples of the Balkans and the Caucasus to revolt. He praised
Catherine's more tolerant policy towards the Muslims of the
Caucasus, and her overruling those who had antagonized them by
zealous Orthodox restrictions. He admitted that Russian attempts
to take common military action with the Greeks, Montenegrins and
Georgians failed in part because St. Petersburg did not understand
that a nation which is "more powerful and more developed" cannot
expect a "less developed" nation to submit automatically to its "way
of thinking." Yet Soloviev concluded that this "did not mean
shrinking from the hard tasks which the greater national interest
required," and that "we will not be too harsh in judging the Russians
of the eighteenth century. They took the first step."

On another occasion he used Alexis Orlov's victory over the
Turks at Chesme to justify Catherine's patronage of the Orlov
family, "something for which she had been reproached continually."
He never alludes to Catherine's longstanding liaison with Grigory
Orlov or for that matter any other aspect of her personal life,
although his extensive citations from her correspondence allow us
great insight into her character and personality.

Soloviev is sharply critical of N. I. Panin's Northern System and,
by implication, of Catherine's continued support of it and its
architect, referring to it as "a fantasy" and "totally unsuccessful."
It was a great mistake to reject the link with Austria, "the most
natural alliance which gave continual security against the Turks."
This meant that Russia must confront the Turks and act in Poland
alone while those who were supposed to be its new allies either were
torn by internal problems, like Denmark, of little real help, like
England, or following their own interests, like Prussia, which
pressed for a partition of Poland which Russia initially would have
preferred to avoid. Nevertheless Soloviev did not criticize Panin
directly and quotes a favorable reference to him by Catherine in a
letter to the king of Denmark.

Soloviev's endorsement of Catherine and her policies is clearly evident in his appraisal of her situation in the autumn of 1769. "Her brilliant legislative accomplishments, her triumph over all hostile forces at home, and her successes abroad in Poland had enhanced the glory of the empress of Russia and given her the reputation of an extraordinary woman." He admitted it was "premature" to accord her the title of "the Great" and attributes her difficulties and discouragement at that moment to "enemies" who had waged "two wars against her." Then he let her justify herself and her reign in long excerpts from letters to Frau Bielcke and Voltaire which paint the progress of the Turkish war in rosy colors. She even claims that "our taxes in Russia are so reasonable that there is not a single peasant who cannot eat chicken whenever he wishes, and who for some time has not preferred turkey to chicken" and that "we are now at war, but Russia long has practiced this profession and is more flourishing at the end of the war than at the outset." Soloviev further let Catherine have "what could be an answer" to a gloomy assessment of Russia by Lord Cathcart, the English ambassador in St. Petersburg which criticized Catherine, and her statesmen, the state of the economy, the lack of progress during the war and the conduct of peace negotiations. He quotes from her letter to Voltaire written June 7, 1770 in which she repeats the same boast she had made the previous year to Frau Bielcke, that "Russia emerged from each war more flourishing than before."

Consistent with Soloviev's endorsement of Catherine and her conduct of Russian policy is his conviction that Russia is a civilized European nation and has a better claim to that designation than other states in Europe. It was not always thus, as Catherine admitted in a letter criticizing Lieutenant General Stoffeln's wholesale burning of villages in the Danubian principalities as "like our old state of affairs on the Volga and the Sura," saying such tactics are "customary for howling barbarians but not for Europeans." In a reply Stoffeln's commander, Rumiantsev, stated that this "kind of barbarism was common to our ancestors and to all savage peoples," and that the Russian forces reverted to this solely in response to the barbarism of the foe.

In every other respect Russia is presented as fully civilized and European. Its formulation and execution of policy was carried out in the same fashion as that of other European powers, and its diplomats moved easily in a world framed by western European standards. In actuality the image of Russia abroad was more complex. While western Europeans saw Catherine, her court and at least part of the Russian nobility as civilized, the Russian empire was regarded as backward and barbarian outside these small circles, and even sophisticated Russian travelers abroad sometimes were looked upon as oddities. Here the limits Soloviev set for his topic allow those vast areas of Russian life still relatively unaffected by western influences to play no part. In this connection see my "L'Europe Occidentale Découvre la Russie. Les voyageurs étrangers pendant la règne de Catherine II" (Western Europe Discovers Russia. Travellers During the Reign of Catherine II), *L'Homme des Lumières et la découverte de l'autre* (Enlightenment Man and Discovery of the Other), ed. D. Droixhe et Pol-P. Gossiaux (1985).

While Catherine remains the commanding figure in these pages, many others come to life, both in the words of their pens or in the eyes of others. We have observed that here Count Panin's service to Catherine was praised, yet his Northern System rejected. By implication Soloviev saw Panin's slow and methodical temperament as the major reason why Russia continued to follow a policy so clearly contrary to its best interests. Soloviev portrayed the clash between Panin and the Orlovs when a council was established at the outset of hostilities and again at the end of 1770 when Cathcart prided himself on having achieved at least a superficial reconciliation between Panin and Grigory Orlov. We also see Grigory Orlov's daring proposal for a Mediterranean expedition and Alexis Orlov's vindication of this gamble in the victory at Chesme as characteristic of the adventuresome spirit of the five brothers who had thrown their lot in with Catherine when she ascended the throne in 1763.

Catherine's commanders also figure prominently in these pages. A. M. Golitsyn originally was entrusted with command of the First Army with primary responsibility for offensive operations, then incurred Catherine's displeasure for his dilatoriness, an impression assiduously fostered by the commander of the Second Army, P. A. Rumiantsev, who resented his secondary role. Golitsyn was replaced by Rumiantsev, whose place in turn was taken by Nikita Panin's brother Peter. Rumiantsev went on to win accolades from Catherine and from Soloviev for his victories over the Turks at Lagra and Kagul, while Panin received merely a perfunctory compliment for the capture of Bender because of large Russian casualties. Alexis Orlov justified, at least to Soloviev's satisfaction, the favor Catherine had shown his family by his victory over the Turks at Chesme.

The various Russian diplomats Soloviev portrays are less personalities in their own right than agents of Russian policy and as such are a perhaps unwitting testimonial to the aggressive and often unscrupulous role which Russia played abroad. I. A. Ostermann in Sweden begged for funds to pay off the pro-Russian party there. First N. V. Repnin and then M. N. Volkonsky interpreted their position as Russian ambassadors to Poland as a mandate to remind the unfortunate Poniatowski that he was a Russian client and his country a Russian protectorate. Volkonsky was brutally frank in dealing with Poniatowski, threatening, for example, to arrest the Czartoryskis or reminding him that "she [Catherine] alone put you on the throne and she alone keeps you on it." Soloviev makes it clear that Volkonsky was not acting on his own but rather following a policy and adopting a tone which came directly from St. Petersburg, as his recounting of instructions to Panin and his quoting a harsh letter from Catherine to Poniatowski make clear.

In fact although Soloviev's loyalties lie with Russia and with Catherine, and he stated that what Russia needed in Poland was "a man who could be respected and feared like Repnin," Poniatowski ultimately emerges from these pages as an honorable and sympathetic character. He is described as "weak-willed" and someone who begged the Russians for money and who wrote to Catherine in almost sycophantic terms, but Soloviev allowed him to speak at length as he attempts to salvage himself and his nation from an impossible situation. We are convinced by his expressions of personal devotion to Catherine and can understand his refusal to jettison his Czartoryski uncles on Russia's orders or submit to other infringements on Polish sovereignty. After reading his poignant letter to Madame Geoffrin which ends with the hope that "with courage and patience everything will end well," the reader must have second thoughts about the rectitude of Russian policy. Even granting the justice of Soloviev's charge that Poniatowski displayed "the fatalism of weak persons and weak peoples," he and his nation still appear as victims, however much their fate may have been deserved. No other foreigner appears in as sympathetic a light as Poniatowski. Soloviev admired Frederick II's astuteness and quickness and his ability "to talk unusually animatedly and intelligently." Yet he portrayed him as fearful and calculating, no longer the "daring, enterprising" leader he had been before the Seven Years War, even accusing him of lying about what he would or would not accept in a peace treaty between Russia and Turkey. Frederick is shown pressing for the partition of Poland against Russia's best interests and cynically using Russia to frighten Austria and Austria to frighten Russia. Undoubtedly Soloviev's negative view of Frederick was colored by his disapproval of the Northern System in which the Prussian alliance was a key element.

His portraits of Maria Theresa and Joseph II are even less favorable. The former is described as a "pious and conscientious old woman" who went against her principles in agreeing to the partition of Poland "but did not cease to protest and to complain," although Soloviev sympathized with her desire "to recover what had been stolen [Silesia] and to preserve the heritage of her forefathers from further depredations." Joseph II is a man "of terrible ambition," blindly following Frederick's lead, while the elderly Austrian chancellor Count Kaunitz is equally determined to enhance Austria's position, even if this meant joint action with the man who had seized Silesia.

Other foreign figures were judged from Catherine's vantage point. Soloviev does not dispute her appraisal of the French foreign minister, the duke of Choiseul, as "dishonorable" and "the cursed enemy of my state and my person." The negative tone of Cathcart's report on Russia mentioned earlier is ascribed to "diplomatic custom," and he is careful to describe the English envoy in Sweden as talented but dishonest. Here, as in the case of other figures from various nations, particularly the Poles and the Christian peoples of the Balkans and the Caucasus, individual traits were subsumed by Soloviev into general national characteristics.

We have noted how Soloviev followed Catherine in assuming that Russia was a civilized European nation. In these pages Russia is even more so when compared to the European nations whose domestic affairs are discussed. Sweden is depicted as a land where members of the royal family were at odds with each other and rival aristocratic factions battled for control. Soloviev described the coercion and bribery practiced by both the French and the Russian ministers, and the reader is left with the image of a weak and unstable neighbor which Russia was justified in attempting to dominate. The situation was even worse in Denmark where as a result of a "deranged" king, a "voluptuous" queen, and what the Russian resident described as "young and foolhardy" favorites, sound policy was impossible and the pro-Russian Count Bernstorff was dismissed.

Soloviev's critique of the Poles is even harsher. Although somewhat sympathetic to Poniatowski personally, he had little use for the "enfeebled body" that was the Polish Commonwealth. His judgment is expressed best through the words of Charles François Dumouriez, then a captain who had been sent by the French to aid the anti-Russian confederates. If he praised the bravery, magnanimity and courtesy of the Polish leaders, he considered their morals "Asiatic" and judged them incapable of effective military or political action. "The body of Polish society, that miracle, consisted of heads and stomachs, lacking hands and feet. The Polish government was similar to the government of sugar plantations which could not be independent." No wonder that in Soloviev's view the issue in Poland was not whether Russia should attempt to impose its authority there but rather how this best could be accomplished.

Even further down the scale of civilization are the Christian peoples of the Balkans and the Caucasus whom Russia hoped to incite against the Turks. Although the Greeks, Montenegrins and Georgians were fellow Orthodox Christians, they were not really within the pale of European civilization at all. In describing a riot in Smyrna, Soloviev stated that two "Europeans" as well as some Greeks were killed. In another place he refers to the "treacherous savagery" and "shameful cowardice and dishonorable behavior" of the Greek allies of a Russian expeditionary force in Morea, behavior which Soloviev quoted Catherine approvingly as attributing to having been "corrupted by centuries of slavery and perfidy." Similarly the Montenegrins, in Soloviev's summary of a Russian report, "lived in the utmost disorder, without sound institutions, laws or customs," while the Georgians were in a similar state.

The Tatars, the Muslims of the Kuban and the Turks lacked even the link of a common Christian faith to mitigate their place outside the pale of civilization and hence, by implication, legitimate objects of Russian expansion and conquest. Whereas Soloviev allowed the western Europeans and the Poles to speak somewhat for themselves, these other peoples, like the non-western Christian peoples, are seen solely through unsympathetic Russian eyes. He called the Crimean Tatars "bandits" and says of the Nogay Tatars that "petty private interests predominated because of the backward and extremely narrow sphere in which they lived." While it is understandable that he could portray nomadic peoples as uncivilized, it is disconcerting that the Ottoman empire is reduced to the level of faceless barbarian hordes. In describing the battle of Kagul, for example, Soloviev called the Russian victory "a phenomenon known from ancient history from the accounts of the struggle between the Greeks and the Persians, of European quality with Asiatic quantity."

As in his other volumes Soloviev's pace here is unhurried, and his customary extensive use of primary sources allows the reader to participate in the gradual unfolding of a complex theme. He once said that "the course of external events" rather than abstract principles determined the development of his narrative. This is certainly the case here as our attention is drawn now to one aspect, now to another, with ample opportunity to explore each one in detail. He does not hesitate to spend time on what might seem to be secondary issues or detours. Thus when describing Russian efforts to incite the Montenegrins to revolt against the Turks he gives a lengthy account of the physical appearance and adventures of Stepan Maly, an impostor who claimed to be the dead Peter III. Similarly we learn of the impression Frederick II's brother Prince Henry made at the Russian court. A letter of Catherine to the Corsican insurgent Pasquale Paoli is reproduced, and we are told what happened to Admiral G. K. Elphinstone's claims that he was unfairly punished for the loss of his ship in the Mediterranean campaign.

In fact, Soloviev let his sources speak, although these are orchestrated in such a way as to create a coherent overall picture with a specific point of view. As in earlier volumes of his History, he combed the Russian archives thoroughly and quoted the relevant material in lengthy excerpts. Most extensive use was made of the Arkhiv ministerstva inostrannykh del (Archive of the Ministry for Foreign Affairs), today the Arkhiv vneshnei politiki Rossii (Archive of Russia's Foreign Policy), from which he excerpted or summarized the reports of Russian diplomats abroad and the replies to these by Nikita Panin or, on occasion, by Catherine herself, and reports of other European diplomats, official correspondence with foreign courts, texts of proposals, and the like. Thus we find a panoramic view of Russia's international concerns ranging from Denmark and Sweden in the Baltic; through the great powers of Europe, France, England, Austria and Prussia; lesser powers such as Venice and Georgia; and, of course, Turkey and Poland. It is above all with the latter that Soloviev's method works to advantage by reproducing the lengthy interchanges between Stanislaw Poniatowski and the Russian ambassador to Poland, M. N. Volkonsky, joined on occasion by the Prussian ambassador, Gédéon Benoît.

Some documents are taken from the former Gosudarstvennyi arkhiv (State Archive), today the Tsentralnyi gosudarstvennyi arkhiv drevnykh aktov (Central State Archive of Ancient Acts), and still others from the archives of the Imperatorskaia publichnaia biblioteka (Imperial Public Library), now the Gosudarstvennaia publichnaia biblioteka im. M. E. Saltykova-Shchedrina (M. E. Saltykov-Shchedrin State Public Library). No use was made of archives outside Russia for this volume.

Soloviev made much more extensive use of published primary and secondary sources in these pages than in many of the earlier volumes of the *History*. This is not surprising since by the time it was written the publication of source collections and scholarly monographs was well advanced. The international scope of this volume and the central role played by such prominent figures as Frederick II and Joseph II also meant that many other scholars, notably German, had turned their attention to Soloviev's concerns, which was not the case for some of his earlier volumes on pre-Petrine Russian history. From the Arkhiv gosudarstvennogo soveta (Archive of the State Council) published by I.A. Chistovich in 1864, we are given a similar range of material on the council established to direct the war against Turkey, including quotations from summaries of its meetings, rescripts and correspondence with commanders in the field or at sea. He also profited from the editions of primary historical sources which had appeared since 1867 in the *Sbornik Russkogo istoricheskogo obshchestva* (Collection of the Russian Historical Society), as well as those in the *Russkii arkhiv* (Russian Archive), which began publication in 1863, and in the *Pamiatniki novoi russkoi istorii* (Memorials of Recent Russian History). He also quotes on occasion from the official newspapers of the time, *Moskovskie vedomosti* (Moscow News) and *Sankt Peterburgskie vedomosti* (St. Petersburg News), as well as from the *Polnoe sobranie zakonov* (Complete Collection of Laws).

In addition Soloviev made full use of the available monographs and separate publications of sources in Russian and other languages, such as the third volume of the *Sochineniia Imperatritsy Ekateriny II* (Literary Works of Empress Catherine II); Volume 26 of the *Works of Frederick the Great* published at Berlin in 1855; the second volume of the *Memoirs of Frederick II, King of Prussia* which appeared at Paris in 1866; and the first part of M. E. Boutaric's edition of the *Secret and Unedited Correspondence of Louis XV*. Other sources include the first volume of A. R. Arneth, *Maria Theresa and Joseph II*, and two works by A. Beer, *Frederick II and Van Swieten* and the first volume of *The First Partition of Poland*. Also cited were M. Duncker, *From the Time of Frederick the Great and Frederick William III;* F. Raumer, *Essays on Recent History, From the British and French State Archives. Part IV. Europe From the End of the Seven Years War to the End of the American War*; and the fifth volume of E. Herrmann, *History of the European States. History of the Russian State.*

By 1878 several works had appeared about the Turkish war on which Soloviev could draw, notably the first part of P.G. Butkov, *Materialy dlia novoi istorii Kavkaza s 1722 po 1803 god* (Materials on the Recent History of the Caucasus from 1722 to 1803); the first four volumes of A. N. Petrov, *Russia's War with Turkey and the Polish Confederates, 1769-1774;* the official *History of the War Between Russia and Turkey* and the *History of the Present War between Russia, Poland and the Ottoman Porte*. Finally Soloviev used William Richardson's *Anecdotes of the Russian Empire*, one

of the many travel accounts of Catherine's Russia that English and
other visitors published during and shortly after her reign.

After Soloviev's death in 1879 primary sources for the period
covered by this volume continued to appear in Russian historical
journals and in separate editions in Russia and abroad, for example,
the two volumes of King Stanislaw Poniatowski's memoirs (1914-
1924) and a massive forty-six-volume edition of Frederick II's
political correspondence (1879-1939). English translations of sources
for topics covered by Soloviev here are still very sparse; one of these
is A. Lentin, ed. and trans., *Voltaire and Catherine the Great.
Selected Correspondence* (1974). Some of the English-language
travel accounts, such as Richardson's *Anecdotes,* have been reprinted
in recent years. Otherwise the student must rely on Soloviev himself
or on secondary works for excerpts in English.

The author's command of this extensive and varied mass of
material is impressive. Soloviev is particularly effective in
juxtaposing different sources on the same topic. We read reports
from field commanders to the council, watch the council's
deliberations, learn of its decisions, see the reaction of foreign
diplomats and occasionally read Catherine's own frank assessment
of events in private letters. When Prince Henry of Prussia visits St.
Petersburg, Soloviev first sets the scene carefully with a review of
the international situation, then quotes from private letters of
instruction from Frederick to Henry. We see the personal impression
Prince Henry made at Catherine's court as through Richardson's
eyes and read Catherine's comment to Alexis Orlov that he "was
as light on his feet as a lead bird, but so intelligent." We read
excerpts from his conversations with Catherine and learn about those
with Panin, Caspar Saldern and Zakhar Chernyshev. Then there is
the more official exchange of letters between Frederick and
Catherine on major issues of the day which were the subjects of less
formal exchanges, notably the Turkish war and the prospects for
Polish partition.

Few historians can equal Soloviev's range of sources or the
volume of his citations from them. Admittedly, his account of Russia
in the years 1768-1770 focused almost exclusively on the wars and
Kabinettspolitik of the period, and his pages are populated almost

exclusively by rulers, statesmen, generals and diplomats. His summary judgments of nations and peoples may strike the modern reader as condescending. Yet it was precisely the players who dominate Soloviev's account who shaped the events he describes, and he succeeds brilliantly in bringing them to life on the political stage. His canvas is broad and he has painted it in full detail, yet never losing sight of the contours of the whole. His picture of the personalities and events of this brief but extraordinarily complex period is enjoyable on its own merits and as one of the final segments of his vast panorama of Russian history.

As these lines are written at the end of 1992 the Russian empire whose formation Soloviev describes in this and other volumes of his *History* has disintegrated before our eyes. The unique insight he provides into how and why it came into being will help us understand the present "Time of Troubles" in Russia's history and its still uncertain prospects for its future.

History of Russia

Volume 46

The Rule of Catherine the Great

Turkey and Poland, 1768–1770

I

FOREIGN RELATIONS
1768–1769

VACCINATION OF THE EMPRESS AND THE HEIR

At the beginning of October 1768 the court and St. Petersburg society were preoccupied. Nobody talked to foreigners about what was foremost in everyone's mind. It was easy enough to find out what the issue was. The empress had decided to vaccinate herself and the heir to the throne [Paul] against smallpox. The terrible scourge already had ravaged Europe, sparing no one. Science was powerless, but finally a remedy had been found, which was vaccination with smallpox toxin. It is easy to imagine what most people thought of taking toxin from a sick person and introducing it into a healthy organism! Doctors clamored against this insane novelty, while preachers denounced it from the pulpit. The effectiveness of the technique nevertheless was proven and was gaining more and more support. So Catherine decided to use personal example to put a stop to public uncertainty and protect her people from the terrible disaster.

The best explanation of her motives came in a letter to Frederick II[1], an opponent of vaccination: "Since childhood," wrote the empress, "I have been taught to dread smallpox, and as an adult I have had to bend every effort to conquer my fear. I thought every minor illness was smallpox. Last spring, when the disease was raging here, I fled from house to house. I was an exile from the city for five whole months, unwilling to expose myself or my son to danger. I became convinced that this was an intolerable situation and that to continue it was a sign of weakness. I was advised to vaccinate my son against smallpox. I answered that it would be shameful not to start with myself. How could I introduce vaccination without setting a personal example? I began to study the question and decided to opt for the less dangerous course. Should I spend my whole life in real danger with thousands of people or choose the lesser danger, one that would pass quickly and save the majority of my people? I thought that by opting for the latter, I chose the surer course."

A skilled doctor, Dimsdale,[2] was sent for from England. Of the six thousand people he had vaccinated, only one, a three-year-old boy, had died. On October 12, 1768 the empress was vaccinated, and the majority of the dignitaries soon followed her example. "Everyone in St. Petersburg," wrote Catherine, "wants to vaccinate himself against smallpox, and those who do so are feeling fine. After the operation I was very surprised to see how the mountains had brought forth a mouse. I questioned how worthwhile it was to protest and to prevent people from saving their lives through such trifling means. I did not lie in bed a single minute and I received people every day. Quartermaster General Count Orlov[3] is a real hero. Like the ancient Romans of the best years of the republic, he is brave and magnanimous. He vaccinated himself and on the second day after the operation went hunting in a terrible snowstorm." A week later the grand duke was vaccinated.

On November 22 the Senate, the Legislative Commission[4] and members of all government offices gathered in the Nativity of the Virgin (Kazan) cathedral. There, after dinner, a decree of the Senate was read which proclaimed November 21 be set aside throughout Russia to celebrate the vaccination of the empress and the grand duke and to commemorate this "magnanimous, celebrated and unequalled achievement."

After the decree had been read and the prayer service concluded the senators, the deputies of the commission and the members of the colleges and chancelleries proceeded to the palace to express their thanks to the empress and to congratulate her on her recovery. The senior senator, Kirill Razumovsky,[5] delivered an address: "Accept from our lips, most gracious empress, the warmest congratulations of your entire people on the recovery of your own personage and that of your beloved son and heir. Accept our sincere gratitude for the salvation of countless of your servants in years to come. Each one, whether young or old, male or female, now falls at your feet to honor the divine mediatrix of his salvation. Following your example, he calls upon God for aid, so that he also might cure his home of the inexorable curse by means of the remedy which you yourself have brought forth."

Catherine responded: "My example was my instrument to save the lives of many of my faithful subjects who, not knowing the effectiveness of this remedy, were frightened of it and thus remained in danger. In this way I fulfilled the duty of my office, or, in the words of the Gospel, the good shepherd lays down his life for his sheep. You can be assured that now and henceforth I will intensify my efforts to provide for the welfare of all of my loyal subjects, wherever they may be."

Gavriil, the bishop of Tver[6] and a deputy of the Legislative Commission, now spoke: "Your intention was to bring Russia through legislation to such a state of perfection that the Russian people would, as far as possible, be the happiest people in the world who enjoyed the fullest measure of justice. Your wise prescriptions are leading us to that goal and fill us with true devotion, love and reverence for your imperial majesty. Your increased happiness makes your life precious to us, but one thing that continued to trouble us was the danger posed by your sore, a danger which this climate makes a danger for all. Your imperial majesty, wishing to perfect and to increase our felicity, gave us consolation in our troubles with her own magnanimity and, by subjecting herself to the dangerous trial, warded off danger from us."

Catherine replied that she accepted the congratulations of the deputies with joy and that she had no doubts about their sincerity. Every day she saw with what fervor and devotion they worked at the task assigned them. They could expect lasting expressions of her benevolence, for she saw how useful their labor was for each and every one. Noble rank was conferred upon Alexander Markov, the seven-year-old boy from whom the smallpox toxin had been taken for the empress. For this reason his name was changed from Markov to Ospenny [smallpox]. Dimsdale was awarded the rank of baron, named personal physician to the empress and senior state councillor and granted a yearly pension of £500. This was done to recognize that for the empress herself, the grand duke and the majority of the people of the capital he "had most carefully, skillfully, and successfully carried out the smallpox vaccination and had destroyed the hydra of prejudice which hitherto had been associated with the terrible disease."[7]

OUTBREAK OF WAR WITH TURKEY

In the midst of these congratulatory festivities the empress was quite preoccupied with the Turkish war, which was completely unexpected and for which Russia in general was not prepared. Catherine wrote to Count Peter Semenovich Saltykov[8] in Moscow: "On November 1 I returned from Tsarskoe Selo where I had smallpox. During that time I was not allowed to conduct business. I now found out that news had come of the arrest of my resident in Tsargrad [Constantinople], Obrezkov.[9] This act could lead to a declaration of war. Thus I was forced to order our forces to assemble at the designated places. I appointed two senior generals, Prince Golitsyn[10] to command the First Army and Count Rumiantsev[11] to command the Second Army. May God grant the former a father's joy and the latter the greatest happiness as well!

"If I feared the Turks I would choose Field Marshal Saltykov with all his laurels without hesitation. Considering the difficulties this war would cause in his advanced age, I decided to spare him. He has enough glory already. I have complete confidence that whichever general I choose would be better than the vizier the foe sends against us. May God bless our undertakings! God sees that I was not the one who started this conflict. It will not be the first time that Russia vanquishes its foes, having been victorious over danger under other circumstances. Thanks to the mercy of God and the bravery of His people, we now can expect a happy outcome."

The letters Catherine sent abroad to Count Ivan Chernyshev were equally animated and filled with hopes for success: "The Turks and the French thought to waken the sleeping cat. I am that cat who promises to teach them a lesson they will not forget soon. When we broke the peace treaty we were freed from a great burden which weighed us down. We had to put up with a thousand coaxings, deals and empty stupidities, so as not to give the Turks anything about which to complain. Now I am done with it and can act with all the means at my disposal. Russia's means, as you know, are considerable, and Catherine II sometimes makes all kinds of dreams come true. Nothing will hold her back. They have wakened the sleeping cat, and see how he has gone after the mice. Now we shall be noticed, and now we shall be talked about. We have sounded an alarm they did not expect, and the Turks will be defeated."

ESTABLISHMENT OF THE COUNCIL

Catherine's first thought after learning that the peace had been broken was to re-establish Elizabeth's conference,[12] and she informed Panin[13] of this. We know how he felt about Elizabeth's conference since he had believed its establishment meant the end of his power and influence. Under these circumstances Catherine wanted no delay. She wrote him, "I want you to advise me who would be best suited for the council about which we spoke. Send me a note right away."

How could this be? There was no avoiding a council! At least it would not be like Elizabeth's conference and it would not be permanent. Who should be appointed? Not to appoint Grigory Orlov would reveal Panin's hostility to Orlov clearly and would incur the displeasure of the sovereign. Not inviting him would mean that everyone would be able to make appointments. Thus he should be appointed but surrounded with friends so as to render him harmless.

"I must inform your majesty frankly," Panin replied, "that it is impossible to establish such a permanent council or conference to conduct business immediately. In the first year it will be unnecessary. It may well be difficult to make judgments in the brief time available. When such a body is created many days may be devoted just to establishing rules of procedure for conducting business. Therefore, would your imperial majesty not wish to convoke an extraordinary meeting in your chambers for tomorrow only? Such meetings already have occurred during your reign and have occurred on all extraordinary occasions under your predecessors, even when Anna I's permanent cabinet functioned.

"For these reasons and in the spirit of true sincerity I would make bold to recommend the following men for this present council. They would then deliberate among themselves and agree on certain matters and then put them before your imperial majesty. The first person who should be named is Grigory Grigorevich (Orlov) because of his special devotion to you and his dedication to the glory, success and tranquillity of your majesty, as demonstrated in his command of the Artillery Corps." Then Panin nominated Count Zakhar Chernyshev on account of his post in his War College; generals who could be named commanders-in-chief; Viazemsky, the procurator general for finances;[14] himself; and the vice chancellor Prince Golitsyn.[15] In conclusion Panin said: "Finally, would it not be fitting to summon Field Marshal Count Razumovsky, although this would reflect more the judgment of your highest dignitaries than general opinion, especially at foreign courts. This will be an even more important and decisive factor since he is perceived as loyal to your imperial majesty by virtue of his conduct at court. For the same reason his agreement with and endorsement of the measures taken by the ruling council can be guaranteed."

PREPARATIONS FOR WAR

At ten o'clock in the morning of November 4 the following assembled at the court in response to the order issued the day before: Count Razumovsky, Prince Alexander Mikhailovich Golitsyn (general-in-chief), Count Nikita Panin, Count Zakhar Chernyshev, Count Peter Ivanovich Panin,[16] Prince Mikhail Nikitich Volkonsky,[17] Prince Alexander Mikhailovich Golitsyn (vice chancellor), Count Grigory Orlov and Prince Viazemsky. They were led into a chamber prepared especially for the council where the empress herself appeared and opened the session with the following words: "Because of the way the Turks have acted, which Count Panin will explain to you, I am forced to wage war with the Porte. Now I have gathered you to ask your advice in formulating a plan: (1) How to wage war. (2) Where the assembly points should be. (3) What measures to take to secure the other borders of the empire. Time does not permit us to go into details. These will be left to the executive bodies such as the War College and the College of Foreign Affairs for matters in their spheres. Count Zakhar Chernyshev will describe the current status of our armed forces and give a short account of their actions in the previous war. There will be an explanation of our financial resources. Some may think we can get by with less of a burden on the people. These resources will suffice for the future, although improvements can be made as things stand now."

When the empress finished, Count Nikita Panin began to read an account of the events leading to the war. Russia had missed no opportunity to resolve all misunderstandings peacefully, and the Porte had started the war. After Panin, Count Zakhar Chernyshev read an account of Russia's war with Turkey under Empress Anna and concluded with a description of the present status and deployment of the army. On the question of precautions for the other frontiers of the empire, Panin asserted that there was not the slightest danger from Sweden on the Finnish border. There a few garrison forces could be left in fortresses. But Chernyshev stated that several regiments should be stationed in the north in view of the proximity of the capital to the border. Two regiments would be stationed on the Estonian border. Two regiments of cuirassiers and three of infantry would be stationed in Livonia. Three cavalry and three infantry regiments would remain in the Smolensk district, and two regiments would be transferred from Orenburg to protect the Astrakhan border. Chernyshev recalled how often there had been alarming news from the Volga region to the east and recommended that a regiment of dragoons be stationed in Simbirsk to maintain domestic order. Catherine added that it was not necessary to use a whole detachment of Kazan Tatars for this. There were always three regiments in Moscow. It was recommended that two of them be left there and that reducing the number of men on guard be considered.

ORLOV PROPOSES A MEDITERRANEAN EXPEDITION

On the conduct of the war, the gathering unanimously recommended taking the offensive, saying it was necessary to put the enemy on notice. Then Orlov made an unexpected proposal: "When you start to wage war, you have to have a goal, and everything should be directed to achieve that goal. If not, it would be better to find some way to avoid the issue." Panin was visibly embarrassed by his opponent's suggestion, the more so because everyone knew Orlov was speaking for the empress and with her approval. Panin did not respond to the question. "It is desirable," he said, "that the war end quickly. The way to do that is to collect all our forces, attack the enemy and conquer him." Orlov remarked that immediate decisive action was impossible. Panin answered, "We must try to wear down the enemy army so that just as the leaders demanded war, so too they will be led to peace."

It was decided to divide the army into three parts. There would be an eighty-thousand-man offensive corps, while the defensive, or Ukrainian, corps would number forty thousand, with twelve to fifteen thousand men in reserve. At the end of the session Orlov suggested sending several vessels on a diversionary expedition in the Mediterranean, but only if the English court agreed. This suggestion was tabled for future decision.

The second session of the council was held two days later on November 6. When the journal of the previous session was read, changes were made. Only two instead of three infantry regiments were left on the Livonian border. Proposals were made concerning the plan of operations. If the Turks together with Polish confederations were to move into Poland on the left flank, the commander of the Russian offensive corps was given permission to leave the general line of battle and deploy his forces to defend the borders. He was also to cover a part of Poland, especially Lithuania, to protect not only his own forces but also Russian allies in Poland. Thus the enemy, forced to march in autumn weather, would be worn down, whether or not he would destroy part of Poland. We would strive in any way possible to prevent him from making use of local resources as he returned to his own borders and to take advantage, when feasible, of his exhaustion. If the Turks delayed an incursion into Poland, Kamieniec should be taken as quickly as possible and a fortress and supply depots be established there. If it happened that the Turkish army was not large and it was possible to gain superiority over it, then Khotin should be captured.

At this session Catherine presented Orlov's question about the purpose of the war for discussion: "For what end should war be waged and, given our advantages, how can we achieve the most favorable results?" Others answered that when peace was concluded, freedom of navigation should be assured in the Black Sea. Thus even during wartime the construction of ports and fortresses should be attempted. Secure borders also must be fixed for Poland.

GOLITSYN AND RUMIANTSEV PLACED IN COMMAND

The senior generals were designated at this session. Prince Alexander Golitsyn would command the offensive forces and Prince Rumiantsev the defensive. Rumiantsev fell on his knees on the spot to express his gratitude for the trust placed in him. The appointment of Golitsyn was seen as a triumph for Chernyshev, who was able to shunt aside generals he did not like. Peter Ivanovich Panin was passed over completely, while Rumiantsev was relegated to a secondary position. As noted above, there was an account of the earlier Turkish war in the previous session. In the third session on November 12 the procurator general again discussed the measures taken in 1737 to provision the army. Count Peter Panin said an historical description of the previous Turkish war was needed. Then the empress asked: "If someone thinks that would be useful in our consideration of current affairs, he can present it." This is why Orlov had asked about the purpose of the war in the first session and why Catherine repeated the question the second time.

ENVOYS TO THE BALKAN CHRISTIANS
Orlov began to read his memorandum "On the Expedition to the Mediterranean Sea." After various observations were made about the memorandum it was decided to send envoys to Morea, Dalmatia, Georgia and all the peoples living in Turkish territory who shared our faith, to convince them to agree that Russia had been forced to wage war for the faith against Turkey. An envoy would be dispatched to the Montenegrins to determine whether an expedition there would be assured of a secure base. The vice chancellor presented a list of peoples who because of their common faith wanted to be under Russian authority. A plan was drafted on the basis of emissaries' reports from various locations.

As early as 1763, when the threat of Turkish interference in Polish affairs arose, Count Grigory Orlov had sent two Greeks, Manuel Saro and the artillery officer Papazuli, to the *Spartans*. Saro returned from his journey in May 1765 and reported that the Spartans were Christian Greeks who, although living in Turkish territory, were not subject to the Turks, did not fear them and even fought against them. They lived in the mountains and in strongholds so that the Turks hardly could move against them. As soon as the Greeks heard Saro's proposal that they rise against the Turks in the event of a Russo-Turkish war, the elders, or captains, Trupaki, Dmitriaki, Kumudro, Mavromikhali, Foka and others summoned a

great assembly. They declared that they gladly would oppose the
Turks with great force as enemies of the Orthodox Christian faith.
One Greek, a rich and respected *nobleman*, Binaki, stated at the
assembly that he would rouse the Lacedaemonians (Spartans) who
were Turkish subjects, only if they could be under the protection
of the Russian sovereign.

There were still other free Greeks who lived in the extensive
district of Karomiro. Their captains were Stafa, Bukuvalo,
Makripuli, Zhudro and others, who as Orthodox did not want to be
subject to the Turks. They gladly would rise against the Turks and
would be able to summon the majority of the other Greeks to join
them. There was also the province of Chimara where the people
were free. It was called Little Albania (although Greek was spoken
there), and they never had submitted to the Turks. They were Greek
Orthodox, they were in a position to fight against the Turks with
considerable force and in fact the king of Naples maintained a whole
regiment of these people. The inhabitants of these districts assured
Saro and Papazuli that in case of war between Russia and Turkey
they would stand as one against the Porte. They could all assemble
in one place, and none of these districts was more than a hundred
and fifty versts apart. "I am convinced," wrote Saro, "that I can
propose sending ten Russian warships with sufficient cannon into
the Mediterranean against the Turks. When the Greeks see them they
will hasten to join the Russians. The Greeks have some fairly large
vessels, but they need to be outfitted with cannon. The Greeks are
a brave and courageous people." Orlov gave Saro a signed affidavit:
"This attests that Manuel Saro was commissioned by me to travel
to Turkish territory in 1763 and faithfully carried out his
assignment." Karazin, a Bulgarian, went on a mission to the Danube
region for the same purpose.

The English ambassador Cathcart[18] described his conversation
with one of these emissaries in his dispatches to his court. At the
outset the empress and her ministers found the project laden with
great obstacles, but then pursued it enthusiastically. In Morea,
according to the emissaries, there were many harbors and seamen,
yet few Turks and few precautions taken. The Greeks yearned for
freedom, and only a little help was needed for them to attain it.
Freedom could be secured by fortifying the isthmus of Corinth.

Albania, Epirus, Zante, Cephalonia and the neighboring islands would follow Morea's example. It would be hard to start a revolt in Candia. There were many Turkish fortresses there, but one or two islands of the archipelago could be fortified, thus hindering Constantinople from sending supplies through the Dardanelles. The Greeks had good reason to hate the Turkish government, but they preferred them to Roman Catholic masters since the Turks were more tolerant. The Greeks never wanted to belong to Austria and hated France. Catherine threw herself into this brilliant undertaking with her usual passion and began to share her hopes with those close to her. "I so flattered our sailors about their profession," she wrote Ivan Chernyshev, "that they are burning with zeal, and I will tell you why tomorrow. If you wish, you can guess. I just visited them and, God willing, you will see miracles." A few days later she wrote: "My fleet is now under excellent care and, God willing, I surely will use it as it never has been before. I already have given orders, I am not saying to which destination. Drunken sailors are saying on the streets, however, that we are going to Azov."

MILITARY CONSCRIPTION

Extensive preparations were made for the war. Resources had to be considered. Regiments were grouped in the south, while other borders and interior districts, including the dangerous Volga region, were left unprotected. On November 16 Field Marshal Saltykov wrote to the empress: "There is robbery in and around Moscow, and the number of bandits has increased markedly. Now that regiments have taken the field there is not one cavalry unit left, and there are no more mounted patrols." "Summon the leading representatives of the various groups in Moscow," answered Catherine, "and take measures with them to assure their security. Establish a cavalry and an infantry unit, maintained by all, and report to me without delay. As you know, many of the Muscovites have a number of men under them, including some hussars. It is possible to form a unit of these, to organize patrols in the city and, once they are armed, put them under the police bureau."

It was also necessary to increase the size of the armed forces on active duty and to replace the losses which had occurred. On October 8 conscription of one recruit for each three hundred souls was announced, and on November 14 an edict was issued to carry out this conscription, including the unemployed sons of priests and deacons. It was calculated that there should be 78,651 serving in the 17,518 churches in Russia. Yet presently there were only 66,025 with 12,627 vacancies. On the other hand, some sons of priests and others of the clerical estate were not being assigned to church duties. Of those aged twenty and older 5916 were not assigned, 6501 of those between fifteen and twenty, and 57,870 of those under fifteen, for a total of 70,287. There were 1472 unassigned priests and deacons and 1565 sextons, psalmists and watchmen. Thus the Senate proposed conscripting a fourth of those aged between fifteen and forty, with three-fourths remaining at their churches. Half of the clerics unattached or under ban or punishment would be taken. None of the 4905 seminarians would be conscripted. The empress agreed.[19]

BANK OF STATE ASSIGNATS

Finally, because of the financial problems occasioned by the Turkish war, a measure was adopted that no one had wanted during Elizabeth's reign, which had been tried under Peter III, but had been repealed at the outset of Catherine's reign. At the council session of November 17 the procurator general discussed the introduction of assignats. A manifesto was issued on December 29: "In an empire as vast as Russia, it apparently is impossible to provide for enough money in circulation to assure the welfare of the people and the flourishing of trade. It is true that in itself the size of our empire is something of an obstacle to full currency circulation. In such a situation every prudent government is obliged, if possible, to overcome natural obstacles. We have become convinced that the burden of copper money valued at its true worth hinders its circulation. Secondly, transporting all metal money over long distances is fraught with great difficulties. Thirdly, we have seen that, in comparison with various parts of Europe, there is a great shortage in Russia of those establishments which could provide for the proper circulation of money and which could transfer private capital without any delay and for the benefit of each person. Daily experience has shown how many states reap benefits from such measures, for the most part through notes issued by banks. Besides the benefits already mentioned, there is an additional advantage. The distribution by various institutions of printed promissory notes in different amounts would furnish a voluntary source of credit people could use as money on hand. There would not be the same problems of transportation and safekeeping, so the circulation of money would be significantly easier. "Thus on January 1, 1769 two banks will be established under our patronage in St. Petersburg and Moscow for the exchange of state assignats. These will be issued at designated state and treasury locations, but only up to the amount of capital on hand at the aforementioned banks. These assignats will be circulated throughout the empire at par with the currency already in use. All state and treasury locations must accept these assignats for state obligations and in place of currency without raising any difficulties. In addition we order that all private persons who henceforward make payments to the treasury shall receive a state assignat for twenty-five rubles as part of each five hundred rubles received. Each private person can at all times, whenever he wishes, exchange his state assignats for currency, presenting Moscow assignats to the Moscow bank and St. Petersburg assignats to the St. Petersburg bank. We further order these banks to make their payments without any delay or loss of time. We solemnly proclaim in our imperial capacity on our behalf and that of our successors that payment for these state assignats will be rendered punctually and faithfully to those who request this of the banks."[20]

It was decided to raise one hundred thousand thalers from Livonia and the island of Ösel, and fifty thousand thalers from Estonia each year of the war with Turkey. The empress sent a handwritten note to the Senate with a view to reducing expenditures: "Stop work on the Baltic port and take care that prisoners sentenced to hard labor[21] there are not set free." The senate ordered them dispersed to other locations. In 1768 expenses for the war reached one and a quarter million rubles.

THE ORDER OF ST. GEORGE
But Catherine had no wish to limit her role merely to material resources. Since she was Montesquieu's pupil,[22] she saw the great importance of a sense of honor in Russia's governmental service. She had to consider her obligation to awaken and maintain this sense

as the source of valor and therefore established the Order of St. George for feats of arms.

ATTACK BY THE CRIMEAN TATARS

Starting in 1769 the council took on a permanent character, and it was most active in that year. Possibly there would be no conflict with the enemy until the spring. Then on January 15 the Crimean khan Kirim Girey[23] (with over seventy thousand men) crossed the Russian border at the small town of Orel planning to invade the province of Elisavetgrad and proceed from there to Poland, where the confederates were waiting to show him the way. The Tatars were met with cannon fire at Elisavetgrad and decided not to capture the fortress. Instead they dispersed to ravage and burn the neighboring villages. The same fate befell the Polish territories when the allies of the confederates appeared there. As was his custom, Kirim destroyed his enemies and laid waste the land. His friends the Crimean bandits, satisfied with the captives they had taken, withdrew beyond the Dniester river. The khan sent a gift of captured women to Constantinople. More than ten thousand people and a large number of cattle were captured from Elisavetgrad province, and more than a thousand houses were burned. A second Tatar force reached Bakhmut and ravaged the environs. About eight hundred prisoners were carried off. But that was the last Tatar attack in our history!

The Russian offensive army had to keep the Turks out of Poland. On April 15 it crossed the Dniester moving towards Khotin. At the outset it was successful, but Prince Golitsyn decided not to besiege Khotin. He had insufficient artillery and provisions because all of Moldavia had been ravaged terribly by the Turks. On April 21 the Russian army left Khotin. The Turks fell on the baggage van but were repulsed with heavy casualties. On April 24 Golitsyn recrossed the Dniester.[24]

Golitsyn sent a report of his movements to St. Petersburg with Cornet Count Münnich[25] who on his own authority reported that things had not gone well at Khotin. Catherine summoned Münnich, and after talking with him for more than two hours, wrote Panin (May 3): "Since I have spoken with Count Münnich for more than two hours, I have noticed many blunders and lies in what he has said. Thus I beg you not to make a judgment before you come to the council tomorrow. Then we shall see from Prince Golitsyn's reports that matters are quite different from Münnich's lies." We do not know what Münnich's "lies" were, but we do know that Golitsyn's recrossing the Dniester spoke for itself.

On May 6 a memorandum was addressed to him: "Based on your first report about your success against the enemy, we hardly could have expected such a speedy and unfortunate turn of events. We were very surprised therefore not to find in your report a detailed account of the reasons why you are now undoubtedly in such a difficult position. Thus very soon you will have lost the glory gained at the beginning of the campaign as well as any advantage gained over the enemy. Since we have lost our previous total confidence in you and your staff, we have decided to order you to convene a council of war to decide upon a second campaign against the enemy. As a result of your campaign, your present unhappy situation has displaced the former glory of our arms, and your hasty retreat has given rise to public discussion."

"Because of serious obstacles," Golitsyn justified himself, "I did not capture Khotin. I could have accomplished this only by an assault which would have cost a large number of men, and I would not have ventured to do so without approval from the highest level. I then was forced to cross immediately to our side of the Dniester, for it was impossible to remain on the other side. I could not risk the otherwise inevitable exhaustion of our undermanned army. There was a hostile threat on various flanks. Above all, I received no information from Count Rumiantsev and no answers to my letters, whether he would come to my aid and take measures to disperse the enemy forces. Necessity dictated withdrawal (beyond the Kalusz river) to nearby supply depots in Poland. I spared no efforts to prevent the burning of the Danube bridge and supplies there, but I was not able to find any men or money for this undertaking. I could not detach a small part of my forces to this end, for that would have meant sacrificing them completely."

Golitsyn's report of May 3 was read in the council on May 18. In it he stated that he had transferred the entire army to our side of the Dniester, removed the bridges and put the infantry and calvary in camps. In response the empress stated that the commander-in-chief should be given some orders. An edict was sent to Golitsyn:

"The glory of our arms demands that changes in our present situation be made. Our goal is not to hold on to previously prepared supply depots. Rather we must anticipate the enemy and prevent him from using to his advantage benefits which we ourselves can gain and defend. Let us repeat our hope, a hope in keeping with the glory of our arms and the genuine welfare of the fatherland, that you act upon these comments efficaciously in pursuing of the goal of this campaign. Proceed to the other bank of Dniester with your entire army, go straightaway against the enemy and press him in every way possible. Not only should you force him across the Danube, but you also should find the opportunity to conclude the campaign victoriously. Thereby you will sweep Moldavia clean and hence open the way to capture Khotin and to occupy winter quarters on the Dniester."

THE SIEGE OF KHOTIN

The concentration of Turkish forces at Khotin and their attempt to cross the Dniester forced Golitsyn to advance to the river again in June. Major General Prince Prozorovsky[26] repulsed two hundred thousand Turks who were attempting to cross. Golitsyn crossed the Dniester a second time early in July and brilliantly repelled a large enemy force. He besieged Khotin, whose garrison was in desperate straits through shortage of provisions and disease resulting from overcrowding. The grand vizier Mahomet Emin-Pasha previously had wanted to invade New Russia. Learning of Khotin's perilous situation, he sent the Crimean khan in aid with forty thousand Tatars. On July 22 the khan fell on the Russian forces at Khotin but was repulsed with heavy casualties and quickly withdrew. A Turkish army appeared, sent by the vizier under the command of Ali the Moldavian pasha. He combined forces with the khan and advanced on Khotin with more than one hundred thousand men. Behind the Moldavian pasha the vizier himself could be expected. At a council of war held on August 1 it was decided to withdraw once more beyond the Dniester.

GOLITSYN REPLACED BY RUMIANTSEV

This second withdrawal beyond the Dniester created considerable dissatisfaction in St. Petersburg, exacerbated by the continual reports of successes Golitsyn had sent during July. "On the very day you crossed the Dniester," Catherine wrote to him on July 20, "I read in all your reports about your continued successes and the defeat of various enemy forces. I congratulate you with all my heart on this. Consequently we gave proper thanks to the Most High yesterday to the accompaniment of cannon fire." On August 4 Catherine wrote him: "I learn from your report of July 23 that the expedition of our matchless forces to Khotin has been defeated. Please express my satisfaction and gratitude to our brave hussars whom you have praised so much. Remind the cossacks of the brave deeds of these lightly-armed forces in former wars. Recall the great kindness they received from our predecessors for their loyalty and devotion. They can expect the same from us. I did not become bored with your sojourn at Khotin, and it is my judgment that you do not have to embark on another effort to take the city with the least possible losses. If the vizier is there to welcome you, then call on God for help and defeat him."

What impression was created by the news that the Russian forces had retreated, having fought not against the vizier, but merely against his vanguard? We saw that Golitsyn complained openly against Rumiantsev. For his part Rumiantsev wrote Prince Mikhail Volkonsky: "You hopefully are unaware that I had to work together with Prince Alexander Mikhailovich [Golitsyn] in all operations. His secret movements always left me perplexed or, to use a better expression, as a blind man who had to grope his way to reach his goal. This was particularly the case with the blockade of Khotin he undertook. The enemy position there made it very dangerous, and there was no way it could be turned to his disadvantage. I had no idea where the operation was headed, so much so that I did not want to make any move to render aid. In fact because of my lack of knowledge I was compelled to remain where I was without budging."

PRINCE PETER IVANOVICH PANIN
Naturally Golitsyn's failure was Rumiantsev's gain. On August 13 Count Chernyshev reported to the council that the empress "in light of various circumstances ordered General Prince Golitsyn recalled from the army. General Count Rumiantsev was to assume command

in his place, and General Count Panin (Peter Ivanovich) was to be named commander of the Second Army." People close to Panin were unhappy that Count Rumiantsev, not Peter Panin, was named commander-in-chief of the First Army. They said that the latter was more capable of offensive operations and of inspiring the army. Rumiantsev was too methodical and wielded such a skilful pen that it would be difficult to send him orders, for he always found a way to explain himself out of them. Rumiantsev's appointment was attributed to feminine intrigue, specifically that of his mother Countess Rumiantseva and his sister Countess Bruce.

"We most graciously have judged it fitting," the memorandum to Golitsyn stated, "under the present circumstances to summon you from the army to our court for personal conversations." The motive behind this was made clear in the memorandum to Rumiantsev: "The circumstances under which I am giving you command of the First Army require some clarification on my part. The army's crossing of the Dniester on August 2, undoubtedly owing to a shortage of forage, gave the enemy cause for rejoicing, although without reason. But I hope that you, with your skill and agility, will not allow the enemy to enjoy this empty glory. When you have the army under your command, an army which in five months has put to flight six times a disorderly mob of countless foes, you must strive in every way possible, not only to regain the advantageous position we have lost, but also to miss no opportunity to enhance it."[27]

CAPTURE OF KHOTIN AND THE DANUBIAN PRINCIPALITIES
Before he left the army Golitsyn was able to take away the Turkish incentive for "empty glory." On August 29 Ali the Moldavian pasha fell on the Russian forces at Kamieniec but was defeated with great losses. The Russians took the offensive and on September 6 inflicted a defeat on the Turks at the Dniester, after which the foe abandoned Khotin and quickly withdrew to Jassy. Khotin, now empty, was taken by the Russians on September 10. On September 16 Golitsyn left the army, and Rumiantsev now took command. On September 26 Lieutenant General Elmpt[28] entered Jassy and administered the oath of allegiance to the empress of all Russia to the inhabitants. "Jassy has been taken," Catherine wrote Bibikov,[29] "and the vizier has retreated across the Danube with a mere five thousand men. Our

forces have advanced to Bucharest. There are more than twenty thousand dead Turkish horses lying on the road from Khotin to Jassy. The new princess of Moldavia salutes you. All Moldavia has sworn allegiance to us, and there are enough cattle for everyone." The new princess of Moldavia expected brilliant results from the offensive. When she learned of the success of the new commander-in-chief of the Second Army, Count Peter Panin, she wrote his brother, Count Nikita, "I particularly am delighted that this occurred as a result of the valiant offensive. Now we shall not be so concerned about the well-deserved destruction of the mob." Golitsyn had been recalled for being too cautious and too careful. The well-deserved destruction of the mob apparently had been unnecessary.

Catherine found it all the more unpleasant to receive reports from the new commander-in-chief of the First Army with complaints about difficulties. She bent every effort to heighten Rumiantsev's sense of pride, stating that everything now was in his hands. He did not have to conform to the campaigns of others. The war now was being fought on a grand scale. The Turks now were being threatened from the east and from the west. Europe looked with fear and horror on the blow dealt to Ottoman power. Catherine urged her commander even more forcefully to intensify his efforts. She reassured him endearingly that he could overcome all obstacles and that she considered him equal to the task.

NAVAL PREPARATIONS

"Our fleet (which is sailing to the Mediterranean)," Catherine wrote Rumiantsev, "has reached Copenhagen safely. Prince Dolgorukov[30] has arrived in Montenegro where great preparations are being made for an attack against the Turks. Count Alexis Grigorevich Orlov[31] affirms that he hopes to raise forty thousand men, and that he has underestimated the number purposely. Three ports have been opened to us. I have sent word to Siniavin[32] that he prepare his squadron for any eventuality. The Georgians have taken the field, Heraclius [Irakli] with thirty thousand and Solomon with twenty thousand men.[33] Thus if everything succeeds and God blesses our cause, we shall see great things in our century, and the Turkish threat will be weakened somewhat. I have been informed also that some Egyptian bey sent word to Venice that he wanted to open relations with us.

He already has dissociated himself in great measure from the Turks, he controls ports, he trades in grain, and he gives rewards to those who bring him news of our victories over the Turks.

"I write about this to you so you can observe the nature of our situation and find out what others think about us. In this way we can have them take a more favorable stance towards us. Europe is watching us. I wish and hope that your efforts have enabled you to find men, and that under your supervision they soon will reach the same state as before. Since everything now is in your hands I do not doubt that you will take the necessary measures to prevent failure and direct all our undertakings to a successful conclusion. I am fully aware of all the difficulties which you described, but I do not doubt that your zeal and your prudence will overcome all obstacles. I have full confidence in you. I want to thank you for the beautiful book you sent. The booty captured from the two leaders was even better. If possible, I would ask you to send me the vizier, or God willing, even the sultan himself."

VICTORIES IN THE PRINCIPALITIES

Bucharest was captured by the Russian forces. The renowned Karazin[34] took it with the help of the Wallachian magnate Cantacuzene,[35] with whom discussions had been held for a long time concerning joint operations to liberate Christians from the Turks. The hospodars[36] of Moldavia and Wallachia were prisoners. The lower Dniester, so important strategically and politically, still was dominated by the powerful fortress of Bender. On September 21 Catherine spoke in the council: "We have not had a similar opportunity for perhaps the last hundred years, and we should take advantage of it. A corps should be detached from the First Army and one from the Second and sent with enough siege artillery to Bender to take the fortress while there is no one to defend it." Catherine wrote Rumiantsev in October: "Concerning the coming campaign, let me tell you the preliminary ideas which have been fermenting in my mind, but which are not yet decided. The coming campaign should be waged on the Danube just as the current one is being waged on the Dniester. If we reach Bender this autumn, I think half our work is done." Bender was not taken in 1769, but the other parts of the general plan were carried out despite all obstacles.

OPERATIONS AT AZOV

The first action of the new year was the capture of Azov and Taganrog. This was a straightforward matter since the Turks had not fortified these locations at the outset of the war. Catherine was concerned about other matters, and she gave the following instructions: "First of all, fortify Azov to defend it against surprise attack, then complete current and all future work speedily and without loss of time." The fortification work was a minor matter. Catherine's major concern was the construction of a flotilla on the sea of Azov, and she pursued this idea with her customary passion. This was evident in her correspondence with Rear Admiral Siniavin who was entrusted with the construction of the flotilla. This correspondence is very reminiscent of the correspondence of Peter the Great on a favorite project. "Alexis Naumovich," wrote Catherine to Siniavin in May, "I am sending to your quarters three drawings which pertain to these locations. (1) Various views of the shores of the Black Sea, all the way to Tsargrad [Constantinople]. (2) The Sea of Azov. (3) A ship which has been built at Voronezh and already launched. I think you will enjoy them and, in addition, you may find them useful. Please let me know if it is possible to raft logs on the Mius river to Troitskoe which is near Taganrog. Please tell me if, in your judgment, there is timber along the Mius suitable for ship building. I think about you more often than I write to you. Please tell me how, in your opinion, the newly planned vessels might perform in the water, and how much time it will take to put them to sea."

Catherine expressed even greater concern about the Azov fleet in a memorandum read in the council session of November 5. "In my opinion, the Taganrog harbor should be put under Siniavin's supervision. Then he could outfit it to shelter as well as build ships, particularly galleys and other vessels that would be useful there. I am giving him an initial sum of two hundred thousand rubles for these purposes and have reached an agreement with him to have the admiralty send the men he needs for his naval forces there. There is no possibility of building, or to put it better, sailing ships along the Don river. It seems our main task on the sea of Azov next year is to complete the newly built fortresses so we can attack Kerch and Taman and capture the fortresses there. Then we will get control of the Black Sea channel, and our ships will be able to cruise to the Tsargrad [Constantinople] channel and the mouth of the Danube. If the Georgians conquer the Black Sea coast, our ships will have the use of a very valuable refuge in case of adverse weather. Therefore, I ask, is the council in agreement with the aforementioned, that we take decisive action to provide that zealous leader Siniavin with everything he might need? I would consider this a great favor, because the Don expedition is a child close to my heart."

"If the Georgians conquer the Black Sea coast." Solomon, the ruler, or as we are accustomed to calling him, the tsar of Imeretia, had been fighting for independence from the Turks since 1755. He fought successfully until enemies appeared in his own domains, drove him out with the help of the Turks and placed his cousin Teimuraz on the throne. In 1766 Solomon petitioned the empress either to grant him asylum in Russia together with some of his princes and noblemen or to intercede on his behalf with the Porte. At the time both requests were denied lest peaceful relations with Turkey be endangered. Nevertheless Solomon, who had been driven into the mountains, sent Maxim, the metropolitan of Kutaisi, to St. Petersburg in 1768 to ask for help. Even before an answer came from Russia he was able to get the upper hand over his enemies and capture his opponent Teimuraz. Since the Russians no longer had to stand on ceremony with the Turks, the empress decided to send a small military unit to demonstrate to the local authorities the superiority of regular military forces. She also decided to send four cannon, two narwhals and fifty thousand rubles in cash. An interesting memorandum written in November 1768 has been preserved which shows Catherine's concern for the Caucasus. The empress sent the following questions to the College of Foreign Affairs: "(1) Why did the father of Heraclius (tsar of Georgia) leave? (2) Does the college have corrected and reliable maps showing where the Georgian domains lie and who their neighbors are? (3) Do the rulers of Georgia have ports on the Caspian or Black Seas? (4) Tiflis on some maps is on the Black Sea, on others the Caspian and on still others lies inland. Please straighten all of this out in the college and report to me. Please note: some time ago there was a rumor that Heraclius had converted to Catholicism. Do you have reliable information on this matter?"

Panin wrote Solomon that he was trying to persuade the Georgian (Kartlian and Kakhetian) tsar Heraclius to take common action against the Turks. Solomon went to Tiflis to meet Heraclius, and both tsars sent prominent envoys to St. Petersburg with a declaration of their readiness to go to war against the Turks. Meanwhile, in the autumn of 1769, Catherine appointed the renowned Count Todtleben[37] to take action against the Turks. He had entreated the empress to take him back into Russian service. Todtleben left Mozdok, crossed the Caucasian Mountains through the Terek and Aragva valleys and took up winter quarters in Georgia.

MUSLIM PEOPLES ENTER RUSSIA

Closer to the Russian frontier in the Kuban and Kabarda the native Muslim subjects of the Porte had to be dealt with. A detachment moved against them under the command of Major General Medem. The main force advancing to the Kuban consisted of Kalmyks who had joined under the leadership of Ubashi, governor general of the khanate. Fighting began in April 1769 with a Kuban attack on the Kalmyks, in which the Kuban forces suffered a serious defeat. After that the Kabardians began to surrender.

An edict was sent to Medem: "A resolution is being sent to you concerning your report about the surrender of the Kabardians. It certainly is necessary to do everything possible to secure the population. Now is the appropriate time to do so since they are afraid of the military forces in the area. Therefore they can be taught to obey like animals instead of chafing against supervision as they have done up to now. Try to keep them down and make them understand that they will be supplied with everything they need here and will retain their previous freedom of action in domestic affairs if they render as much service as their circumstances permit. Now they are asking you for an officer to command them. This is only because of their present need. Perhaps they intend to send him away when the danger is past. But henceforth they always should have a resident officer to whom they submit willingly, without any loss of freedom. This is contingent in the first instance on the person sent to them exercising his command as sympathetically as possible. His actions should be gentle. He should conduct himself in their affairs justly and give clear explanations in response to unnecessary demands.

"Our granting asylum to their runaway serfs along our border has caused trouble between them and us. It seems that in the settlements in Mozdok their serfs habitually run away from them and, after they have left that place [Mozdok], they settle closer to Turkish territory. This proximity creates dissent and draws the attention of the Crimeans. The Kabardians have very few Christian slaves, Georgians and Armenians. They prefer not to take them prisoner themselves but rather acquire them from Crimean slave traders. Balancing the loss of a few Christians against the rescue of many, one must not opt for (the granting of asylum to slaves) in preference to the present necessary concessions to the Kabardians in the matter of their serfs. Future circumstances may create a more favorable situation."

In July Medem, after joining forces with the Kalmyks, inflicted a serious defeat upon the hostile peoples of the Kuban. The outcome of the battle can be judged by the fact that the victors acquired thirty thousand head of cattle. Catherine followed these campaigns attentively. A handwritten note she sent to Count Nikita Panin has been preserved: "The son of the late Bekovich, who is married to Tefkelev's daughter, is here. He is a commissioned officer even though he is a Muslim. I know he is not very clever, but it would not be a bad idea to meet with him and see if he could be useful in Kabardian affairs. He is related to all those mountain princes, he is loyal to us, he is peace-loving and prosperous, and all his domains are on Russian territory."

Part of the Kalmyks moved into the Kuban, while the other part stayed with the First Army. Catherine raised the question whether the Kirghiz would take advantage of the situation to attack the remaining Kalmyks. She wrote Panin: "The question is whether the Kirghiz-Keseks have ever harmed the Kalmyks after Orenburg was built in its present location? When and how? Please find out all about this. If harm has been done, then our maps are completely wrong, since they indicated that the Kirghiz-Keseks of the right bank are protected by the Yaik and Orsk fortresses. I would like to have a clear picture of those locations. "

TURKS INCITE RUSSIA'S MUSLIM SUBJECTS

At the same time the Russians wanted to use the influence of a rich and prominent Muslim who was a Russian subject to win over the inhabitants of Kabarda, measures were taken to organize a widespread insurrection of the Christians in Georgia and Greece against their Muslim oppressors. Meanwhile news was received of unrest among the Muslim population under Russian rule. The natural conclusion was to remove the pretext for such disturbances by abolishing all previous restrictions on the Muslims. While emphasizing the dismal situation of the Christians in Turkish territory, St. Petersburg did not want to call attention to the similar status of Russia's Muslim subjects. Thus the privileges granted to the Muslims during Catherine's reign were the result, not just of the spirit of toleration which Catherine owed to the general philosophical tendency of the time, but also of political considerations stemming from the war with Turkey. An edict sent to the governors of Orenburg and Siberia stated that the College of Foreign Affairs learned of correspondence between Muslims of the provinces of Orenburg and Kazan and the Crimean khan. He intended to come to their aid because their faith was being persecuted.

Chicherin, governor of Siberia,[38] wrote to the empress: "It is impossible for the Muslim inhabitants of the province of Siberia to undertake anything. The distances are too great and they lack the necessary means. Let me report that they are completely loyal to your imperial majesty, particularly under the new system of collecting the tribute and because of the peaceful life and many rewards which they have received through the infinite kindness of your imperial majesty. I cannot say that they do not suffer persecution for their beliefs. The preachers of the word of God, and particularly their growing families, are those most responsible. I wish that useful people would multiply as rapidly as those under the protection of the authorities. When the clergy travel around they inflict great persecution, damage and ruin on the people. Although

I do everything I can to prevent this, I can only oppose the clerical authorities with written statements. I have had no success in this. It is impossible for them to win converts to Christianity, because the clergy do not know one word of the non-believers' languages, nor do the non-believers know one word of Russian." Chicherin requested: (1) That the useless clergy be removed and that schools be established so that they might learn the languages of the peoples to whom they would preach. Neither should they go out to convert before finishing their studies. (2) That those working among the inhabitants of Bukhara and Tashkent be allowed to live in those cities unimpeded. (3) That permission be given for mosques to be erected should the local inhabitants persist in asking for them. If there are but a few mosques, they will be of little use. If there are many mosques, that will not hurt the treasury or cause harm to society. If mosques are allocated in the previous manner on the basis of population, the wide territorial spread of the Muslims will cause problems.

This report put the empress in a difficult situation. On one hand, both for reasons of principle and because of the particular circumstances, she wanted the greatest relaxation possible. On the other hand curtailing Christian evangelization, even temporarily, might give rise to rumors about Catherine's relationship to the church, something she did not want to allow. She answered Chicherin: "We order: (1) That you discuss with the bishop of Tobolsk how the preachers should approach the non-believers in your province, for he has been given directions in this matter by the synod. (2) That those who go to the inhabitants of Bukhara and Tashkent conduct themselves on the basis of the policies of our ancestor Peter I. (3) We put the construction of mosques entirely under your supervision. You are to answer to no one except us. We hope that you will grant such permission according to the policies established by Tsars Ivan and Peter Alekseevich[39] (that mosques not be allowed near Orthodox churches and not be built in Christian areas).

THE PORTE WOOS THE ZAPOROZHIAN COSSACKS
The Muslims who according to the College of Foreign Affairs were Russian subjects were in communication with the Crimean khan.

But it was obvious from the start, as soon as war with Turkey was declared, that Catherine intended to detach the Crimea from Turkey, not to annex it to Russia, but to make it independent. "Her imperial majesty orders that four of the most reliable and most prosperous Kazan Tatars be selected to be sent to the Crimea" stated the protocols of the council for November 6, 1768. The Porte anticipated this policy and sent envoys to the Zaporozhian Cossacks[40] to win them over, threatening them with destruction if they refused. The Zaporozhian Cossacks, however, informed St. Petersburg about the offer and their rejection of it.

Rumiantsev wrote the empress about the matter: "I have learned through long experience to understand the Zaporozhian Cossacks. In the present situation they have shown themselves worthy of the esteem which always has been given them. Just as their military force is important for the defense of our borders, so too it is attractive to other powers. I fail to understand how the sultan could send as an emissary openly, without any prior assurance, someone who under their customary law would be seen as the worst criminal. They would put him under the authority of their commanding hetman[41] and send him under escort to the governor general in Kiev and thus put a stop to any further attempts of this kind. The cossack commander forwarded a report to Voeikov[42] (governor of Kiev) and sent the emissary back to the sultan a few days later with a written reply. I do not know how the correspondence continued between our subject and the enemy, a correspondence which is so suspicious in the present circumstances. Since the Zaporozhian host consists of men not from one but from many nations, I believe this could damage your majesty's best interests." Precisely because of the "present circumstances" it was not considered necessary to require a reply from the Zaporozhians regarding the breach of their duties as subjects.

PLAN TO WIN THE TATARS AWAY FROM THE PORTE

We do not know if the Zaporozhians made similar overtures but, if so, they were not carried through. On October 16, 1769 an order was sent to Count Peter Panin, commander-in-chief of the Second Army: "We are inclined to attempt to induce the Crimea and all the Tatar peoples to waver in their loyalty to the Porte and to plant the idea of establishing their own independent government. Enclosed is the model for a letter from you to the Crimean khan. A letter to the Crimea is best sent through Tatar captives. If you do not hear anything from the Crimean leaders, attract the attention of the Tatars by disseminating copies to various places. At least this might stir up dissension among them."

NAVAL EXPEDITION TO GREECE

Inciting revolution among the Christian subjects of the Turks promised greater success. Thus it was decided to send a squadron to the Mediterranean. This was an unusual endeavor for the Russian fleet and presented great difficulties. As Catherine herself had observed recently, the condition of the fleet was unsatisfactory. It had been impossible to make significant improvements over the past three years for, as Catherine said in 1765, there was neither a fleet nor sailors.

The squadron was to consist of three ships of the line, one frigate, one bomb ship, four pinnaces and two packets. Ten companies of twenty-five men each would be sent on the ships, as well as three to four thousand weapons, including a thousand carbines and five hundred dragoon muskets in the expectation that these would be needed by their allies. It was decided to send thirty cannon as well.

Admiral Grigory Andreevich Spiridov[43] was named commander of the expedition and received the following instructions: "Do not stop or inspect any Christian merchant vessels but give them provisions and all assistance, especially Danish, Prussian and English ships. The first stop on your voyage will be Denmark, on which you can rely completely, because we have a close alliance with the king of Denmark. Then comes Holland, with whom we are on good terms, and whose harbors certainly will be open to you. The case of England is much more delicate. On one hand we are very friendly with the English and share common interests concerning the general European state of affairs on the continent. On the other hand, because of the attitude of its government and its dominant naval power, it easily might happen that England, jealous of all foreign naval operations, might view our expedition with an envious eye, or at least follow it closely. But you can expect that, although the English will not make trouble openly for you in their harbors, they sometimes might find pretexts for doing so in actual practice. We have only formal relations with the Bourbon rulers of France, Spain and Naples, and we are sure that they wish no success for our arms. Nevertheless you should wait for them to oppose your voyage openly. Except in the case of dire necessity, you should avoid their harbors. By their own written indication we have the right to expect all possible aid from the Order of Malta. You should present yourself to the grand master to ask if he will add his ships to your squadron and use the opportunity to share the glory of a great victory with us."

As late as April Catherine still was keeping the goal of the undertaking secret. On April 17 she wrote [Ivan] Chernyshev: "Promise me you will find the foundry for cast iron cannon that I have wanted. For this, sir, I thank you. But if it is rather expensive, what is to be done? It only matters if it can cast cannon with fewer defects than our foundries can, and that it can cast a hundred cannon because we need them far more than ten. Sir! Sir! I need many cannon. I am sailing against the Turkish empire from four sides. I do not know if I will be burned or if I will burn them, but I do know that their cares and troubles have never been turned against them. My army is either now before Khotin or has been repulsed. We have cooked a lot of kasha,[44] and someone will find it tasty. I have an army in the Kuban fighting against the Turks, and I have an army opposing the brainless Poles, ready to do battle with Sweden. Beyond this, I have three half-formed plans *in petto*[45] which I cannot reveal. Send me a naval map of the Mediterranean and the archipelago, if you can do so confidentially. I pray to God that He order everything correctly. Farewell, I wish you good health, and keep silent about this letter."

The more hopes were raised about the impression the appearance of the Russian squadron in Turkish waters would make, the greater was the irritation and chagrin felt when its condition proved unsatisfactory and its voyage slow. The fleet set sail from Kronstadt on July 26. In August the newly-built *Sviatoslav* returned to Reval from Gotland, unable to continue the voyage because of construction defects. In the council on September 7 in the presence of the empress Admiral Mordvinov[46] and Rear Admiral Elphinstone,[47] who was supposed to follow Spiridov, examined a plan of the *Sviatoslav* to discover why it failed. It was decided to correct the defects as soon as possible. Spiridov spent a long time on the voyage to Copenhagen and tarried a long time in the roadstead. He justified himself by citing poor health. Catherine's reply sympathized with him but mentioned the slowness of the voyage to Copenhagen, the lengthy stay there and the growing number of sick men in the fleet, so that many Russian sailors had to be left on shore when the fleet left Copenhagen. The empress also demanded that strict discipline be enforced.

"Unfortunately," the Russian ambassador in Copenhagen, General Filosofov,[48] wrote to St. Petersburg, "our sailors are so ignorant and so ill-disciplined that the rear admiral constantly has great difficulty in dealing with the resentment, grumbling and protests of the officers against the regulations. Moreover he is very distressed to see that most officers want to turn back rather than continue the expedition. Whatever is reported to him about the inadequacy of the ships and suchlike is done solely from this motive, and this has caused all the trouble. For this reason the lower ranks and the entire crew have lost hope, and hope is so necessary for such a difficult expedition." Filosofov gathered all the captains and told them that the rear admiral had full authority over them.

Ivan Chernyshev also noticed the same "loss of hope" among the Russian sailors when the squadron reached England, although Chernyshev did not portray the situation in such a negative light. More importantly, he explained why the squadron, anchored at the mouth of the Humber twenty miles from Hull, was in such bad shape.

Chernyshev wrote Panin: "I did not find that what the admiral had done was as bad as I had heard, but things could have been handled better. But let be done now what can be done! I was displeased above all to see him so depressed, making subordinates unhappy too. Although I could not put right what he had done, I tried to approve and to praise his actions and so correct matters by talking with the soldiers and sailors and visiting all the ships. His depression was caused by the obstacles he had encountered during the voyage, which prevented speedy progress. That was the main reason for the large number of sick men. Up to seven hundred were sick, and more than eight hundred to some degree weakened. Thanks to God's mercy, however, only a few died.

"Since the squadron set sail only forty men died out of more than five thousand. Most of the sick are suffering from flux and fever, which is not surprising since (1) half the crew is made up of conscripts from the Moscow region, who not only have been away from the plow for only a few months but also are quite unused to the sea, ships and naval rations, (2) the sailors were exhausted by the great efforts required to outfit the fleet. Few precautions were taken, and sick men coming from hospitals mingled with healthy recruits, almost all of whom in turn fell sick, and (3) from the crowding on board ship because of the extra crew members. On the other hand they have begun to recover because they have been at anchor and have had fresh meat and green vegetables."

"I have inspected ship No. 2 and the packet *Letuchy*," Chernyshev wrote from Portsmouth. "I found them in very good condition, the crews clean and in good order. They merit this praise, of course, because their commanders have made it possible. There are a great number of sightseers, many from London specifically to see our ships, among them the duke of Cumberland. They are good men, with a lot of veteran sailors and also some recruits. All are from Archangel, all are in uniform, all are happy and all are healthy. Does this not demonstrate the correctness of the regulations based upon the collected instructions of the naval commission to which you agreed and which received the highest approval? Does it not confirm as well the decision taken then to replenish the fleet every year independent of the general conscription? This was based on the indisputable principle that conscripts cannot be made into sailors until they have completed several campaigns at sea. Only the men of Archangel are ready for that.

"The fleet has cost Russia more than one hundred million rubles since 1700, and what do we have to show for it? Perhaps more than nothing, but not much. Had everything been in accord with the wise and generous care our sovereign exercised sending this fleet out, what could not have been accomplished? It has to be admitted with regret, sorrow and disappointment that none of this was evident in the execution of the plans, reminiscent of sending Stepan Fedorovich

Apraksin[49] to the army in 1756 so as to get rid of him. We cannot praise our reception by the English people enough, for they showed us many kindnesses and courtesies besides entertaining us. They accepted Russian copper money at our usual rate, not for its monetary value but as commemorative tokens of the Russian fleet's stay in their ports."

Even so, Catherine could not tolerate Spiridov's slowness and wrote him: "I am very distressed to see how slowly you proceed with the squadron entrusted to you, and how you loiter in various places for God knows what reason, even though the success of your undertaking depends completely on the speed with which you execute it. Although you do not write about it, I have heard that you have many sick men. Judge for yourself whether this is the result of your loitering. When you eat all the provisions on the way and half the people die, the whole expedition becomes shameful and disgraceful for both of us. This is despite the fact that I spared neither money nor effort nor anything else that I could think of to provide you with everything necessary to achieve the desired success. I beg you before God Himself to gather your wits and not allow us to be disgraced before the whole world. All of Europe is watching you and your expedition. For God's sake do not stop, nor think of wintering except in the assigned location."

ORLOV LEADS CHRISTIAN REVOLT

Morea was the assigned location. We have noted that Count Alexis Orlov was supposed to travel to the south for a definitive cure after a dangerous illness.[50] He and his brother Fedor[51] travelled under the name of Ostrovov and spent a long time in Italy. At the same time that his brother Grigory in St. Petersburg proposed inciting the Christian peoples in Turkey to revolt, Alexis Orlov proposed to the empress that she "make use of him together with the Greek and Slavic peoples in the service of the fatherland."

"I have found many of our faith here," he wrote his brother Grigory from Venice, "who would like to serve under our command in the present action against the Turks. We have considerable information that all of Montenegro and the neighboring areas, which are now under Ottoman rule and share our faith, will take up arms. I can report that if I do what I can in this situation, the results will be good. In my opinion this is the only way to disrupt the flow of supplies and to create divisions within the (Turkish) army. If we advance we should advance to Constantinople and free all Orthodox and God-fearing people from the heavy yoke they now bear.

"I will say what was said in the declaration of Tsar Peter I, that the Muslim infidels must be driven out into the fields and into the empty and sandy steppes where they lived before. There the fear of God will reign again, and we shall say 'Glory to our Almighty God.' It seems to me that it will not be difficult to incite this people against the Turks. They will obey me. They are brave, and they love me and my comrades because we share the same faith. They are eager to do everything I command. You advance with one goal in mind, but I do so with another. In my opinion, if anything is to be accomplished, it should follow the example of Tsar Peter I. The court should send them a very friendly declaration with an upright, reliable and talented man. Be as wary as you can of the imperial [Habsburg] court. As far as I have been able to observe myself, and from what I often have learned in various conversations, they are our greatest enemies. Accordingly I sent men out to talk with the common people and merchants, and I can say that all of them want our army to be defeated. No one envies as much as they do the greatness and glory of our people."

"On the basis of your brother's proposal," Catherine answered him on January 29, "we have considered making a significant diversion against the enemy, both on the Greek coast and inland, as well as on the islands of the archipelago. We now have more recent information from you that the people there are inclined to revolt against the Porte, and that has confirmed our opinion. Thus we are fully confident of your loyalty to us, of your talent and your ardent wish to be a useful citizen and son of the fatherland. It is with pleasure therefore that we grant our approval of your request and entrust you with the preparation, command and direction of this entire undertaking."

RELATIONS WITH THE BALKAN CHRISTIANS

The empress informed Orlov of the men who would be sent to incite the Christians of the Balkan peninsula to revolt. Colonel Ezdemirovich and Lieutenant Belich would be sent to Montenegro.

The former had served for a long time in Russia and had led a large number of their countrymen and their families into New Serbia.[52] The latter recently was sent by the Montenegrin reformer Stepan Maly[53] to ask for help against the Turks. Catherine wrote: "We have decided to use Belich's arrival to our advantage and to make him a weapon in our cause." The Venetian Greek Petushin was sent to the Albanian chief Bukoval and to the Maina chief Mavromikhali. Some years earlier he had brought a letter from them to St. Petersburg expressing their willingness to be of service to Russia. The famous Lieutenant Colonel Nazar Karazin was ordered to the Danubian principalities and other interior Turkish districts.

Catherine described the plan of action to Orlov: "Our guiding principle and basis of our conduct must be to consider the insurrection of each people separately. Moreover we cannot make the same preparations on behalf of and do the same things for neighboring peoples at the same time, or at least very soon after taking arms. It is not to our advantage that none of us be powerful enough to accomplish anything but an isolated victory; that is, just a temporary devastation of some portion of the neighboring territory. As a result each victory of this kind neither deals a significant blow to the enemy nor creates a useful diversion for our benefit, the only way to reach our main goal. This would do nothing but open the eyes of the Turks and impel them to acquire what they needed to defend themselves as quickly as possible against further attempts. It is much easier to prevent one spark from catching fire than to take action later and quench a roaring blaze.

"Therefore our primary and greatest task is to forge a firm mutual understanding and mutual agreement among all of those peoples, or at least among a great number of them. We must convince them of the general benefit and general hope of freeing everyone from the infidel yoke. We must also convince all Orthodox Christians that they must defend the holy church and the cause of religion. You should make your preparations and carry out your measures in strictest secrecy so that taking arms occurs everywhere at the same time as much as possible, or at least with one group rising quickly after another. They should take concerted and effective action against the enemy from various sides, because it will not be possible to execute a planned surprise attack with small and scattered units from each group. We further must decide how to continue the campaign and where to set up a reliable assembly point. An assembly point is needed to assure the necessary provisions for those gathering, and as an occasional refuge against attacks of superior forces."

Orlov was supposed to circulate the following appeal to the Christian peoples of Turkey: "We, by the grace of God, Catherine II, and so on, make the following proclamation to all the Greek and Slavic peoples of the Orthodox faith, both to the inhabitants of the mainland and of the islands of the archipelago. The present state of those ancient and pious peoples now under the yoke of the Ottoman Porte is a cause of great regret. The innate cruelty of the Turks and their hatred of Christianity is mandated by the Muslim faith which strives at once to ruin both the souls and the bodies, not only of Christians who are their subjects and slaves, but also of those who are their neighbors. Force is the only way to curb these sons of Hagar in their evil ways, for until now they have known no bounds. The Ottoman Porte is accustomed to show its malevolence towards our Orthodox church because of our efforts to secure the privileges long established for the church by treaties in Poland. These privileges now are being taken away from the Orthodox by force. The Turks thirst for revenge, and they scorn not only all human rights, but even truth itself. To mention only one instance of their treachery, they have broken the perpetual treaty of peace concluded with our empire, and they have begun to wage a most unjust war against us without any legal justification. This now has convinced us to use the weapons God has given us. This is happening at the same time that Christians groaning under their yoke feel their oppression all the more keenly....

"As we consider the pitiful condition of the pious sons of God's church, it is our most gracious judgment and our wish to deliver them from this condition as speedily as possible. Given what our armies have done already, it remains only for them to take action themselves. We call upon them individually and collectively to take advantage of the present war to throw off their yoke and regain their former independence. They must take up arms whenever and wherever necessary against the common foe of all Christians and try to do him all possible harm. Thus they will help both the common cause and themselves. This common cause will be strengthened and will be a sacred and indissoluble bond when our haughty foe, the Ottoman Porte, is forced to ask us to conclude peace. It will be our greatest pleasure to see the Christian lands delivered from base slavery and see their peoples under our leadership follow in the footsteps of their ancestors. Henceforth we shall use every means available to achieve this goal. We shall extend to them our protection and our favor to safeguard what they achieve by their brave deeds in our war with the treacherous foe."

RELATIONS WITH MONTENEGRO

The call to action was proclaimed to the Greeks and Slavs of the Balkan peninsula. Among the Slavs the Montenegrins were more familiar to the Russians than the others. There had been frequent contacts, especially during the reigns of Peter the Great and his daughter Elizabeth. We have observed how Alexis Orlov made special mention of them. At the end of Elizabeth's reign Collegiate Councillor Puchkov was sent to them with fifteen thousand rubles. He was supposed to explain to their leaders that if the Montenegrins were able to reach agreement among themselves and establish order, arm themselves and wage war on a regular basis with good discipline, Russia would send them fifteen thousand rubles a year. Puchkov was supposed to deliver a letter and money to Metropolitan Savva[54] in the presence of several lay leaders. He was supposed ascertain the current state of affairs, their loyalty to Russia and whether they might be useful to Russia. In addition, he was to determine whether the payments sent from St. Petersburg with the Montenegrin prelates actually had reached the people.

Puchkov returned in 1760 and reported to the College of Foreign Affairs that the Montenegrins lived in the utmost disorder, without sound institutions, laws or customs. They existed in a state of internecine strife and mutual hostility and did not obey their leaders. These leaders cared nothing for the welfare of their people but only for their own profit. Thus the prelate Vasily used every kind of cunning and deception to cheat Puchkov of the money he had brought. To give credence to his swindle he sent commoners to Puchkov, claiming one was a prince, another a boyar and the third the son of a boyar. The Montenegrin leaders said little or nothing about Russia and distributed the Russian funds to a few of their relatives. Justice was unknown in Montenegro because each house and family was a law unto itself. Disputes were decided by representatives who stabbed and shot each other, then fled into neighboring lands. Powerful families oppressed weaker ones; when a murderer belonged to a large family, he lived at home peacefully and settled the matter with a cash payment. The prelates and their associates functioned as peacemakers, but in such cases they looked to their own advantage and sometimes even fanned the flames. The Montenegrins were a very unsettled people, inclined to brigandage and very willful. They were quite ignorant of the teaching of their religion, doing no more then bowing while making the sign of the cross and keeping the fasts. Puchkov concluded his report by stating that, although the Montenegrins were a savage people, "with good leadership and moral formation it is possible in time (although with difficulty) to make something worthwhile out of them. No one would be able to do this better than their two prelates, the so-called Montenegrin sovereigns, provided that the prelate Vasily, who by nature is a restless, highly ambitious, money-grubbing, trouble-making slanderer, is not one of them."

In 1762 when Catherine was already on the throne the Montenegrins Nikolay and Ivan Petrovich travelled to St. Petersburg and delivered a letter from their prelates Savva and Vasily Petrovich. In this letter were requests that Vasily be allowed to travel to Russia, that Montenegro be liberated from the Turkish yoke and that an edict be issued directing how the Montenegrins should deal with their enemies, the people of Ragusa,[55] who were slandering them to the Porte.

On the basis of Puchkov's report the College of Foreign Affairs informed the empress that order had not yet been established in Montenegro, and that it would be difficult to establish it. Moreover Russia could expect nothing from these people except unnecessary trouble and worse relations with the Turkish court and the republic of Venice. Therefore it was the judgment of the College of Foreign Affairs that the envoys be sent with a letter from the chancellor back to the Montenegrin prelates. This letter would state that the Montenegrin people should live peacefully and quietly and not afford the Turks or their other neighbors any occasion for hostilities.

The prelate Vasily should not be allowed to travel to Russia because he was needed in his own country. With the letter the Petroviches took two gold medallions commemorating Catherine's coronation and a hundred gold pieces. Despite the letter Vasily Petrovich appeared for the third time in St. Petersburg in 1765 under the pretext of congratulating the empress upon her accession to the throne. As was customary he asked for assistance in church restoration and for a chasuble and miter for himself. The chasuble, the miter and the five hundred rubles, however, were sent to Metropolitan Savva, because Vasily died in St. Petersburg in March 1766. Relations cooled noticeably. Catherine said openly that the College of Foreign Affairs was quarrelling with the Montenegrins. Meanwhile a new reason for dissatisfaction came to light.

THE STEPAN MALY AFFAIR

As a result of unusual intelligence received in 1768 a circular was sent to the governors of the border provinces informing them that an impostor had appeared in Montenegro who was passing himself off as Emperor Peter III.[56] "It is not enough that this impostor has taken refuge among the Montenegrins and gathered a band around him, with whom he has begun to rob merchant caravans. He has taken it into his head to send emissaries in various directions to publicize his claims."

Reports from various quarters revealed that a man named Stepan Maly had come to Montenegro from Bosnia at the end of 1766. He claimed to be a physician and treated the wounded. At the same time on every suitable occasion he spoke as an inspired prophet about the necessity to improve the morals and customs of Montenegro, to reform family life and to stop the blood feuds among the clans. A Russian officer was in Montenegro who had brought the effects left by the late Metropolitan Vasily in St. Petersburg. Stepan became acquainted with this officer and conversed with him frequently. As a result of these conversations he conceived the idea of passing himself off as the Russian emperor Peter III. The powerful appeal of this title would bring about the transformation the Montenegrins needed to wage a successful battle with the Turks.

In 1767 Stepan went from Montenegro to Bocca da Cattaro where he worked as a stonemason. There he persuaded one of his comrades, also a stonemason, to take a letter of his to Russia. Then he went to the town of Maina where he lived with the workmen employed by a certain Marko Bukovich Bovar, whose wounded brother he treated. He began to make secret pronouncements. "When the Lord God returns, then I shall act so that no one of you shall bear any kind of weapon." Rumors spread among the people that Stepan Maly was no ordinary man. It was said that the stonemason whom he sent to Russia cried when he saw a portrait of Peter III in a monastery. According to other reports he claimed to be Ivan Antonovich,[57] who had been saved from death. People recalled that during his exhortations he had said: "You are close to the sovereign." Also when someone once leaned against him he said: "If you knew against whom you are leaning, you would run from him as from a fire."

In the meantime it was rumored that the Russian emperor Peter III was alive and lived in Asiatic lands. People were found who testified to Stepan Maly's likeness to the portrait of Peter III, and suddenly almost everyone began to recognize him as Peter. Metropolitan Savva and the popular assemblies sent elders to Stepan Maly to ask him who he was. He answered: "When you acknowledge the true God and establish genuine and lasting peace among you, so that henceforth there will be no disagreement or shedding of blood, you will know who Stepan Maly is." Then he summoned the metropolitan before him and chastised him for allowing the people to live as animals. He demanded that the metropolitan gather all the inhabitants of Montenegro and establish universal and perpetual peace among them. They should pardon each other's offenses, and henceforth everyone who had a grievance should seek satisfaction from the court and not take private vengeance.

A popular assembly was held on October 1. Marko Tamovich, who had accompanied the late Bishop Vasily on his trip to Russia, was the first to speak. He affirmed that Stepan Maly was the real Peter III whom he had known in St. Petersburg. When they learned of the demands of the supposed Russian emperor, the assembly agreed to conclude a general peace which was to last until the spring of 1768; that is, until the convocation of a new assembly on St. George's day [April 24]. Maly became angry when he was informed that the assembly had rejected a perpetual peace in favor of one for just six months. When the elders told him of the decision of the assembly he said: "Whoever takes another man's wife must give her back. Whoever sends his wife away and marries another must take the first one back and send away the second. If you do this neither God nor the Russian court will abandon you."

A new assembly was summoned on October 8, where a beginning was made towards achieving a general and perpetual peace. All swore not to renew internecine conflict. They elected Stanishich governor, and the elders again went to Maina to inform Stepan Maly what had happened. Maly met them with a drawn saber at the head of an armed detachment and thanked them for their obedience to his counsels. The elders fell to their knees, recognized him as the tsar and called upon him to manifest himself openly. "Hear, O Montenegrins and neighboring peoples," Maly answered, "the voice of the most high God and the glory of the holy Jerusalem. I did not come hither of my own accord but was sent here by God, to whose voice I hearkened. Arise, go forth, and go about your tasks, for I will aid you." In conclusion Maly promised to make the Montenegrins happy forever.

From that time on Emperor Peter Fedorovich, his consort Catherine and his heir Paul Petrovich were remembered in church services. Metropolitan Savva recognized Maly as Peter III. Later, when Savva realized that he was losing all authority to Maly, he began to oppose him, but quickly made his peace with Maly once again. Maly appeared to be a little more than thirty years old, thin and of medium height. He had an oblong face and a fair complexion, light brown hair with a broad and prominent forehead and small, grey, deep-set eyes that darted here and there. His nose was long and narrow, his mouth was large and he spoke in a feminine voice. Besides Serbian, Maly could speak German, French and Italian.

When the Montenegrin monk Sofrony Plevkovich travelled to Kiev he reported that Stepan Maly lived at first with Marko Bukovich as a holy fool,[58] but then revealed himself as Peter III. He did not want to be called by that name, but rather as Stepan Maly.

When Marko heard this he fell to his knees and kissed Stepan's feet. Then Maly summoned the metropolitan and the elders and proclaimed to them that he was Peter III. He added that if they did not obey him the funds from Russia would be cut off. Sofrony said that Maly had begun to raise a regular army and to give them military training. Maly summoned Sofrony and asked him to go to Emperor Joseph [II][59] in Vienna. When Sofrony asked Maly who he was, the latter answered: "If you are questioned about this great secret, it will be enough to say that you have heard that I am Stepan Maly. I have been sent neither by Caesar nor by the tsar but by the Lord God of Hosts Himself to save the Christian people, since for ten years the Turks have fed upon my bread."

Sofrony was supposed to ask Vienna to send warships and armed forces. Sofrony was detained and questioned in Glatz.[60] He was told that he should return home and that the emperor could not send forces to aid Maly. Sofrony, unable to pass through Turkish territory, went to Russia. He embellished his previous description of the pretender's appearance. Stepan's lower lip was thick and protruding. He had a thin black mustache and dark brown hair. He had some smallpox scars, and his whole forehead was covered entirely by a linen band, concealing two prominent veins. According to Sofrony, Maly knew many languages: Italian, Turkish, German, French, English, Greek and some Arabic, in addition to Serbian.

The empress wrote Alexis Orlov concerning Stepan Maly: "Major General Podgorichany has reason to suspect that Stepan Maly is the same Italian Vandini whom the chancellery here dealt with. He got diamonds from a Greek merchant by fraud, pawned them, took the money and made his escape. Podgorichany said that the descriptions of the figures and the faces were identical. Although Vandini was pockmarked while the other was not, Podgorichany wrote that when Stepan came to Montenegro he had smallpox and so he is now pockmarked, even though he was not when he was in St. Petersburg."

At first the Russians wanted to use Sofrony by sending him to Montenegro to incite the local population to revolt against the Turks in concert with Stepan Maly, persuading the latter to abandon his imposture. Instructions for Sofrony already had been drafted, but the matter was reconsidered, and a notation on the document indicates that it was not implemented. Sofrony set out with Admiral Spiridov's fleet. Count Alexis Orlov wrote the empress that he could not approve those chosen to go to incite rebellion among the Turkish Christians: "It is most desirable that everything be done as we wish, and that we win fame in this epoch by saving thousands and thousands of our coreligionists suffering under the barbarian yoke. Although this may not be accomplished as speedily as you and I would want, it is essential for the success of this great venture that you have begun as you have described it to me. For that I give you great praise. Those who were sent from here, however, deserve no praise, and it is apparent that the undertaking is marked by a certain carelessness. Almost from the very beginning of the war when Count Grigory Grigorevich [Orlov] proposed sending a fleet to the Mediterranean we thought that we could win over the same people with whom we now are dealing. The College of Foreign Affairs now believes that we presently are on bad terms with the Montenegrins.

"It should be recognized that the majority of the Greek, Serbian and other Orthodox adventurers now are beginning to push ahead with plans, projects and negotiations. Lieutenant Colonel Ezdemirovich has landed in their midst. He made a very good impression, because earlier he led several hundred people from various ethnic groups to settle in New Russia. They had begun to negotiate with Ezdemirovich when Efim Belich, who stayed in the same camp with Ezdemirovich, arrived. Belich revealed that he was sent by Stepan Maly. We previously sent a public manifesto to the Montenegrins saying that Maly was a deceiver. But since they thought Maly was so powerful they decided to use him [Belich] and forbade the use of the deceiver. They sent out Ezdemirovich and Belich because they were the best at hand. I think they also used the Greek Petushin on a similar mission since they could not find anyone better."

Sofrony was not sent to Montenegro lest he add to the number of "adventurers" there. But the choice of the College of Foreign Affairs turned out to be unfortunate. In the summer of 1768 Merck, a councillor at the Russian embassy in Vienna, was sent to Montenegro to appeal to the local inhabitants not to believe the impostor. On August 9 Merck reported that going to Montenegro meant death because the Montenegrins were committed totally to

Maly. Catherine made a note on the report. "If a captain of the guards were sent with a circular to the Montenegrins, it certainly would be delivered, but this would-be politician brought it back undelivered because he thought it over too much. My advice is to recall him from Vienna, because here obviously he will be very useful in important matters, but there he will be just a drain on the resources of the college."

RELATIONS WITH VENICE

Major General Prince Yury Vladimirovich Dolgoruky was sent to Montenegro with a circular calling on Christians to rise against the Turks. He was armed and travelled as a merchant named Baryshnikov. Good relations with Montenegro required agreement with the Venetian republic. It seemed that Venice, a long-time opponent of the Porte, would be quick to sympathize with the Russian cause. But Venice was a rotting corpse, no longer the courageous ruler of the southern seas. The Venetian government feared that change of any kind might harm or even destroy the slumbering body politic. Venice feared everyone and everything; Turkey, Sardinia, Austria, and now particularly Russia, or any Russian impetus towards peace between the Slavs and the Greeks, and therefore feared its Slavic and Greek subjects might revolt.

Marquis Maruzzi[61] had acted on Russia's behalf with the republic of Venice since 1768. He was supposed to persuade the Venetian government that it would be advantageous to ally with Russia against the common foe. Any territory conquered would go to Venice, since the distance was such that Russia neither wanted it nor would be able to hold it. Maruzzi wrote Panin that the Venetians nevertheless were terribly afraid of the Turks since all their wars with the Turks had been disastrous for the republic. Russia was far away and could render no aid. Maruzzi did achieve one result, having the Venetian senate establish naval links with the Montenegrins.

Concerning Montenegro, Maruzzi wrote that Metropolitan Savva was the one most responsible for the current troubles and for the prominence of Stepan Maly. Maly was convinced that the present war between Russia and the Porte was being waged solely to make him ruler of the lands between Scutari and Ragusa. In September

1769 Maruzzi reported to Russia that Prince Dolgrouky had gained entry to Montenegro, that he had captured Stepan Maly and that he had received permission from the governor at Cattaro to take the impostor under guard through Venetian territory to Russia. The governor received permission from the senate to allow this. Maruzzi also wrote that the Venetian government had agreed to Maly's arrest.

The Venetians were not happy at other news. They found out that when Count [Alexis] Orlov was in Venice he invited Slavic subjects of Venice to arm corsairs against the Turks. Ships for this purpose were being outfitted at Leghorn. The Venetians were very angry at this, fearing it would lead to enmity with the Turks. The governor of Cattaro informed the senate that Dolgoruky was inciting the Greeks, particularly those who were the subjects of the Porte. The governor suspected that Dolgoruky was carrying on secret negotiations with Greek subjects of the republic. Every day soldiers were deserting Venetian regiments. These deserters were going to Montenegro, where they received fifteen solidi a day in addition to provisions. Only Slavs were enrolled, while no notice was taken of Italians. The governor reported Dolgoruky's boast that the Russian squadron soon would be there. Dolgoruky was advising Turkish subjects to live peacefully and pay tribute while awaiting the proper time to revolt. Armed forces were already in action in Montenegro. The governor thought that Venetian districts would be in great danger when the Russian squadron appeared. He noted that many settlements already sympathized with the Russian cause, and that many people were implicated in clandestine disturbances.

When this information reached the senate one of its members stated that the matter had to be dealt with carefully, and that they should not wait until it was too late to opt for the side which offered the greater advantage. The Russian squadron soon would be in Venetian waters. All of the republic's harbors were unfortified and lay wide open. Russian vessels could enter the Cattaro channel easily. Once the Russian squadron arrived the Montenegrins would become even bolder. Venice should think in advance about its army, its fleet and its finances, for all were in very bad condition.

The other senators replied that they should wait to see what the Venetian envoy who had been sent to Moravia for negotiations with Kaunitz[62] wrote. No decision should be made until an answer had been received from Kaunitz. The situation was in fact critical, but it was necessary to ascertain the opinion of the Viennese court. An answer came from the oracle of Vienna. When the Venetian ambassador told Kaunitz about the situation in Montenegro and about the senate's decision not to allow foreign vessels to enter the harbor of the republic, Kaunitz replied that Austria and the duke of Tuscany[63] would follow the same policy. The senate then decided to strengthen the fleet.

PRINCE YURY DOLGORUKY'S VISIT TO MONTENEGRO

In October [Alexis] Orlov summoned Maruzzi to Pisa to discuss Montenegrin affairs and instructed him to obtain permission from the Venetian government for Russian officers to cross the territory of the republic en route to Montenegro. When he returned from Pisa, Maruzzi found a letter sent by Prince Dolgoruky from Ancona stating that he had been forced to leave Montenegro and hand over authority to Stepan Maly because of the natives' unstable character and barbarian mores!

Dolgoruky saw Maly for the first time on August 2 at the Burchel monastery. Maly had arrived on horseback accompanied by a number of Montenegrins. Let Dolgoruky describe his impressions of the impostor in his own words: "His speech, his actions and his manner prove he is a ridiculous comedian and a windy, totally undisciplined vagabond. He is of medium height, clean-shaven with a fair complexion. He has curly light brown hair which he combs back. He is thirty-five years old. His white silken gown is long in the Greek style. He wears a red skullcap. A narrow golden chain holding an icon about the size of a Russian ruble hangs from his left shoulder, attached to an embroidered case under his right arm. He carries an ordinary Turkish pick in his hands. His voice is thin, like a woman's, and he speaks quickly. He speaks for the most part like a vagabond. His utterances are obscure, verbose and senseless. Yet the Montenegrins fear him and submit to him because of his elegant prophecies. He usually smoked a pipe while drinking a glass of vodka and water, a longstanding habit." When Dolgoruky set out for Cetinje he received a letter from the metropolitan that Stepan Maly was traveling through various villages inciting the inhabitants to revolt. Dolgoruky sent the governor an order to arrest the impostor and take him to the Cetinje monastery. According to Dolgoruky the governor held the principal hereditary rank in Montenegro, but this meant nothing, given the anarchy which reigned there. At the time the governor was a young man, twenty years old.

People began to gather on the field at Cetinje after dinner on August 6. A proclamation from the metropolitan exposing the blindness of the Montenegrins about Stepan Maly was read to the assembly. The proclamation called him an impostor, a flatterer and a vagabond. The metropolitan exhorted the Montenegrins to repudiate the pretender and to atone for their sins through devotion and service to the imperial Russian court. When they heard the proclamation the governor and other authorities asked Dolgoruky to give them a written copy of the proclamation with a seal. Dolgoruky issued a statement that Stepan was an impostor who was not recognized in Russia. This statement was read to the people, who listened to it calmly. After dinner a proclamation from the empress was read, and the people were invited to swear an oath of allegiance. Then wine and money were distributed.

At five o'clock in the morning of the next day, August 7, Dolgoruky was awakened by a noisy disturbance. Stepan Maly had appeared, and people flocked to him from everywhere. Dolgoruky went and ordered the people to disperse and that Stepan be seized and taken to prison. This was done. The people who originally had flocked to Stepan now suddenly began to shout that he be hanged, and Dolgoruky had great difficulty in calming the crowd. Under questioning, Maly revealed that he was a Turkish subject born in Bosnia, who had left Bosnia as a youth and wandered around in many countries, finally arriving in Montenegro.

Dolgoruky's troubles did not end with the imprisonment of the impostor. Dolgoruky so little understood and so little sympathized with the mores and customs of the Montenegrins that it was impossible for him to reach an understanding with them. It is not surprising that in all Montenegro he found only one man he could understand and who could understand him. That man was Stepan Maly, precisely because he was not sympathetic to the Montenegrin way of life and was trying to transform it, following models he had seen in foreign lands; but Stepan knew how to deal with the

Montenegrins and began to take advantage of their religious feelings. He gained influence as a prophet and struck another responsive chord in his effort to gain power by inciting the people to believe that this secret reformer and prophet was none other than the emperor of Russia. He was careful not to reveal himself openly and ceremoniously as Peter III.

This game led him to prison and almost to the gallows. He did not spend long in prison. Dolgoruky, despairing of accomplishing anything in Montenegro, cursed the savage mores of the people there and left. Before his departure he freed Maly and convinced him to swear that he would serve Russia loyally and diligently. He gave Maly a Russian officer's uniform and supreme authority over Montenegro. Subsequently Maly, dazzled by his success, perished as a result of his treachery.

RELATIONS WITH PAOLI

Maruzzi was also instructed to open relations with Paoli[64] who, after the French purchased Corsica from the Genoese, raised the standard of revolt on the island to overthrow French rule. Catherine wanted to aid in this struggle and, in assisting Paoli, to support a useful ally in opening new prospects in the Mediterranean. Together they could pay back the duke of Choiseul[65] for inciting Turkey against Russia. "I pray every morning," Catherine wrote to Ivan Chernyshev, "that the Lord rescue the Corsican from the clutches of the dishonorable French." On March 21 Paoli replied to Maruzzi's letter that the best thing for him would be to proclaim the coincidence of Russian and Corsican interests. Paoli told Maruzzi's envoy that he hoped Russia would aid him with warships. "With twelve ships and my infantry," he said, "I can drive the French out of Corsica." But relations with Paoli soon had to be broken off. His allies abandoned him and he had to flee Corsica.[66]

CATHERINE'S SITUATION IN 1769

This little setback could not dim Russian hopes raised by the appearance of the Russian squadron in the Mediterranean. Maruzzi wrote [Nikita] Panin: "Now that our fleet is in the Mediterranean we can help all the Greeks who have taken up arms. It is a sign of our approval. The fleet can capture Turkish vessels carrying grain

С. Торелли: Екатерина II.
(Собств. кн. К. Э. Бѣлосельскаго-Бѣлозерскаго).

S. Torelli: L'Impératrice Catherine II.
(App. au prince C. Bélosselsky-Bélozersky).

S. Torelli

Empress Catherine II

from Egypt to Constantinople. Since the Turkish navy is in bad condition, it will not be difficult for the Russian fleet to reach Constantinople. This should be done in the initial campaign before the Turks have the chance to improve their warships." Thus it is easy to see why the squadron's tardiness so exasperated Catherine, and why she wrote the letter she did to Spiridov. She was exasperated likewise with the tardiness of the land forces when they recrossed the Dniester under Prince Golitsyn.

It must be remembered that success was much more important for Catherine, who had reigned for less than ten years, than for sovereigns who had come to the throne by ordinary means. Her brilliant legislative accomplishments, her triumph over all hostile forces at home and her successes abroad in Poland had enhanced the glory of the empress of Russia and given her the reputation of an extraordinary woman. But her enemies had been able to put a great obstacle in her path by waging two wars against Russia. How could Catherine, who already was being called the Great, escape this difficult situation? Failure proved that this title was premature. Her reputation was diminishing both abroad and at home. Both abroad, and especially at home, this could have the most serious consequences. Catherine lived through hard times until autumn. She found the triumphs of her foes unbearable. The French newspapers exaggerated the Russian defeats, and they celebrated the supposed victories of the Turks and the Tatars. The *Cologne Gazette* echoed the same theme.

CORRESPONDENCE WITH BIELCKE AND VOLTAIRE

"Let us proceed with courage!" Catherine wrote Bielcke,[67] a close friend since childhood. "This has been my motto in good times and in bad. I have lived for forty years, and how can the present misfortunes compare with those of the past?" Describing the defeat of the Turks at Khotin, Catherine continued: "Azov and Taganrog have been taken. Both were razed in 1739 by French mediation,[68] but I restored them without mediation. Since work was begun on those cities not one foe has appeared. Since the winter the Tatar leaders have lost their appetite for raids against us. In three attempts they have had no success anywhere, thanks to General Rumiantsev's orders. They may have fired off cannon in Constantinople to celebrate the khan's successes, and the *Cologne Gazette*, thanks to the papal nuncio and the French minister, may have killed off seventy thousand of our men in New Serbia, which according to us is called New Russia. But it is also true that this campaign cost the khan his life. The Porte ordered him to set out with five of the most important members of the Turkish gentry class [murzas] and attributed his failure to penetrate our frontiers to bad intentions. The comedy of firing off the cannon in Constantinople was staged to encourage the army, which had shown no great desire to set out on a campaign."

In June Catherine wrote Voltaire: "Not all of your compatriots share your opinion of me. They like to persuade themselves that I cannot do anything well. They bend every effort to convince others of this, and woe betide their underlings who dare to think otherwise. My glory depends not on them but on my principles and on my deeds. I find comfort in their censure, and I forgive as a good Christian should. You tell me that you agree with my opinions on my various affairs and that you take an interest in them. You will be interested to know that my beautiful colony in Saratov already numbers twenty-nine thousand inhabitants and, despite the *Cologne Gazette*, is not at all afraid of Turkish, Tatar or other raids. Each canton has a church of its own denomination. The fields are cultivated peacefully, and no taxes are to be paid for thirty years.

"Besides our taxes in Russia are so reasonable that there is not a single peasant who cannot eat chicken whenever he wishes, and who for some time has not preferred turkey to chicken. It is also true that the export of grain, which is permitted under certain limitations to prevent abuses without restricting trade, has raised the price of grain and has given cultivators more resources. Thus agriculture is stronger every year. In the past ten years the population has increased ten percent. It is true we are now at war, but Russia long has practiced this profession and is more flourishing at the end of the war then at the outset. Our laws are following their course, and work on them is continuing without fanfare. While they are now only of secondary concern, nothing is lost thereby.

"Since the beginning of the war I have completed two projects. I built Azov and Taganrog, where there is a harbor, begun and then destroyed under Peter I. As you please, the Turks were beaten on

April 19 and 20. I thought we made a decent beginning of the affair. It can be said that human intelligence is the same for all. The absurdity of the Crusades did not prevent the Polish clergy, under the influence of the papal nuncio, from preaching a crusade against me. These insane self-styled confederates took the cross in one hand and signed an alliance with the Turks with the other to lay waste their own provinces which the Turks had promised them. Why? In order to prevent a quarter of the Polish population from enjoying the rights of citizens."[69]

The treaty about which the empress spoke contained the following terms. A defensive and offensive alliance was concluded. Poland would raise an army of one hundred thousand men and the Porte one of two hundred thousand. The borders would be those of the Treaty of Carlowitz,[70] except that Poland would cede the region of Kiev to the Porte and take Smolensk, Starodub, Chernigov and Livonia from Russia in return. Poland, in gratitude for services rendered, would hand over freely all Russian Orthodox peasants to the Porte, particularly in those areas where revolts had broken out. Poland also would hand over all dissidents, their wives and their children, except for the leaders of the revolt, whom the Commonwealth[71] itself would try and punish. The Porte would not forbid its subjects, Muslims included, from settling in Ukraine and Podolia.

Catherine also would have been able to inform Voltaire about the vizier's reception of one of the leaders of the confederation, Joachim Potocki.[72] When he was invited to a council of war Potocki stated that he was asking the Porte in the name of the Commonwealth to put a certain number of troops under his command. With this force he would drive the Russians and all their allies out of Poland and restore its former liberty to the Commonwealth, the liberty to which it was entitled under the Treaty of Carlowitz. Hearing the word "Carlowitz" the vizier flew into a rage and told the interpreter: "Tell that dog not to mention Carlowitz again. The Carlowitz agreement no longer exists, and it is they who have broken it. According to the law whoever makes an alliance with our enemy himself becomes our enemy. My all-powerful autocrat, the refuge of kings, who hands out crowns as he pleases, is not the servant of these dogs and has no need of them to lead our armies. But if he (Potocki) wants me to send him with a seraskir,[73] then he can bow down to the ground and kiss my feet. In that case as one who has sought our protection, no harm will come to him. Mercy will be shown to all who submit to us with a noose around their necks, but the sword will fall upon others who ally themselves with the Russians. The mighty sultan wishes to hear nothing about this cursed liberty which they have lost, and they and the Russians can go to the devil!" Potocki replied mildly that he would obey the seraskir completely and that he would unite the confederates under his authority. The vizier was satisfied with the answer and said, "Speak thus, but do not betray us!" Then turning to one of the pashas he said, "If the Poles adopt the Muslim faith we shall help them willingly."[74]

RELATIONS WITH POLAND

The Turks were unable to help the Poles, and the latter did not have to adopt the Muslim faith. But magical events occurred in Poland as soon as Russia declared war on Turkey. People quickly began to stir, and fantasy ran riot. An enfeebled body which could do nothing for itself waited until the very end for salvation from outside. Their dream was that the conflict would not be limited to Turkey. A European coalition would emerge and France, Austria, Prussia, Saxony, Sweden, Austria and even England would take up arms. Russia would be defeated and forced to renounce all its Polish acquisitions. King Stanislaw Augustus, then sovereign of Poland,[75] also began to stir. He was a brilliant devotee of the ideas of the age, with broad and, in theory, sound political views. He sought to remake Poland and to give it an *active* role among the other powers. Stanislaw Augustus, however, was very weak-willed, completely unable to initiate action and to make any kind of firm decision. Here was a man who wanted to give Poland an active role; who according to his compatriots was passive in character, hence his habit of looking for salvation from circumstances rather than from his own will and energy. He was wont to shrink from difficulties and wring his hands. In fact he constantly said that happy days came of their own accord, and he would use them to accomplish something wonderful. Fate had exalted him for a purpose, and fate would accomplish everything. This is the fatalism of weak persons and weak peoples.[76]

PANIN'S FOREIGN POLICY QUESTIONED

At first it seemed as if Poland and its king were right. St. Petersburg was not totally firm when tested by the Turkish war. There were signs of wavering and some changes occurred in the way Polish affairs were conducted. A mistake was made which stirred the Poles even more, causing resistance and suffering, but nonetheless led to increased difficulties and irritation. As usually happens, given the difficult situation caused by the two wars and the lack of preparedness, people began to look for someone to blame for the troubles, someone on whom they could vent their spleen. Why not look to the man in charge of foreign affairs? Panin had to prepare for the storm. He had irritated the Poles, he had irritated Austria and France, and the result was the upheaval of Turkey. He had changed the wise and longstanding system whereby Russia was the constant ally of Austria. This was the most natural of alliances, one which gave continual security against the Turks. Panin thought up some kind of Northern System which had been totally unsuccessful. He concluded a firm alliance with Prussia, but how could the king of Prussia render the kind of help against the Turks that Austria, given its geographical position, could? The most important thing was that with an Austrian alliance there never could be a Turkish war, since the Porte would not dare take arms against two empires.

Of course these complaints soon were on the lips of Panin's enemies. Less prominent voices joined those of such powerful enemies as Grigory Orlov and Ivan Chernyshev in a loud chorus of criticism. Solms[77] wrote his king that there was talk of removing Panin, who was blamed for the present difficulties of the state. The English ambassador Cathcart reported to his court that Panin had only a very few friends with whom to resist the pressure of the Austrian and French parties. In Cathcart's opinion Panin would be unable to withstand the deluge. Orlov, Chernyshev, Razumovsky and both Golitsyns, the vice chancellor and the general, all of whom were dissatisfied with the new system and the abandonment of the Austrian alliance, were against Panin.

Roslin, 1777

Count Nikita Ivanovitch Panin

Opposition to Panin appeared in the council. On November 14 Prince Mikhail Volkonsky expressed his opinion: "All possible domestic preparations are being made at home, but what is being done abroad is unknown. I would dare to ask, have we reliable allies in the present time of need? Besides, one would consider the present situation in Poland more dangerous than favorable for Russia. Count Grigory Orlov then asked for an explanation of the causes that led Poland to rise against Russia. Count Nikita Panin explained these causes and stated those which resulted from the confusion there. After that the question was raised whether it was possible to find some way to restore order in Poland and win it to our side. In response Count Nikita Panin read a declaration which had been sent to Poland to restore peace and to which an answer was awaited. Various political arguments were expressed on the issues."

RUSSIAN PRESSURE ON POLAND

Catherine supported Panin. She could not give in to irritation or appear to be fainthearted or timid at the first setback and betray the man who had acted with her full approval. She could not admit the bankruptcy of her policy and the superiority of the previous one, and though still supporting Panin she dissociated herself from the man who had been active in Warsaw. She sacrificed Repnin[78] who had been the target of complaints that he had acted too hastily and had exasperated the Poles. It was decided to recall Repnin as a concession to the Poles. and replace him with someone more conciliatory. We saw how Repnin, comparing himself to an exiled convict,[79] had asked Panin to recall him from Poland. On one hand he had been dissatisfied with the conduct in St. Petersburg of military affairs. On the other hand he was very upset that as a result of the Turkish war the Poles began to assert themselves and demand that he begin to undo the very thing he already had completed with such strenuous efforts. Now he was given a difficult new commission. To wage war successfully with the Porte and to prevent the Turks from forcing their way into Poland to join with the confederates, it was important that the Russian army seize two Polish fortresses, Zamosc and Kamieniec-Podolski, especially the latter. A proposal concerning Kamieniec was made in the council on December 8. If the campaign depended on the capture of this fortress, then the means necessary to take it had to be used. Count Grigory Orlov stated that, as far as it was known, Kamieniec occupied such a position of natural strength that it was impossible to take by force. Fifty thousand men would be unable to overcome a garrison of only a thousand. Count Peter Panin said that if the fortress could not be taken by force, then military strategy would have to be used. It was finally decided "to make every effort to capture the fortress." We have the empress's handwritten statement on the matter: "It seems to me a courier should be sent to Prozorovsky and Saltykov with an order that they try to take Kamieniec either by money, by a ruse or by some other way. They should not attempt an assault or a formal siege because nothing could or should be achieved that way."

Zamosc was on the domain of Zamoyski,[80] who was married to the king's sister. Therefore Repnin, acting unofficially, turned to the king's brother, Lord High Chamberlain Poniatowski.[81] He asked Poniatowski whether the king could write privately to his relative asking him not to prevent the Russian forces from taking Zamosc. Instead of responding privately, the king summoned his ministers and told them the Russians wanted to capture Zamosc. As a result Repnin was sent a note that the ministry of his majesty and of the Commonwealth found it necessary to request that Zamosc not be taken. Repnin did not accept the note, replying that he had not demanded anything concerning the fortress. He remarked however to Crown Chancellor Mlodziejowski[82] that Russian forces had been summoned by the Polish government to restore order to the country. Why not give them the same advantages that the Polish forces enjoyed?

When Repnin began to reproach the king why he did not distinguish between action taken *candidly and confidentially* and action taken *in a ministerial capacity*, Stanislaw Augustus said bluntly, "I will not do this unless you take Zamosc." Repnin replied in equally blunt fashion that the capture of Zamosc was necessary to assure the safety of Warsaw in event of a Tatar attack. In that case the king would not prevent him from taking the fortress. "I will take it by fire if necessary." "This capture is very important," the king continued, "one need only begin." "Don't you mean Kamieniec?" asked Repnin. "Exactly," answered the king. Then Repnin told him, "We will not leave Poland and cross the Turkish frontier unless and until we have Kamienic in our hands as a place to establish a supply depot and drill field. Thus if you want the war to be fought not on your territory but on Turkish soil, give us Kamieniec. How is your majesty getting along with his uncles?[83] Have they expressed their opinions on the current situation?" The king was taken aback somewhat and answered: "Formerly they were cold towards me, but they say that mediation by foreign powers is necessary in the present situation. The only way to calm the nation is for Russia to give up its role as guarantor and its involvement with the dissidents. The dissidents should be allowed religious freedom only, but should not be permitted in the law courts or the diets."[84] "The medicine is worse than the disease, and of course we will not use it;" answered Repnin. "It is not becoming for you, a friend of Russia who owes his throne to Russia, to ruin our common project. You should remain loyal to Russia, especially when you see that everyone is trying to topple you from the throne. Everyone is angry with Russia because we are supporting you." "I would leave my place gladly," answered the king, "if that would bring peace to my fatherland quickly and give the nation what it so desires; that is, an end to the Russian guarantee and the dissidents' turmoil."

KAMIENIEC AND OTHER POLISH ISSUES

Voices hostile to Russia echoed loudly in the royal council. Crown Marshal Prince Lubomirski[85] and Count Zamoyski, both on his own behalf and that of the Czartoryskis, proposed that the army of the Polish government, which had been put under the command of the young Branicki[86] to act against the confederates, should disperse into temporary quarters. Otherwise the Russians would win him to their side and use the army against the Turks. The sultan could conclude that Poland was acting in concert with Russia against Turkey.

Lubomirski and his comrades protested violently against the latest decision of the senate to ask Russia for help against the confederates. Branicki opposed the dispersal of the army. He said this would cause dissatisfaction among the people and arouse suspicion on the part of the Russian government. Zamoyski continued to insist upon the dispersal of the army. He also recommended a system for dealing

with Russia in the future. Do not refuse Russian demands outright
but continually find reasons why it is impossible to fulfill them.
Flatter them but do nothing. The king neither should become
involved to any degree in the current disturbances nor move against
the nation. He should not take up arms against the Turks but should
wait for events to take their course. The king was silent the whole
time. He agreed in general with Zamoyski's advice but sided with
Branicki in opposing the dispersal of the army. Finally they
proposed that the army not be dispersed, but that it be forbidden
to approach the Russian frontier. It could ask for Russian help and
to coordinate its movements [with Russia] only against rebellious
peasants. It was not to operate jointly with the Russians, nor to
reveal that the Polish government was acting in concert with the
Russians.

Naturally there was no hope the Poles would give up Kamieniec
once these decisions were made. Realizing that the king once again
had turned to the Czartoryskis, Repnin approached them, saying that
Russian forces must take Kamieniec. The Czartoryskis answered:
"It is better to have that entire district devastated completely than
to give the Turks a reason to declare war on us. This is even more
the case because it is still uncertain whether the Turks will move
toward the Polish frontier. Even without these reasons it would be
unpatriotic to give up Kamieniec." "In your opinion," Repnin asked
them, "would it be better for Russia or for the Porte to get the upper
hand in the present war? Your course of action depends upon the
resolution of this question." "Neither one nor the other;" answered
the Czartoryskis, "it would be best for us not to get entangled at
all in this matter." "The dignity of your king is suffering from the
scorn of the Porte," said Repnin. "Where there is nothing, there is
no dignity either," the Czartoryskis answered, and the Lithuanian
chancellor[87] said: "It is better not to act at all than to act in vain."

REPNIN AND STANISLAW AUGUSTUS

Repnin turned to the king and received the same answers. Repnin
told him that the king had his own perspective, and that it never had
been so necessary for him to be in full agreement with Russia. That
was the only way he could save himself from the downfall the Porte,
France and the majority of the Poles were preparing for him.

"I see all this very well," answered the king, "but there is that period of disasters which is susceptible to every kind of danger. We are now in such a period, and that is why I am leaving my fate to the course of events." "I entreat your majesty to consider," responded Repnin, "that now you still have an army, albeit a small one, but that in March there will be nothing left with which to pay for it. Then if you want to make a decision and come to us, there will be nothing you can do." "It seems I already have demonstrated my zeal," answered the king, "and because of this zeal I have lost all credit in my nation and have become impotent through no fault of my own." "Certainly," said Repnin, "your former friendship will not be forgotten, but you must continue it, for as soon as you give it up, everything is finished." "If her imperial majesty," answered the king, "gives me the opportunity to be useful to her, if she agrees to renounce completely the role of guarantor and to abandon to some degree the cause of the dissidents, thus enabling me means to regain the love and trust of my subjects, I will prove that no man is more devoted than I to her imperial majesty. If she does not do this I will continue to be her friend, but a totally inactive and insignificant one." Repnin replied that the empress could not renounce her rights without loss of dignity. When the king again definitively refused to surrender Kamieniec, Repnin ended the conversation by saying that the king himself was to blame for everything. The Russians would take all necessary precautions.

The king brought up the possibility of his imminent downfall in conversation with Repnin at the beginning of 1769. Repnin remarked that although it always was unpleasant to abdicate, it was shameful to be forced off the throne. "Of course they will not force me off the throne," answered the king. "I will perish, shot in my palace, but I will not abandon my place, and I will defend myself here." "It is better not to wait for such an extremity," retorted Repnin. "It would be more glorious to die on the battlefield than in your chamber. I will help you if you just will take the manly step of joining your forces with ours. Glory and happiness do not come of themselves; rather one must go out to meet them and search them out." "In my situation one cannot think about glory," answered the king. "I consider duty more important than glory, and duty forbids me to alter my conduct."

St. Petersburg wanted to join the confederation which would be established with Russian aid to uphold the decision of the previous diet that the king ally himself straightaway with Russia. Benoît[88] wrote to his court at the beginning of 1769: "St. Petersburg is seriously mistaken in imagining that Russia still has a party in Poland. All here agree with me that everyone, from the most prominent magnate to the lowliest subject, hates everything Muscovite with a deadly passion." Stanislaw Augustus shared Benoît's opinion and so asked Repnin on December 9, 1768, "What do you want from us?"

Repnin: That you wind up the mainsprings of your government so as to prevent your complete destruction.

King: That is, you want a diet or confederation to which you will say: If you do not maintain order, we will consider you treaty violators. You will force us to adopt measures harmful to us as you did at the last diet.

Repnin: That is not our intention, but if we were to act that way, then you should say *"no"*, and say it manfully and in a true patriotic spirit. Then it would be apparent that we really were infringing on your independence and national sovereignty. Then you would have grounds for calling on Austria and France for help. Then the hour of revolution definitely would strike for you.

King: Why should we decide to take such a risk when we can foresee it?

Repnin: But why even contemplate it?

King: We have learned from the past. Prince Repnin is an honorable man, but the ambassador uses everyone. He tempts both the venal and the ambitious, and he frightens the patriotic.

Repnin: So you will not summon a diet or a confederation for twenty years if things remain as they are now? Why should I remain here if no one is able to or wants to do anything? It would be better to recall me and send someone else.

King: It is better to do nothing than to do something foolish. You, Prince Repnin, have caused me more suffering than anyone else in the world. But I am certain that you cannot hate me and hold me in contempt. Therefore I will gain nothing from your recall.

The king concluded by asserting that not a single Pole would make any agreements unless conditions improved.[89]

CATHERINE AND STANISLAW AUGUSTUS

Stanislaw Augustus wrote the empress on January 26, 1769 (New Style) concerning these matters. "When your majesty wished to make me king, she certainly intended that I fulfill my royal duties. Therefore I owe it to your majesty to the same degree that I owe it to my fatherland to present to you a true picture of Poland's condition. I have an obligation to do this particularly after the demand made in your name by the Russian ambassador that I form a confederation. During that time my frankness and my patriotism led me to report to the Russian ambassador constantly and continually about everything happening here that I considered contrary to the welfare of Poland, of me and also of you. I never tried to incite enemies against you nor make any political alliance without your consent.[90] Others demanded I comply with what would be very harmful to me and my state. I do not regret what I have done, for it has kept me the title of your tried and true friend. My conduct however has caused the estrangement and even aversion which the greater part of my people felt towards me. Since they are not aware of all my objections to what they consider oppression, they see me as responsible for that oppression.

"To justify to the citizenry as a whole what they did for personal advantage, many magnates found it useful to assert that I wanted guarantees and equality between dissidents and Catholics. Your majesty knows full well that I fervently desire that you not want these two things, and that I refused to carry them out myself. All the confederations which have been destroyed by force and all the confederations which appear every day despite continual defeats are proof of the general dissatisfaction. There would be immediate and general dissatisfaction if I established a confederation that was not based upon abrogating the guarantees restricting the dissident statute. I dare to assure your majesty that I would render you no service by such a course of action, but only increase the present difficulties.

"There are not thirty men in Warsaw who freely would subscribe to such a confederation. Such an insignificant number would arouse the scorn of the provinces and impel them to oppose such an impotent effort of the capital and the king. Were I to use force to increase the number of subscribers, that would strengthen the conviction of the popular majority that I was acting contrary to their wishes and their interests, and that I was declaring myself their enemy. When I made reference two years ago to the very great difficulty the dissident cause was encountering, what resulted merely from my familiarity with the thinking of my compatriots was ascribed to different motives. Events have proven me right. From beginning to end I have betrayed neither the truth nor my loyalty to your majesty. It is up to you and it is important for you to bring peace to Poland and to restore the love of my people to me, and thus do what really is to your benefit."

"It would be unheard of," answered Catherine, "if I freely agreed to abandon that which force of arms alone could take from me. The more I realize the duties of my position, and the more I attempt to carry them out in regard to the dissidents, the more culpable I would be if I abandoned them. The pacification of Poland and your own safety are closely linked with the success of my forces. God alone can give victory, but just as He demands effort, vigilance and firmness, which alone can prepare for it, so neither will I spare any effort to prepare for it." This answer was dated March 26.

VOLKONSKY REPLACES REPNIN

As early as March 31 Catherine signed a letter of instruction to the new ambassador in Warsaw, Prince Mikhail Nikitich Volkonsky. The change of ambassadors necessarily heralded a new course of action. It was done in such a way as to leave doubts about the need for it, and was a mistake. It was precisely Prince Repnin who was the indispensable man in Poland at that time. He knew the country well, he knew the people and he was able to deal with them. At the outset of any undertaking he would weigh the difficulties involved and take a clear look at anything that might have negative consequences. As soon as he became convinced that action was needed or received a definite order from his court, he set to work without wavering and without retreating a single step. It was possible to hate Repnin, but impossible not to respect him. Considering the character of most of the Polish men of affairs, a man who could be respected and feared like Repnin was indispensable. The change of ambassadors naturally and necessarily led the Poles to think that the Russian court was repudiating what

Repnin had done. They had recalled him to preserve appearances and wanted to blame him for not acting as he had been instructed. "Poland," the instructions to Volkonsky stated, "is in a state of extreme disorder with the mere vestige of a moribund government. You must support and encourage this government, for it still is a positive force for advancing our interests. It is no less necessary to have a single representative body, a center that in time could revive somewhat the whole body politic of the Commonwealth. This is particularly so when our troops have the advantage over the disorganized Turkish forces and have not allowed them a foothold inside the Polish borders during this first campaign. There is good reason to hope that Polish affairs can be managed and again can be regulated as expected to aid our war with the Turks. Therefore we charge you to use all possible force and all possible means to give public support to this vestige of a Polish government, whether the king or the ministry of the Commonwealth. We are trying to give it, if not domestically, then at least internationally, greater trust and respect among nations. We are trying to strengthen and encourage the Poles by extending them our strongest possible protection lest they lose heart and in their despondency neglect to do everything possible to save their fatherland.

"We have reason to be satisfied with the current actions and thinking of the king. It is necessary therefore to deal with him openly and consult with him about your joint undertakings with the goal of pacifying the nation and restoring order as soon as possible. For the time being that should be the principal and only goal of all your negotiations. Of course the king, for his own benefit, will be ready to share in your efforts and successes and will not refuse to follow your advice in distributing the awards at his disposal. We require that the king become beloved in his own nation and, since his power is limited, the only way he can do this is to hand out titles and awards."

Volkonsky was supposed to follow six *general* guidelines. (1) Maintain the Polish government, even if in appearance only. (2) Find the most suitable means to pacify Poland. (3) Give full support to the dissident cause throughout the country. (4) Affirm the Russian guarantee of the integrity of the territory of the Commonwealth and the inviolability of the decrees of the previous diet. (5) Do not allow the Poles to make an alliance with the Turks. (6) Keep the king secure upon his throne.

Concerning the second guideline it should be noted that the empress would spare neither effort nor money to achieve this goal without abrogating the guarantee. Volkonsky was supposed to frighten magnates by telling them that if a Russian policy of moderation did not make the required impression, then fire and sword would return, not just to those stirring up sedition openly, but also to those engaged secretly in criminal activity. Volkonsky was supposed to threaten that not only Russia, but also all the Protestant powers had an interest in the dissident cause. The involvement of Catholic powers would mean a war disastrous for all Christendom, in which Catholicism could be annihilated completely in Poland. The possibility of compromise on the dissident question was explained to the ambassador: "While not entering into or taking part in any modifications of the existing advantages enjoyed by the dissidents, keep silent about those compromises which they occasionally agree to make among themselves for the sake of achieving the earliest possible peace and harmony with their fellow countrymen."

On May 22 Volkonsky arrived in Warsaw. He took up where Repnin had left off; that is, with Kamieniec. The king told him that the fortress would not handed over to the Turks, and should it be attacked, there were orders to defend it. "Based on what your majesty has said," answered Volkonsky, "I will ask for a formal assurance from the Polish government." "Ask for it," said the king. Volkonsky sent a proposal to the ministry for a note containing assurances that the Kamieniec garrison be ordered to defend the fortress against the Turks, that they not surrender and that they take the necessary measures to defend it with the help of and in conjunction with Russian forces. The ministry sent a draft reply stating that the Kamieniec commander was ordered to defend himself against an attack and allow no force not under the Commonwealth's command into the fortress. Volkonsky insisted in vain that the answer include the words "to defend themselves against the Turks," even if the words "with the help of Russian forces and in conjunction with them" be omitted. The Poles did not agree, and Volkonsky decided not to exchange the notes.

VOLKONSKY PLAYS A STRONG ROLE

The number of confederates increased, and communications between Warsaw and the commander of the Russian army crossed paths. Volkonsky, seeing that it was impossible to pacify Poland with the small Russian force available and that the insurgents were closing in on Warsaw, sent an order to Count Peter Apraksin to come to the city from Poznan and for Major General [August] Czartoryski to come from Thorn. The ambassador did not know if his orders would reach their destination since communications had been interrupted. The addition of Apraksin and Czartoryski would increase the Russian forces to four thousand men. The king assured Volkonsky of his immutable loyalty to the empress but reiterated that calming the upheavals would require compromises in the guarantee and the dissident question. He was undecided when he spoke about this.

The king promised nothing and refused nothing. Volkonsky repeated that there would be no concessions, and that there would be no discussion of this means to pacify the nation. Since in fact there was no government this aroused great resistance. Volkonsky remarked that the king depended completely on his uncles and did not dare initiate anything without them. The ambassador added, "the truth is that he himself has no credit at all and so does nothing." The Czartoryskis played the same tune about the guarantee and the dissident cause. The primate said that Poland could not be happy under a Piast king, that the nation hated Stanislaw Augustus and that unless he were overthrown there was no way to pacify Poland. Volkonsky told the primate that he had forgotten about that, and that Russia would not tolerate the defeat of its cause. The primate[91] persisted in his opinion and said: "I have stated frankly what I think; nevertheless I will do everything the empress commands." "From all of my conversations with the magnates here," Volkonsky wrote, "I have noticed that they do not want to wait for changes in our dealings with the Turks. The court and the ministry are estranged from us and make it evident to the people that they have no communications or agreements with us. In fact we learn nothing from them and have no contact with them."

PLANS FOR A CONFEDERATION

Volkonsky was confused. The thought that a general confederation would be formed in Poland at the first setback of Russian arms in the war with the Turks frightened him. At the end of June Bishop Massalski of Wilno[92] and the Pomeranian military commander Count Flemming[93] presented a plan for a confederation to him. These well-wishers proposed Russian concessions in the guarantee and the dissident question as necessary conditions for their participation. They presented a plausible way to achieve this, whereby the entire Polish nation would petition the empress for these concessions. Massalski and Flemming also asked that Russia not block an increase in the size of the Polish army.

Two other well-wishers soon appeared. The first was the young Count Branicki, son of the famous hetman, and the second was the royal master of the kitchen Count Poninski,[94] long considered a partisan of Russia. They now put together a plan for a confederation. They asked that Russia promise to cede Bessarabia and Moldavia to Poland if the Russian army captured them from Turkey, if the confederation was successful. This Branicki, as noted earlier, had been named commander of the royal forces which were supposed to take action against the confederates under Brzezinski's command.[95] Branicki was to operate jointly with Colonel Prince Golitsyn. Since there was no money in the Polish treasury, Volkonsky gave three thousand ducats to send this army into the field. But we saw that it was decided not to allow the Polish royal army to campaign with the Russians.[96] It is strange that Volkonsky did not learn about this decision from the reports of his predecessors. Branicki had not yet reached Brest Litovsk when he received an order to return immediately to Warsaw with his corps. The king sent for Volkonsky and told him that unfortunately he could not have done otherwise but was unable to explain the reason for his action. Branicki kept six hundred of the three thousand ducats, which sum thus was lost with nothing to show for it.

"After this episode," Volkonsky wrote Panin, "you can conclude how consistent the behavior here is and how much hope can be placed in all the oaths and assurances which are as changeable as the wind." In speaking with Prince Czartoryski, the Lithuanian chancellor, Volkonsky informed him that insurgents were gathering in Lowicz and around Warsaw. Czartoryski replied drily that possibly they were forming a general confederation. Volkonsky asked what they, the Czartoryskis, planned to do in this eventuality, for a general confederation would oppose the king and consequently oppose them, and that it would bring ruin to Poland. They replied, "we do not know what will become of us, but Poland will always remain Poland." The Russian commander arrived. Volkonsky asked him what orders he had given for the Polish forces in Warsaw. Czartoryski answered that there was nothing to be hoped for from these forces, because they themselves said they would not fight against the confederates.

On July 26 the king invited Volkonsky to dine and after dinner began a conversation with the usual assurances about his devotion to the empress. He ended with a question. Would it not be better to do away with the treaty of alliance[97] and the most recent constitution in its entirety and write a new treaty in its place? Volkonsky answered that such thoughts should be dismissed. Russia would never renounce the treaty because the Commonwealth had sent a ceremonial delegation to petition the empress for the guarantee, and the treaty had been based upon this petition. "All that was done by force," said the king. "Not true!" answered Volkonsky. "That kind of ceremonial delegation could not have resulted from coercion."

At the same time the king asked Volkonsky if he could help him in his extreme poverty by lending him ten thousand ducats, because all his income had been taken by the confederates and he had almost nothing. Volkonsky gave him five thousand, while Repnin earlier had given him thirteen thousand ducats. Stanislaw Augustus asked that this loan be kept secret. He was ashamed, and afraid people would say he had been suborned by Russia. A little while later the king asked for another five thousand ducats; otherwise he would have to disband his guard. Volkonsky gave the money, knowing that this guard was waiting for the first opportunity to join the rebels, which would happen when the king disbanded them because he was unable to pay their salaries. The king asked the empress directly for money through Psarski, his resident in St. Petersburg. Catherine approved a sum of ten thousand ducats, paid by Volkonsky. She remarked that with the enormous current expenses of the Russian court, she could give no more help.

Panin informed Volkonsky about a plan for a confederation presented by the bishop of Wilno, Massalski. "This ingenious prelate has one thing on his mind. He would like with our help somehow to become and be considered a man of means. While in no way daring to be his own man, he would like to play his own role. This would leave him freedom to deal on all sides as circumstances change. In all previous matters he acted in his own frivolous style." Panin reported that Massalski had sent the Abbé Bodo and Colonel St. Lô as emissaries to St. Petersburg. They brought a proposal to form a confederation in Lithuania. St. Lô returned from St. Petersburg with the response that Massalski should discuss everything with Volkonsky. Bodo stayed and made new proposals for concerted action with France to restore order in Poland. Panin suggested that Volkonsky not put Massalski at the head of the undertaking but rather to insure that he worked with others also favorably disposed, but not as vain and haughty.

St. Petersburg was much more pleased with the proposal made by Poninski and Branicki because both were considered men of proven loyalty. Panin called Volkonsky's attention to the possibility of compromise in the dissident question. "The dissidents themselves must make a precise evaluation whether the preservation of all the rights they gained at the last diet would be worth civil war and their total ruin. Would it not be better to sacrifice part of their advantages to restore general order and to safeguard their other gains? The glory and dignity of her imperial majesty do not allow us to suggest the necessity and utility of such a step. The dissidents must decide this themselves or at least be led to it by very skillful and discreet intervention on your part through some third party."

St. Petersburg agreed to Poninski's and Branicki's request to annex Moldavia to Poland. Annexing Moldavia to Russia was not considered worthwhile, and its distance from the Russian border would make it burdensome for Russia to defend. On the other hand annexing Moldavia to Poland would strengthen Russia's influence there. The Moldavians were Orthodox, and their nobility constituted a separate body which, with annexation to Poland and under Russian protection, should gain the same rights the Polish gentry enjoyed. Besides it would be advantageous if a new confederation seeking Moldavia would enter into clearly stated mutual obligations with

Russia. The confederation could put Kamieniec at Russia's complete disposal for the duration of the war.

What happened in Poland depended on the course of the war. When news came in August that things were going badly for the Russians, the Russian commander Czartoryski said to Volkonsky: "I will tell you frankly, not as ambassador but as my old friend, that we will side with whoever gains more power here. I will not leave Warsaw, but the king must be rescued. You are not strong enough to defend us."

News came to Warsaw in September of the Russian defeat of the Turks and the capture of Khotin, and this was received with displeasure. Rumors spread that the Poles wanted to convoke the senate. Volkonsky asked for a meeting with the king but was refused on the pretext of lack of time. The ambassador came to the palace on Sunday, the customary day for audiences, and was able to engage the king in conversation. Stanislaw said nothing directly about convoking the senate, but began the old refrain about the need to manage the nation. Unsuccessful here, Volkonsky went to the Russian commander as if on an ordinary courtesy call, because the latter was ill. Czartoryski said that convoking the senate was necessary to justify themselves to the nation. The confederates considered the Czartoryski party Russian supporters and were laying waste their villages. On parting Volkonsky told him that his party would regret it if the results of the convocation went against Russia, while at another meeting he said bluntly that the Czartoryskis would answer with all their domains.

Volkonsky heard the old complaints from the king that he was hated only because of Russia, and that he had discovered a malicious plot against him. He knew who the guilty were but did not want to identify them. When Volkonsky said that Russia could deliver him from these enemies the king answered that that could wait for the proper time. For all these reasons he had to show the nation that he was doing everything possible on its behalf. Volkonsky suggested that not only would this sham of a nation, the term he applied to the confederates, not keep him on the throne, but no one else in the world would either, if his behavior forced Russia to depose him. The king answered that he did not expect that from the empress, but that as a Pole he could not act against his fatherland.

Since the Czartoryskis had brought senators of their party to Warsaw, and thus would have a majority, the primate thought it better not to go to the convocation at all and persuaded his friends not to go either. Depending on the results of the convocation a protest would be issued that it was illegal because it deliberated about state affairs, the resolution of which was the province of the Commonwealth as a whole. The convocation, which Volkonsky called a divan, ended on September 25 and demonstrated the consequences of Repnin's recall. The senators resolved to send complaints about Repnin to the Russian court. They also resolved to request England to direct its minister in Constantinople to present excuses for the king and the Polish Commonwealth stating that Poland did not break the peace with the Porte and that all previous actions had been done under Russian coercion. The king was authorized to send ambassadors to all the courts he saw fit with these complaints.

"It seems to me," wrote Volkonsky, "that the time has come to tame the Czartoryskis. We have spared them even under critical circumstances, but they have not abandoned their intention to make Poland an active power through their efforts. They are preparing for this more energetically than before. They are trying to abrogate the most recent treaty, which they see as an insurmountable obstacle to their goal. They have gained such power over the king that he cannot take a step without them. He is weak beyond measure and, with all his weakness, his plans to be strong and masterful in the realm are also beyond measure. He knows that we will not permit this, and he is going against us.

"The Czartoryskis suggested to him that we never will depose him. I will take the liberty of presenting my opinion, whether it would not be useful to frighten the king away from us. We should decide that if he does not mend his ways we will depose him. Since the Czartoryskis have assured him that the Prussian king will not permit him to be overthrown, it would not be bad to influence the Prussian king to state his agreement with us. We must take measures quickly against the excesses of the Czartoryskis and against the French intrigues."

In addition to the need to frighten the king, Volkonsky again suggested the necessity of a confederation which would act under

Russian supervision and requested three hundred thousand rubles for it. "If we initiate this," he wrote, "then it should be done without fail in November, so that matters could be brought to conclusion before spring."

Perhaps Volkonsky raised the Polish question at the council in St. Petersburg on purpose to call Panin and Repnin to account. Perhaps he took the latter's place in Warsaw convinced that a diametrically opposed course of action would correct what Repnin had spoiled. But now he was criticized harshly for that, since he was forced to adopt Repnin's course of action and tone and compelled to justify his predecessor.

On October 1 Volkonsky informed Panin about his conversation with the king. "Is not your majesty ashamed," said the ambassador, "to attribute everything done in the last diet to the use of force by Prince Repnin when you know that everything was approved by the empress? That is why you and the diet ratified the matter. Let ordinary people fear some use of force by Prince Repnin, something he could not order without the permission of his court. But what does your majesty fear? Prince Repnin would not capture you, would he? Besides, why have you been silent until now? Now when you especially should be grateful to it for delivering you from the Turks and from your domestic evildoers, you intend to break with Russia. You complain about Prince Repnin and you demand the withdrawal of the Russian forces, the only thing that keeps you on the throne. You are sending ministers to precisely those courts which are trying to ruin you. Hitherto you have called the confederates fanatics, but now you are talking their language as if we were causing faith and freedom to falter in Poland.

"Based on your majesty's own reasoning, what should our court conclude about your conduct, and what would be the consequences for you? I will say only that those who are leading you into this abyss are not in a position to rescue you from it. You will regret it, but perhaps too late."

The king at first was dumbfounded but then, recovering, began to affirm his loyalty to the empress and concluded with the usual declaration that as a Pole he had to demonstrate to the nation that he was looking after its welfare. Volkonsky remarked afterwards that the king was not dejected but happier and more content than before. The ambassador repeated his statements that the Czartoryskis were leading the king to ruin. He added that the Prussian king advised Poniatowski through Benoît to hold fast to Russia and that therefore he could not be satisfied with the king's present course of conduct. The king said nothing in reply but merely left with a smile.

Stanislaw Augustus Poniatowski

STANISLAW AUGUSTUS SEEKS INDEPENDENCE

The Czartoryskis made the obvious response to this that they never had had such a firm footing as they had now. When they told the Russian commander [August Czartoryski] that Russia would not be grateful to them, he replied: "It is true that we really might feel the first blow, but everything will calm down in time." They were convinced and assured their supporters that the Prussian king was no true friend of Russia. The king began to speak loudly against Russia. The one who shouted the loudest among the king's advisors,

Vice Chancellor Borch,[98] preached everywhere that the last convocation of the senate had been a very happy occurrence for Poland and was creating an epoch of national prosperity.

One day the bishop of Kujawy mentioned to Borch that they would bring ruin upon themselves and upon others if they acted openly against Russia, which was Poland's only source of help. It was particularly foolhardy to irritate Russia now that it had the upper hand over the Turks. Borch answered not to fear Russia, despite the victory over the Turks in this campaign, for it would be defeated in the future. Even if that did not happen all of Europe would intervene on Poland's behalf to prevent an increase in Russian power. Austria in particular would not look with equanimity at Russian victories over the Turks but would intervene on Poland's behalf. Borch added that although Russia held ascendency it would not dare touch either their persons or their estates, because hitherto it had done them no harm.

At that time Stanislaw Augustus wrote Geoffrin[99]: "There are people who attest that in earliest childhood I had a presentiment of great eminence. When I became king I said, See, terrible misfortunes soon will befall me. Everything I undertake will be spoiled and half destroyed. Nevertheless I will survive misfortune, I will build anew, and I will emerge at the end. Even now that hope warms my heart, despite the fact that I am in very great difficulty. My affairs are going extremely badly, but I say, Now God must deliver me from misfortune, and in that expectation we will do our duty. I have done my duty by signing the senate's resolution, according to which an official delegation has been named to bring complaints to the Russian empress about everything that has been done here for the past two and a half years. These things have been done against my will by a man acting in her name, but who apparently gave her false information. I cannot imagine that the empress is angry with me for that. But if she is angry, then I suffer because of these same confederates who lay waste my domains and who steal my revenue. Some of them are trying to take my crown from me and even my life. But never mind; with courage and patience all will end well."

The primate told Volkonsky that the king had sent a Frenchman, Saint Pol,[100] as his agent to Versailles. The missive which Saint Pol carried said that the king would declare himself against Russia if the French would take him under their protection. This missive was given to Choiseul, and as a result there was veritable chaos. Volkonsky could not verify this information, but Podoski[101] affirmed that he knew about the matter from a reliable source and promised to provide a copy of the missive.

Panin wrote Volkonsky that the primate should be controlled with an iron hand. It was understood that Russia was his only hope, and for that reason he was loyal to it, but he also was devoted heart and soul to the house of Saxony. St. Petersburg understandably was very dissatisfied with the senate meeting. A proposal was made not to receive Prince Oginski,[102] who had been designated to go to St. Petersburg with complaints against Repnin. Panin wrote Stanislaw Augustus two letters, one in the empress' name and one in his own, presenting the same points which Volkonsky had made to him orally. Meanwhile money was set aside for the loyalist confederation. Panin wrote to Volkonsky that it was absolutely necessary to bring the king over to this confederation and to Russia. The elder Czartoryskis should be excluded, and their reputation among the people destroyed along with any hope of reviving it in the future. Mniszech[103] and the Potockis should be won over, but they must not be allowed to depose the king.

In the extreme eventuality that Stanislaw Augustus became unable to rule because of frivolity, inconstancy and foolhardiness, Russia would have to depose him, and the new king would have to be a Piast, also put on the throne by Russia. Thus France would not be able to show the world that Russia had no basis for placing Poniatowski on the throne and that Russia's domestic weakness left him helpless against French intrigues. Action had to be taken because of the agreement with Prussia, and because Russian influence in Poland had been endangered seriously by raising the elector of Saxony to the throne.[104] Saxony's position between the rivals Austria and Prussia, and its relationship with France, meant it would shift itself and Poland from one alliance and one side to another. This was totally incompatible with the independent Northern System which her imperial majesty would adopt as a permanent policy.

Panin's letters had no effect on the king. Volkonsky saw not the slightest change in him after he had read them. Stanislaw Augustus insisted that duty required that he show his concern for the nation, and that he also acquire a good name in the world. When Volkonsky asked if he hoped to remain on the throne even for a little while if the empress removed her support, he said nothing, but only *huddled up.* Every day the king held a council consisting of his Czartoryski uncles and his confidants; that is, Marshal Lubomirski, former Chancellor Zamoyski, Vice Chancellor Przezdiecki[105] and Borch.

At the end of November Volkonsky went to the king with the demand that he dissociate himself from his advisors and surround himself with such good patriots and impartial men as Count Flemming and Branicki. These men loved the fatherland, were devoted to the king and had no family interests, unlike the Czartoryskis, who had reason to exacerbate the confused state of affairs. If they could bring the king to the point where the empress withdrew her support and he lost the crown, they would not hesitate in the least to sacrifice him for the benefit of Prince Adam Czartoryski and Marshal Lubomirski. "They are my relatives," answered the king, "and I cannot dissociate myself from them, but I will do as you wish."

Volkonsky began to reprimand the king for his lack of candor and for concealing his intention to convoke the senate and to enact the well-known resolution. "Then we were hanging by a thread," the king replied, "thank God the war took such a favorable turn." "But how would you be saved," objected Volkonsky, "if the Turks defeated us, and what would be the use of your senate's resolution? You know that the nation hates us, and that it is only our forces that keep you on the throne." "I prefer a patriot's duty to all else," answered the king. "I am bound to act in the interests of the nation." "Whom do you mean by nation," asked Volkonsky, "unless it is those who revolt against you under the pretext of faith and freedom, those from whom the empress defends you? Your action will not awaken in them the slightest gratitude. Even if it did, and even if the subversives joined you, would you take up arms with them against your benefactors?" "I would not take up arms," answered the king, "but I would persuade them to adopt peaceful ways." The next day Volkonsky went to Poniatowski together with Benoît, who urged him in the name of his sovereign not to forfeit the friendship of the Russian empress, since his royal happiness depended on that alone. Stanislaw Augustus answered Benoît that he would do nothing against the empress, but would act as duty required, for he put that above all else.

Volkonsky asked St. Petersburg for approval of the plans for a new confederation. Panin replied at the beginning of December that it was necessary to wait, especially since Moldavia had been conquered without the Poles. Nor could a decision be made about the king's conduct before it could be seen what impression the empress' displeasure with Oginski's mission would have on the *vacillating soul* of Stanislaw Augustus. Even before receiving this answer from Panin, Volkonsky was invited by the king on December 13. The king began to speak to him: "Benoît in the name of his king offered me the friendly advice that I take refuge only with the empress. I do not want to do anything hostile, but since I do not know what this is all about, I do not want to put myself blindly in her hands." "What it is all about," answered Volkonsky, "is keeping you on the throne and bringing peace to Poland. Her imperial majesty sees your unexpected behavior and knows that you have been forced to act this way by your cunning advisors. Because of her magnanimity, she has not yet ceased her concern for your deliverance. It is only your advisors whom she has excluded from her protection.

"Your majesty must take advantage of this and lose no time in thinking of yourself. Abandon your evil advisors. I shall not be able to clarify the measures we will take to save you until I see that you have forsaken these advisors and that you seek your sole salvation in the empress's protection. Otherwise your advisors would learn of these measures and would obstruct them." "The Czartoryskis," answered the king, "are my relatives, and I cannot abandon them. Neither can I promise to carry out your will in all things. Perhaps you would like to abolish all the decrees made for the benefit of Poland during my reign?" "You can treat your uncles as relatives without listening to their advice or asking their permission," answered Volkonsky. "The empress will not retreat from her treaty with Poland or from the dissident laws. She will explain that the guarantee is not at all dangerous to Polish independence. She has withdrawn her protection completely from your uncles." "Then who will our friends be," asked the king, heatedly, "except the Potockis, who have shown us such ingratitude?" "I do not know," answered Volkonsky, "whether the Potockis are grateful or not. I only know that the Czartoryskis are ungrateful, and that several times we sacrificed the Potockis for the benefit of the Czartoryskis." "What are you doing with the Czartoryskis," asked the king incensed. "Will you arrest them as you did Soltyk?"[106] "I cannot vouch for that," answered Volkonsky, "if they do not change their ways." "In that case it would be better to arrest me," said the king. "I hope that the empress in her magnanimity does not force me to abandon my relatives," he concluded.

Mediation was discussed. The king proposed choosing a Catholic power, France or Austria, since it was a religious matter. "It is not a religious matter at all," answered Volkonsky, "and there is no need for mediation. There is no need for intermediaries between the empress and your majesty, because she alone put you on the throne and she alone keeps you on it. Mediation is impossible between Russia and the rebels, whom you call a nation."

Meanwhile Psarski, the Polish resident in St. Petersburg, told the king that the Russian court intended to abandon the guarantee completely and had agreed to exclude the dissidents from the legislative process if they came voluntarily and requested it. The king showed Psarski's dispatch to Volkonsky. The ambassador answered that he had no orders to abandon the guarantee. The guarantee could be clarified only by a declaration or supplementary agreement. Volkonsky thought that if the dissidents wanted to renounce some rights voluntarily, the Russian court would not object. When the king heard about a supplementary agreement he was elated. "Marvellous," he said, "we must set to work!" But Volkonsky restrained the king's elation, remarking that the Czartoryskis and the other royal advisors definitely would be excluded. Henceforth the king would distribute awards not on their recommendation, but on the ambassador's advice.

"I rather would allow myself to be torn to pieces than to agree to this," answered the king angrily. "In that case," said Volkonsky, "if we must proceed with the establishment of a confederation, we will be forced to do so even without your majesty." "I will not renounce my advisors," continued the king, "because if I dissociate myself from them, the nation would see that I discarded them because they opposed Russia." "The conclusion," said Volkonsky, "is that it is your majesty himself who is trying to appear as an enemy of Russia. In my opinion your throne would be more secure if you assured the nation that you are with us." The king, realizing that he had said too much, made no reply.

RELATIONS WITH PRUSSIA

Along with Volkonsky, the Prussian minister Benoît also tried to persuade Stanislaw Augustus. Frederick II continued to play the role of Russia's faithful ally. We also saw that sometimes he felt this alliance was a burden, and he regarded Russia's efforts on behalf of the dissidents with annoyance as something that might increase Russian influence excessively.[107] Frederick was disturbed by the thought that the allies were not equal, and that he was serving Russian aims, quite apart from his irritation that the Russian court wanted to bind him to its Northern System which he considered senseless and constraining. The growing Polish disturbances, the war of the confederates and finally the Turkish war, had caused greater difficulties for the Prussian crown. According to the treaty of alliance Prussia must help Russia, at least monetarily. Prussia also had to try to halt the Polish disturbances and the Turkish war as soon as possible. Finally Frederick contemplated the serious consequences of a European war from which he would be very fortunate to escape unscathed.[108] In any case he clung firmly to the Russian alliance, which was his only protection.

In a letter to Catherine the king expressed the wish to implement an article of the 1764 treaty to renew the alliance for another eight years. The empress answered that she was very anxious to receive a proposal renewing the treaty which "in the present circumstances could be even more useful for both powers and for all of Europe." In the same letter Catherine confided to her "most faithful ally" that she would leave Poland to its political slumbers for a certain time and would act only to prevent the constant brigandage from developing into a general uprising.

Although Catherine's letters to Frederick continued to express her fervent wish that the alliance be renewed and strengthened, the matter dragged on from January to October, 1769. Important people in St. Petersburg were convinced that the existing alliance with Prussia was not as advantageous as the previous alliance with Austria, which had been based on their joint relationship to Turkey. The current Turkish war was clear proof of this. When the alliance with Austria was in force, either the war would not have happened, or the Turkish forces would have been deflected by Austrian armies. Frederick was well aware that there were supporters of the Austrian alliance in St. Petersburg. He feared the overthrow of Panin and a change in policy. For that reason he proposed a renewal or, properly speaking, an extension of the alliance. Simultaneously, a memorandum was prepared in Berlin which demonstrated that an alliance with Prussia was more beneficial than one with Austria. An alliance between Russia and Austria would lead to an alliance between Prussia and France. In that event Russia could not receive significant help from Austria, which would fear French attack in Italy and the Netherlands. On the other hand a Prussian alliance would be very advantageous, because Prussia and Denmark would restrain Sweden.[109]

The strenuous objections to the Prussian alliance naturally forced its supporters and the empress herself to be more demanding, and to want to obtain as many advantages and as many guarantees from Prussia as possible, in order to derive the greatest benefit from the alliance. Thus Panin demanded a major commitment from Frederick, particularly in the event of a general war. These demands irritated Frederick. Once again he saw that equality was being negated, and that the Russian court was trying to get more from Prussia than it could give.

Finally the treaty of alliance was renewed for eight years on October 12, with March 31, 1772, considered the start of the term. A supplementary stipulation to the second secret article of the treaty stated that if the Saxon court sent an army into Poland to further its interests, the Russian empress could call upon the Prussian king, depending on circumstances, to use his army to oppose the Saxon force or to send his army into Saxony. The third secret article stated that in the event that Sweden attacked Russia and the constitution of 1720[110] were overturned, the Prussian king was obligated to create a diversion in Swedish Pomerania.

An interesting note from the empress to Panin about this article has been preserved. "Would it not be better not to mention Swedish Pomerania by name, because acquisition of this territory would give the Prussian king a number of useful harbors, and consequently possession of Danzig would offer the possibility of launching a fleet on the Baltic? Please tell me if I am mistaken. But I have heard from you more than once that if Danzig or some point like it, as for example Stralsund, were in Prussian hands, it would be harmful for us. Perhaps a diversion could be indicated without mentioning Swedish Pomerania." Catherine of course was not mistaken, but it was easy to show Panin that even if Swedish Pomerania were not mentioned, a diversion could be made only in that area. St. Petersburg became anxious about Pomerania and stopped being anxious about Saxony, reserving the right to demand that Frederick enter Saxony with an army. Frederick was exultant, for he would no longer be irritated by the protection given to Saxony. The Northern System disappeared the first time actual international relations were involved, although St. Petersburg still thought that it existed.

Only a Russian alliance could provide firm support and protection for Frederick, so it is understandable that all the efforts of France and Austria to wean him from this alliance were in vain. As a result of France's efforts to ingratiate itself with him, he resumed diplomatic relations, but always dealt with cold disdain the way one would deal with an aged beauty who had lost her charm and kept only laughable pretensions. He eagerly approached Austria, because he wanted above all to prevent its rapprochement with Russia. He wanted to use Austria to frighten and restrain Russia. He wanted to be the mediator between the two empires and use the arms of both to achieve his own goals. He succeeded completely.

In the middle of 1768 France initiated diplomatic contacts with Prussia under the pretext of concluding a commercial treaty. To bring Frederick over to his side Choiseul told Frederick that France would not oppose Prussian annexation of Danzig and Hamburg. A French emissary [Adrien-Louis] Prince de Guines came to Berlin at the beginning of 1769. Colonel [William Bernhard von] Goltz was sent as the Prussian emissary to Paris and told his king that Choiseul offered Prussia Warmia and Courland.[111] But Frederick laughed at these proposals, realizing that he could obtain rich booty from Poland, but not through the mediation of France.[112] At the same time France's emissary reported to his court that the Prussian king was planning a great undertaking in Polish affairs.

RUSSIA, PRUSSIA, AUSTRIA AND THE POLISH QUESTION

Austria felt the need even before France did for rapprochement with Prussia with a view to restraining Russia. At the very beginning of 1768 Kaunitz gave Maria Theresa[113] a memorandum in which he said that Austria could not intervene in Polish affairs without affecting the European political system in general or the powers allied with the Commonwealth in particular. This was now the case. Russia, using the guarantee, would have exclusive control over all of Poland's affairs, making it, according to Kaunitz, into a Russian province. It would be dangerous for Austria to incite a war, one it would have to join, or to take some step or other which could harm its position. There would be no danger if Austria could have confidence in the Prussian king. Possibly the Prussian king not only would not oppose an undertaking intended to restrain Russia, but would be glad if others did something that under the circumstances he himself could not. Kaunitz advised asking the Prussian king whether he would agree to make a joint proposal with Austria to the Polish diet to add their guarantees of Poland's free institutions. This would restrain Russia, which no longer would be the sole guarantor, but instead would have to share influence with two other neighboring powers.[114]

Thus Russia would not be able to put an end unilaterally to its ancient feud with Poland. A plan was drafted in Vienna to share influence among the three neighboring powers. It would not be necessary to wait for the plan in order to divide territory. It would be executed immediately, thanks to the Turkish war. "War between Russia and Turkey," said Frederick II, "has changed the entire European political system. A new field of action has been opened. To profit from such favorable circumstances, one should neither be too cunning nor be rooted in one spot. I read a wonderful allegory by Boiardo,[115] and I seized the opportunity which was offered. Aided by negotiations, I achieved a result which compensated my monarchy for its former losses by incorporating Polish Prussia into the lands I long had possessed."[116]

Thus Frederick changed his first opinion about war between Russia and Turkey. He now saw the war as a *beneficial occasion* which could enlarge his own territory. Kaunitz also saw it as a beneficial occasion which could "change the European political system," to Austria's benefit of course. The Austrian chancellor already had been able to change this political system once, for he had been able to bring together two states, Austria and France, which had been inveterate enemies. Why not therefore succeed in bringing together Austria and Prussia and achieve what the death of the Elizabeth of Russia had prevented the Seven Years War from accomplishing—the return of Silesia![117] A triple alliance of Austria, Prussia and Turkey would restrain Russia, for while Frederick would cede Silesia to Austria to strengthen the alliance, he would take Courland and part of Poland and even might receive money from the Porte. Frederick should agree to this because he could not but see how harmful it would be for him to promote an increase in Russian power.[118] In the last analysis Poland would have to pay, Poland which counted for nothing (*res nullius*) and was the supply depot of Eastern Europe.

Emperor Joseph II did not share Kaunitz's hopes for the success of this plan. He did not think that Frederick preferred an alliance with Austria and Turkey to one with Russia. He did not think that the Prussian king would exchange Silesia for Courland and part of Poland. In Joseph's opinion, Frederick could exchange Silesia only for Saxony. But the emperor also recognized the need to seek rapprochement with Prussia, and this initiative could be carried out most speedily by a personal meeting between Joseph and Frederick. The latter eagerly agreed to the meeting. "Prussia," he said in his memoirs, "had to fear lest its ally (Russia), which had become too powerful, in time would want to dictate laws for it as it had done for Poland. The Viennese court would have to fear almost the same thing. This common danger in time would make them forget their previous enmity." The meeting between Joseph and Frederick took place in the Silesian city of Neisse in August 1769.

"The king," wrote Joseph to his mother, "showed me every courtesy and showered me with expressions of friendship. He is a genius. He is a wonderful speaker, but even while talking he is able to see through a rogue. In his conversations he expressed fear of

Russian power, a fear he wanted to instil in us as well. He spoke to me about our Greeks (Orthodox Slavs) in Hungary,[119] saying that our merchants of that religion in Breslau celebrated a public holiday to honor Russian victories. He said it was necessary to treat them well and be patient with them lest they become even more attached to Russia and make trouble. He told me all of Europe would have to take up arms to restrain Russia, because Russia was the most powerful of all. Sire, I answered him, in the event of a general war you will be in the forefront, and therefore we can sleep soundly. As far as we are concerned, rest assured that you can deal with the Russians in any way that is to your advantage. He did not agree, admitting that he was afraid of the Russians, and that the alliance with them was necessary, even though it was a burden."[120]

According to Frederick, Joseph cleverly made him realize that he did not have enough influence over his mother to insure that his wishes would be carried out. He did not hide the fact that, in the current European situation, neither he nor Maria Theresa ever would allow Russia to keep Moldavia and Wallachia. Frederick wrote Solms in St. Petersburg about the meeting. "The emperor is very amiable and extraordinarily courteous. He assured me in the strongest possible terms that never had he forgotten about Silesia, and I heard protestations how they were entitled to it. I turned his attention to Russia. He admitted that the Russian empress was a great woman, *gran cervello di regina*[121] to use his expression. This man is consumed with ambition. He contemplates doing something great. At present he is held back by his mother and bears the yoke impatiently. As soon as he is free of her he will take some major step or other. I was not able to find out exactly what he had in mind, Venice, Bavaria, Silesia or Lorraine; but I can affirm with certainty that Europe will be in flames as soon as he becomes an independent sovereign." Frederick ordered Solms to show his letter to Catherine.

Frederick used Russia to frighten Austria, and Austria to frighten Russia. He wrote to Catherine that the Viennese court would not intervene in Polish affairs as long as Russian forces were successful against the Turks. At the first Russian setback, however, Austria would try to put one of the Saxon princes, Albert of Teschen, on the Polish throne. It was easy to see why Frederick followed the events of the war so closely. On August 30 (New Style) he wrote to Solms: "Although it always must be supposed that the Turks would make every effort to save Khotin, I confess that I did not expect such a speedy lifting of the siege. In any event we now must consider the consequences of the retreat, and whether there will be a decisive battle between the Russians and the Turks. I would like this to occur for the good of the Russian cause. This seems even more desirable because postponing the battle further could result in Russian supply shortages. I will not conceal from you that in my opinion Prince Golitsyn delayed the capturing this fortress too long, and that if misfortune befalls his army he alone is to blame for this and for the food shortages incurred in recent victories over the Turks."[122]

RELATIONS WITH FRANCE

Austria informed the court at St. Petersburg that it would observe neutrality in a war between Russia and Turkey. France said nothing, continuing to use every means to estrange Russia, though avoiding any publicity or open rift, desiring to make use of what was considered Russia's mistake. The latter, seeing resistance to its plans from the king and from the Czartoryskis, formed the Confederation of Radom. The confederates agreed to act in Russia's interests only because they hoped they could depose Stanislaw Augustus. When they saw that Russia definitely wished to keep Poniatowski on the throne, they turned against it. Because of Russia's declaration that it would support Poniatowski, France took the opposite view of the Confederation of Bar and the Confederation of Radom. Choiseul believed that this turn of events was to France's advantage and considered it necessary to support the Confederation of Bar. He put little hope in the Poles, incited Turkey against Russia and tried to prolong the war by using various means to aid the Porte.

He sent a colonel of the dragoons, Valcroissant, to Constantinople with the following written instructions: "The lack of a clear policy in the Turkish councils has led the king [of France] to hope that Count Valcroissant can find some means or other to influence their decisions. If Turkish pride and prejudice make this plan impossible, then Count Valcroissant should render every possible service to the Turkish cause against the Russians."

A dispatch dated February 1928 from Choiseul to Gérard, the French *chargé d'affaires* in Danzig, stated: "The king is deeply interested in the fate of Poland, and so you may not exaggerate anything in your conversations with the patriots. You should limit yourself to commonplaces which do not commit us to anything. You should make them realize at all times that the pitiful and incoherent actions of the Polish nation, unable to maintain itself, give its friends no means to help it. You should say that the Poles must reach agreement among themselves and with the Tatars and the Turks to take up arms for the Commonwealth. The patriots should realize that from now on salvation, independence and the very existence of the Commonwealth depend on arms. In the present circumstances the main goal is to do all possible harm to the Russians and not to shrink from any temporary inconvenience this creates. This policy is part of the grand design of the king's present system.... The frivolity, the lack of agreement and the national character of the Poles give no reason to hope for any significant effort against Russia on their part. We can look only to the Turks and the Tatars, and our counsels and our views should be directed toward facilitating their success."

Public relations between the courts of St. Petersburg and Versailles were not particularly friendly either. On Panin's instructions the Russian *chargé d'affairess* Khotinsky[123] was supposed to make a curious declaration to the duke of Choiseul that the Russian court was very displeased with the continual interception of dispatches from St. Petersburg to the Russian *chargé d'affaires* at the court of Versailles and of those sent in the opposite direction. Official orders and private letters also had been intercepted. Khotinsky was supposed to ask Choiseul what good it was, after this had occurred, for the Russian *chargé d'affaires* to remain in France and for the French *chargé d'affaires* to remain in Russia. Russia and France were not in such a position that purely external proprieties needed to be maintained. Choiseul gave his word of honor that the dispatches had not been intercepted in France. If they had been opened in France, then why hold on to them?

At the same time news came that Châtelier, the French ambassador in London, took precedence over the Russian ambassador,

Count Chernyshev, in a most unseemly manner. When Khotinsky complained about this to Choiseul, the latter answered: "I do not understand why Russia now intends to contend with France over primacy. I know, not from rumors, but from my own experience, that the ambassadors of Empress Elizabeth gave way to the ambassadors of France. I myself was ambassador in Vienna together with the late Keyserling,[124] who never quarreled with me about precedence and who sat below me. France already occupied the most important place in Europe at a time when Russia was completely unknown, and it would be unjust if Russia now took precedence. When the Russian rulers were called tsars, they had no pretensions of precedence. It is only since they have been conceded the imperial title that difficulties have arisen, probably because an emperor is considered the chief of sovereigns. But France had no need to concede, needing nothing from Russia, and if Russia persists in such pretensions we will end this dispute at once by denying the Russian sovereign the imperial title. The king will proclaim this in a manifesto, and Spain will follow our example. It was foolish of us to grant the title, but one day we will set things right permanently." Khotinsky replied that Russia neither claimed precedence nor conceded it to anyone else, but merely demanded equality. "Such equality is impossible," objected Choiseul, "for where there is a first, there certainly must be a second."

France was a close ally of Austria, and Choiseul felt it necessary to state his views in a memorandum which he gave to Count Mercy, the Austrian ambassador to the French court.[125] "It is no fantasy that France's relations with Russia are hostile. Since the first months of her reign the sovereign who rules St. Petersburg has revealed her ambitious system. It was impossible not to see her intention to arm the North against the South. One of the bases of our alliance with Austria is the avoidance of a continental war. But if a northern alliance led by Russia and Prussia and funded by England were established, this necessarily would cause difficulties for Austria and France, which would have to wage a major land war. Thus an effort had to be made to prevent this dangerous alliance by all means, and to do so by dealing with Russia before dealing with England, which was at peace. The Russian empress helped us by being drawn into undertakings beyond her strength. Sweden will not join an alliance against France and the Viennese court, and will restrain Denmark. Unhappy Poland tears itself apart. The Russians are occupied with the Porte, and Poland only can be a burden to its allies. Of course the Polish king wants war so he can fish in troubled waters, but he does not dare threaten our alliance because he is restrained by Austria. The best thing for our alliance would be for the Turkish war to continue for several years more with equal success on both sides. Let them wear each other out, and if we gain time that will be to our advantage."

These views were not shared in Vienna. "Unfortunately the Turkish war has taken such a turn for the worse," Kaunitz replied, "and with so little prospect that things will improve in the future, that the remedy not only has not diminished but rather has intensified the illness and the danger. It now is apparent that the coming campaign will not favor the Turks, and that they will be forced to conclude a hasty peace, giving up Azov, Taganrog, and even Ochakov and the Crimea. If that happens Turkish power will collapse but Russia, on the other hand, will become the greatest threat to all the other continental powers.

"Therefore a prolonged war between Russia and Turkey poses a terrible risk. Only the threat of the danger she would incur if she does not limit her grandiose plans can restrain the ambitious soul of the Russian empress. To do this we have assembled forces in Hungary and Transylvania, forces which initially were insignificant and were only a protective measure. Since then we have increased them enough to make Russia think twice and, if necessary, we would use them in earnest."[126]

At the end of August news came from Versailles that the Russian vessels bound for the archipelago had sailed through the English Channel. Afterwards Khotinsky called on Choiseul who received him with his usual vivacity and, with a happy expression, said with a smile: "Well, you can board your fleet." Khotinsky said that if the rumor of the squadron's passage through the English Channel were true, he hoped that the Russian vessels would not be denied refuge in French harbors in case of danger or need. "I will report to the king about the matter," answered Choiseul, "and I hope that aid to the fleet in these harbors will not be denied." Khotinsky wrote to Panin about this conversation. "I confess that the restraint and the opinions of the duke of Choiseul surprised me. He was in every way a new man. His manner was calm, gentle and peaceful, and more courteous than usual. He seemed frightened to me, and the news that he had heard with such interest so affected him that he had not yet composed himself when he talked to me about it. The ministry here always thought that the equipment of our squadrons was as useless as that of Danish vessels, fit only to cruise the Baltic, give a stern warning to the Swedes and return home." Apparently Choiseul was very courteous and calm, but Khotinsky knew that shortly after news arrived of the squadron's passage a courier was sent from Versailles to Constantinople. The Prussian ambassador Baron Goltz recounted his conversation with Choiseul. "Did you hear about the new phenomenon, the Russian fleet?," he asked the minister. "A new naval power has appeared!" Members of the diplomatic corps talked about nothing but the Russian fleet. They were amazed that Russia had been able to outfit twenty vessels in such a short time, something that would have been difficult even for France. Khotinsky heard about the following comment by Choiseul: "This is a romantic adventure, but there is something behind it, and it must be watched carefully. It is expensive, and I do not think much can be accomplished, but nevertheless it is a dazzling expedition."

Khotinsky also reported to St. Petersburg about the hopes, plans and conversations of the Poles in Paris. Gamolinski, an emissary of the confederates, was in Paris at the time and he offered the Polish crown to Prince Karl of Saxony,[127] who refused the dangerous gift, and only expressed the desire to recover the duchy of Courland. Therefore the confederates decided to choose the duke of Teschen as king. It was said in Paris that the confederates had decided to proclaim an interregnum and send Wielhorski[128] as ambassador to France from the general confederation. Wielhorski was in Russia, and apparently the French king had promised to receive him with full honors. The confederates did not limit themselves to Poland, for they wanted to incite Lithuania to revolt as well. They based this possibility on the great dissatisfaction of the gentry there, caused by demands from the Russian government for wartime monetary assistance.

Choiseul finally revealed the king's decision on the Russian squadron to Khotinsky. In certain dangerous circumstances France, on humanitarian grounds, would not deny the necessary assistance and would not forbid Russian vessels from entering its harbors, since France and Russia had an agreement. The vessels must enter the harbors singly, and not as a united squadron, because France conducted a significant amount of trade with Turkey, which must be protected. Khotinsky said this was not good enough, for if an entire squadron were overtaken by a storm and sought safety in a harbor, was it really the intention that only one vessel be allowed to enter and the others be destroyed? The duke answered that it was impossible to change the decision, for those were the laws of the sea. An entire squadron could be allowed into a harbor only from a power allied with France. It would be the same in Spain. The fleet could be permitted to seek refuge from the winds in the roadsteads, except off Corsica.

On November 1 Khotinsky reported the curious news that an Italian Count Tomatis, who was serving as the master of ceremonies to the Polish king for court spectacles, had arrived in Paris and was saying that, based on their successes in Turkey, the Russians already were talking about a division of the conquests. They would keep Azov and Taganrog for themselves, as well as the right to free trade on the Black Sea. The Polish king would receive Moldavia and Wallachia. Since the courts of Vienna and Berlin might oppose this, the former would receive that part of Wallachia which it had lost in the previous war with the Turks. The latter would receive the bishopric of Warmia. Tomatis affirmed that both courts already had agreed to this, and that a treaty of friendship had been concluded between Russia, Austria and Prussia.

RELATIONS WITH DENMARK

We saw that Choiseul believed that Denmark[129] was no longer under French influence and thought to use Sweden to restrain it. Denmark hoped to restrain Sweden, and Choiseul could not tolerate this. Bernstorff told Filosofov that Denmark was ready to take the most extreme measures to oppose French plans in Sweden. Denmark made a commitment to send from one hundred to one hundred and sixty thousand thalers to Stockholm to this end. Filosofov urged that, in addition to providing money, Denmark outfit a fleet to deter Sweden. When he learned about this the duke of Choiseul suggested to the Danish ambassador at the French court that France could not forbid the Danish king to use money and threats in the current Swedish situation. France was giving notice in advance, however, that if Denmark took direct action in Sweden, both the French and the Spanish kings would not look upon this with equanimity. They would regard this as a complete rupture of friendly relations and as a first step would occupy Danish colonies in America.[130] In response the Danish royal council immediately decided to outfit a fleet and to prepare land forces for a campaign.

Choiseul made a formal inquiry to the Danish king, asking the motives behind the Danish mobilization. "The king, my sovereign," wrote Choiseul, "regards the kingdom of Sweden as an independent state, and no other state has the right to restrict Swedish national power. For example, the king thinks that no nation should act in Sweden the way Russia acts in Poland." Bernstorff instructed the Danish ambassador to reply that it was far from the intention of the Danish king to restrict or disturb Sweden, and that he hoped that the extraordinary Swedish diet would not engage in undertakings with consequences greatly harmful both to the existing tranquillity and the vital interests of the northern powers. The Danish king would be forced to fulfill his longstanding obligations and take action to ensure the safety of his own domains. At the same time the king did not hesitate to give his most Christian majesty[131] his most complete assurances that Denmark's modest armament represented no danger whatsoever and posed no threat at all to any nation on earth, least of all France. In the event of war with Sweden, the Danish court feared not just the hostile states of France and Spain, but also its own ally Prussia.

On July 4 Filosofov wrote to Panin: "Full participation by the Prussian court in our joint action in Sweden by issuing a declaration is not considered necessary here at present. The court here, of course, believes that in the event of war the Prussian king's agreement with us and with the court here is of the utmost importance. It is recognized that the Prussian king will not take action unless he benefits. He believes that the most important way to strengthen his state and to assure his own security and the tranquillity of the north as a whole for the future is to increase his holdings on the Baltic coast or his dominance of Polish commerce.

In order to be circumspect and to gain proper respect we should consider when it would be useful and necessary to open negotiations to find him some satisfaction from Poland, although not in the country itself." That was the way the natural and unavoidable question of compensation for the Prussian king at Poland's expense was discussed in Versailles, Vienna and Copenhagen. And why? That is what shaped the interests of each of the courts.

Filosofov was satisfied with Bernstorff but reported about the unsatisfactory state of affairs at the court: "The internal situation of the court here," he wrote, "has become somewhat unsettled. Court intrigues are increasing by the hour. The chief intriguers are the former favorite Count Holck, a boy of nineteen; Warnstedt, whose influence is growing steadily; and Mesdames Gobel and Bille, two ladies living at court, each of whom is striving to be the royal mistress.

"Unfortunately the king, surrounded by such contemptible people, is young and susceptible to all kinds of influences and, what is most unfortunate, his ministers are timid. Since none of the aforementioned trying to get control over the king interferes very much in state affairs, the ministers are content that the government is in their hands, so they offer no opposition to the court chicaneries. My goal is to prevent the French and Swedish ministers from becoming involved in court intrigues, since they are attempting to win Count Holck to their side."

SWEDISH AFFAIRS

The most heated contest between Russian and French ministers took place, as previously, in Sweden.[132] On January 8 the French party spread the rumor in Stockholm that a revolution was underway in Russia. "An evil band," wrote Ostermann,[133] "has so deceived its accomplices that they have overstepped all bounds. There is every evidence that they are playing a most desperate game. Colonel Baron Horn went to the senate and very threateningly and impudently reproached the senators for their behavior and praised the king's conduct." The senate, out of fear of its opponents' desperate game if a diet were to meet in Stockholm, ordered the diet to be convened in Norrköping. Then the opposition party circulated threats that Norrköping, which consisted for the most part of old houses, would be burned. The king stated that he did not intend to be separated from his family, and that the senators therefore should provide suitable lodging in Norrköping for the court and allot the necessary funds for this. Ostermann gratefully reported about the friendly cooperation of the English and Danish ministers. The Prussian minister Cocceji, however, responded coldly to an invitation to cooperate, saying that peace soon might be concluded between Russia and the Porte, and that the hopes of the French party in Sweden would be deceived.

On February 21 Ostermann asked Panin for 207,250 rubles for expenses for the diet. This sum was determined together with the Danish ambassador and sympathetic leading figures. "All the opinions of the leaders of the French party," wrote Ostermann, "proved with certainty that the attempt which they and the court which is favorably disposed to them have made in regard to the diet is a last desperate effort. If they fail, those who are loyal will have peace for a long time. That is why, if they risk their gamble, we must make an equivalent defense. Because of the well-known corruption of the national spirit here, it is hard to guarantee in advance that we will obtain supremacy when the diet is opened. But I can assure you that our opponents will pay very dearly for their supremacy."

At the end of March the king requested in the senate that, in the event a Danish fleet was armed, orders be given to outfit a certain number of ships and frigates in Karlskrona.[134] With two exceptions the senators refused to agree to this, stating that the Danish government had given a satisfactorily friendly answer to the Swedish inquiry about their mobilization, and that it therefore was dangerous to pit Sweden against Denmark. The diet should be convened quickly; thus any measures taken by the senate would be useless. One of the senators, Baron [Friedrich von] Friesendorf, said plainly that in his opinion the Danish armament was intended for intervention only in the event of a threat to Swedish liberties or for self-defense in case of an attack from Sweden. Since he could not attribute either of these intentions to the future diet, he did not see that there was any threat from Denmark. This argument so disturbed the king that he stood up and left without bowing to the senators.

The French proposed the following plan to the king. (1) The king should rely on the fleet. (2) He should send a secret emissary to Constantinople to ask for money. (3) Conclude the diet in three or four months in anticipation of a peace between Russia and Turkey. (4) The Porte should make Swedish independence a condition in its peace treaty with Russia, and should assume a guarantee of the new form of Swedish government.

The extraordinary diet in Norrköping began under very unfavorable auspices for the Russian party. The speakers for the clergy and the peasants were chosen from the partisans of France. Count Fersen,[135] who held the rank of general, was elected land marshal, or president of the diet, by a majority of 604 to 372. Naturally the first consequence of the triumph of the French party was that Russia's followers lost the majority in the senate. Ostermann held England responsible for this misfortune for not having sent the necessary money to Stockholm to support the Russian cause in the diet. When she heard the news of what had happened in Norrköping, the empress wrote to Panin: "Give orders to Ostermann to explain to everyone and anyone that, even if there is only one Swede to defend freedom, I will support him. Also have a short article written so as to seem it came from a foreigner explaining this, and have it printed and disseminated as soon as possible."

In May a secret commission dismissed all but one of the senators, accusing them of attempting, not to advise, but to exercise authority in opposition to the fundamental laws. The main instigator here was Crown Prince Gustavus, who conversed with peasants daily on the main square, urging them to decide which one they wanted to save, the king or the senate. The diet was transferred from Norrköping to Stockholm. Ostermann had to acknowledge that his bribes had been ineffective. Pechlin, the most prominent member of the Russian party, told the ambassador that he would vouch only for the preservation of the constitution and for tranquillity. Ostermann did not trust Pechlin completely because of his dual role and wrote that in all probability Sweden, fearing Russia's close alliance with Denmark and Prussia, would not initiate a war with Russia. As far as the change in the constitution was concerned, the French party foresaw great difficulties in this delicate matter. The queen requested that the king be given complete authority over promotions. The king and the crown prince, however, were satisfied with the full restoration of the constitution of 1719, excluding in perpetuity the article whereby official ranks were interpreted according to the basic laws. It was decided to take up the constitutional question after the financial matters were decided. If this could not be decided, secret instructions should be given to the senate, and the diet would be prorogued at the end of October, because the French minister told his friends that his sovereign did not intend to subsidize his party after that date.

Ostermann was ordered by his court to uphold the constitution of 1719 to the utmost. In September the ambassador reported that Mayor Kerning had brought deputies of the burgher estate to the queen, and that she had converted them to her views. The crown prince had invited lower-ranking officers to dine with him with the same goal in mind. All the remaining members were called together on September 30 (Old Style), and all reports agree that about this time it was agreed to decide the constitutional question at the forceful insistence of the queen and the demands of the French minister. The officers were enticed by the promise of a thousand plots for each vote and the circulation of assurances written in the queen's hand that each would be raised one degree in rank. At the beginning of October the French party was thrown into confusion by the news of Russian victories over the Turks, but quickly recovered and began to proclaim that the Russian victories were to Sweden's advantage. The victories would delay the conclusion of peace and thus give the Swedes more freedom to settle their domestic affairs without interference. This was how the queen talked, adding that since it now was winter Russia and its allies were in no position to use armed force to hinder them. Meanwhile it would be possible to take better defensive measures.

The prospect of changing the constitution met strong resistance, since the French party felt it had to strike a deal with members of the Russian party. The French party proposed bringing a certain number of the latter into the senate and the secret commission, if the Russian party would agree to strengthen the queen's power. It goes without saying that Ostermann's entire efforts were directed towards nullifying this arrangement. He was successful, and the Russian party gained the ascendancy in the nobility so that it was forbidden to raise the question of changing the constitution. The same decision was made by the burghers and the peasants. The *operation* cost Ostermann four hundred and fifty thousand thalers in copper money. Those who were loyal received three hundred thalers a month, and the *operators* were paid double. Ostermann requested another hundred and fifty thousand rubles to take advantage of the fortunate turn of events and conclude the diet in accord with the desires of the Russian court.

RELATIONS WITH ENGLAND

We have observed that because of an article about subsidies to Sweden, a treaty of alliance was not concluded between Russia and England.[136] Russia desired that if England did not want to help in the Turkish war it at least should help monetarily to prevent a Swedish war. "If England by giving subsidies to Sweden could free Russia from a second war instigated by France," the empress wrote to Chernyshev, "will it do so? It is possible that the French party will be able to have an extraordinary diet convened and having the king abdicate. If England does not give subsidies to Sweden, the odds are ten to one that Sweden will be stupid enough to declare war on Russia. Then England because of its false economy will undergo war with an empire which for many reasons it now should regard as its only friend and support. I think that if my argument were brought before parliament, then, regardless of the opposition of the lower house, there would not be a single good Englishman who would not vote for subsidies. If the nation decided not to give, then private citizens would. If they do not give, then henceforth I would regard the friendship and the enmity of England as empty words, devoid of meaning, because they lead to nothing."

The only response received from England was that parliament would agree to pay subsidies in peacetime. Catherine was angry and wrote to Chernyshev in March 1769: "Listen, sir! When you find out everything that I have done and undertaken against the enemies of the Russian empire, then you will say that, after Ivan Chernyshev, no one dislikes sound and fury more than Catherine. Don't think that I am ranting and raving. Granted that I have been suffering from chills and fever and all the fluxes in the world for three weeks, but I am of sound mind and good memory. If necessary I can deal with the Swedes as I would with bugs who bite, but at the risk of being squashed. Your Englishmen now have the joy of being insignificant, and I hope that they will remain so until the French and the Spaniards fall upon them. May God grant this the day after this letter is received."

It remained to influence England to give some money to counteract the French party in Sweden. When Count Ivan Chernyshev proposed to Rochford[137] that in order to regulate Swedish affairs England could send at least £40-50,000 to Sweden, the latter replied in strictest confidence: "I still do not know if we will agree to pay one sum or another. I have only one thing I must tell you, that the question to whom the money can be entrusted might cause very great difficulty in the royal council. They do not want to entrust it to Goodricke.[138] Everyone knows he is dishonest, though he is the best of our ministers at foreign courts and can be trusted with everything except money." After a while Rochford told Chernyshev that it had been decided to send an order to Goodricke to spend a designated sum of money to strengthen the loyalist party in Sweden, but he did not say exactly what this sum was. From this Chernyshev deduced that it was not large. Rochford assured him that France had sent only one hundred thousand livres to Modein, its ambassador in Stockholm.

In March Chernyshev informed Panin of an interesting statement by Rochford. "I know for certain," said Rochford, "that the Prussian king was determined not to permit the Swedes to go to war with Russia. As regards their change of government, not only will he not become involved, but perhaps he will not regret it if they succeed." At the same time Chernyshev wrote: "I am beginning to worry that there is some kind of coquetry between the court here and Vienna. In order to frighten Rochford, I read him the conclusion of Ostermann's latest letter, where he mentions the possibility of a proposal about the conclusion of an alliance of the Austrian, French and Spanish courts with Sweden. At this all of a sudden he indiscreetly blurted out 'Would the Austrians want to deceive us this way?' No matter how much I tried to get him to say more about this, I was unable to do so."

Chernyshev blamed the English ministry for the failure to conclude the treaty between Russia and England. "You can be completely certain that as long as this ministry is in place no definite action can be expected that would harm France in the slightest. If it came to that, they would not remain in office, and they are ready to do anything to avoid that." Rochford told Chernyshev directly that he held the Prussian king responsible that the treaty between Russia and England had fallen through. Through his minister Frederick II attempted to spread the news everywhere in London that it would be foolhardy for the English to give any subsidies to Sweden.

At the end of August Chernyshev told Rochford about the dispatch of the Russian squadron to the archipelago. Rochford could not restrain himself from saying, "What a daring enterprise! How I wish we were at war with France! Two allied fleets could accomplish wonderful things!" Chernyshev also did not restrain himself in conversation with the Englishman: "If the present ministry were more secure at home," he said, "the English now could acquire some possessions in the archipelago the way the French seized Corsica, and with a firm base there could destroy the profitable French trade in the Levant. England could find a stalwart helper in Russia, not only on land but also at sea, when Russia becomes accustomed to the local waters." "How mistaken are they," answered Rochford, "who think that the Russian fleet cannot help us in case of need!"

The English ambassador at the Russian court, Lord Cathcart, reported to his ministry about a project in St. Petersburg to transform the Crimea, Moldavia and Wallachia into independent states as buffers against Turkey. Similarly Finland was to be transformed into an independent grand duchy for protection against Sweden. Rochford told Cathcart that such a plan was not completely consistent with the restraint of the court of St. Petersburg and its unwillingness to extend Russia's frontiers. It was quite evident that such independent states in reality would be completely dependent on Russia. Rochford remarked to Cathcart that he was not convinced completely of the lofty character of the Russian empress and some of her ministers, but instead ascribed to them a certain degree of ambition.

II

FOREIGN RELATIONS
1770

CAMPAIGNS AGAINST THE TURKS IN THE DANUBIAN PRINCIPALITIES
There was discussion in St. Petersburg about the conditions for peace, a peace very much desired. But the Turks had not been pushed to the limit by the previous year's campaign and did not ask for peace, so it would have to be won with strenuous new exertions and new victories. "Victory is the enemy of war and the beginning of peace," wrote Catherine. "I repeat," she wrote to Voltaire, "a wise Europe will approve my plans only if they are successful. You have compared the plan for an expedition to the Mediterranean, which has been attributed to me incorrectly (I have decided to name the author of the plan when it succeeds),[1] with Hannibal's enterprise. But the Carthaginians were dealing with a full-blown colossus, while before us is a feeble ghost which will fly to pieces at the first touch."

Seeing that the Porte did not intend to make peace proposals, Catherine hoped that the people would induce the sultan to do so and wrote to Rumiantsev:[2] "In the Levant it is said that everything is prepared to throw off the shameful yoke. I hope that there will be even more disorder among the Turks, if you spread the rumor imperceptibly among them that their furious sultan does not want peace, which he could have if he wishes. You know that Russia never wanted war but will defend itself with all its might, as experience has shown. As a consequence, the Turkish empire easily might fall."

We saw that in 1769 the Russian forces captured both the Danubian principalities and their principal cities.[3] But it was a disadvantage that the Russian forces were scattered over a wide area, while the Turks still had two fortresses, Zhurzha and Brailov. As early as the end of 1769 Lieutenant General Stoffeln[4] had begun preparations for the capture of Brailov, to Catherine's great interest. She saw the significance of the places on the map and could not conceal her uneasiness from Rumiantsev, because considerable time had elapsed and Brailov was not yet in Russian hands. The commander-in-chief did not consider this necessary for the security of the Russian army in Moldavia that summer. At the very beginning of the year the Turks anticipated Stoffeln. A sizeable detachment moved from Ruschuk to Focsani to split the Russian forces which were between the two main cities of the principalities, Bucharest and Jassy. Major General Podgorichany and Potemkin[5] with comparatively small forces decisively defeated the enemy after an unusually bitter struggle. But even before the report of the victory at Focsani arrived, the name of this small locality was mentioned in another sad report. The plague had appeared in the surrounding areas, and newspapers hostile to Russia were saying that it would wipe Russian army out. "In the spring," Catherine wrote Voltaire, "the plague victims will rise from the dead to do battle."

An enemy attack on Bucharest was repulsed. After a successful battle with the Turks, however, Stoffeln was forced to retreat from Brailov since it was too strongly fortified. During his retreat he burned two hundred and sixty villages to deny the enemy the possibility of attacking Focsani again. Upon receiving news that there was another threat to Bucharest from Zhurzha, Stoffeln went there, routed the Turks at Zhurzha, and burned the city and one hundred and forty-three villages. The area extending along the Danube for two hundred and fifty versts, from the Pruth to the Olta, was laid completely waste again to protect Bucharest from a new attack.

These movements occupied the first two months of 1770. Rumiantsev remained in Podolia and wrote the empress that he would have crossed into Moldavia long ago had there not been shortages there of provisions and forage, which would have to be brought from Podolia even for the small detachments operating there. Rumiantsev complained bitterly that Brailov remained in Turkish hands, that the Turks had sizable forces and supplies and that the Russians had few of either. Catherine reassured her commander-in-chief: "Now that Zhurzha has been taken," she wrote, "do not doubt that this will enable you to wipe out the swarms of enemy again. It seems to me that the fortress at Brailov has not been that important since, so to say, it has been surrounded by our forces and positions. I am much more disturbed by the difficulties in setting up supply depots in the territory already under our control. For God's sake, do everything to eliminate any deficiency there. Perhaps there is still some grain in Wallachia. When the Moldavians return from the mountains and from their hiding places, live peacefully in their homes and our army maintains order, then at least horses and oxen will be available to transport provisions. These will be useful, thanks to our usual efficiency in such matters. Having saved themselves, the Moldavians will have to comply because the Turks threaten to wipe them out, and you will not shrink from discussing this with them. The countless Turkish forces will be repulsed completely in the coming campaign, because apparently the confusion which existed in the army during the last campaign will not recur. The Asiatics will stay at home to oppose the Georgians. According to the news, there was nothing more to be heard from the vizier since forty thousand of his troops were beaten at Focsani, Brailov and Zhurzha. Don't imagine that their supply depots are that outstanding. Everything of theirs is in a state of total disorder. Last year they got a lot of grain from Wallachia, which we won't give them now."

Catherine was quite indignant over Rumiantsev's report of Stoffeln's actions. "I confess that I find Mr. Stoffeln's exertions in burning city after city and hundreds of villages completely distasteful," she wrote to Rumiantsev. "I find it unnecessary to have recourse to such unlimited barbarism. When this is done unnecessarily it is like former days on the Volga and the Sura. I know that you, like me, do not find satisfaction in such events. Please calm Stoffeln down. The destruction of all those places will not win him any laurels or bring us any profit, especially if these are Christian habitations. I am afraid that a similar fate may befall Bucharest and other places on the pretext that it is impossible to hold them, and so it can happen. You can see from all of this that I am giving you my candid thoughts. I leave you to do what neither more nor less than prudent caution and, even better, your military knowledge and skill dictates. I have full confidence that you will do what will advance the cause entrusted to you. Perhaps my natural inclination is to create rather than to destroy. I react to such unpleasant events too passionately, but I felt it useful that you know exactly what I thought."

In fact Rumiantsev informed the empress that "he found no satisfaction in such events," but he tried to justify Stoffeln, whom he valued very much. To this end he already had written to Count Grigory Orlov: "Thank you most gratefully for the advice you have given me. Put aside any thoughts, most gracious Count, that our explanations were anything but the most gracious kind of guidance. I beg you to give me the experience of your candor. That is, inform me in friendly confidence how our present victories are received, not as the judgment of the sword but as the judgment of fire. I conclude from your words, and I of course am of the same opinion, that burning villages, and even more, burning splendid buildings is customary for howling barbarians but not for Europeans. But on the other hand we must point out the special character of this war.

"Different measures are used, and this war takes a different form from that on battlefields elsewhere in Europe. How do the enemy customs differ from European ones? Everything he does is marked by atrocity. It is impossible to follow the same policy towards villages, which in any other war would be preserved because of the benefit they would bring. If the enemy does not succeed in clearing out with all his possessions, he destroys them himself, so that nothing is left for us. If the village is left intact but deserted, there is the danger that the enemy, to whom humanity is foreign, will infect it with a cruel plague, something he has done more quite a number of times to the ruin of the human race."

When he received the aforementioned letter from Catherine, Rumiantsev wrote to her: "Truly the present war is characterized by the kind of barbarism which was common to our ancestors and to all savage peoples. Thus it is difficult to use gentle measures against this kind of enemy, whose actions are nothing but savagery and inhumanity. We quickly realized during the Prussian war[6] how harmful it was for us to burn and exhaust the district where we were waging war. Following the example of our opponent, therefore, we improved our old customs. When we fought against the Turks, the examples of their barbarism so embittered our forces that they showed them no mercy. Lieutenant General von Stoffeln, from what

I know of his character, certainly would not have put enemy dwellings to the torch had he been in a position to make use of them himself, or if he could employ other means to weaken the enemy. Leaving the villages intact would give the Turks a firmer base on their side of the Danube and help them ravage Wallachia and exhaust our forces with constant sorties.

Count Peter Alevandrovich Rumiantsev

"The ability to cross to our side of the Danube now has been denied them as much as possible, neither will they find anything they need in the devastated villages on their bank to facilitate their movement. Up to now this has ensured the security of the borders of the subject principalities and of our armies which now are in both principalities. This military necessity was less of a burden to the inhabitants than the Turkish tyranny which so had dispirited them. When the announcement was made, they took all of their possessions to Wallachia and Moldavia for the duration, losing only the walls of their dwellings to the flames. Besides, the dwellings that were burned were inhabited for the most part by Muslims, who crossed the Danube at the approach of our forces. Thus I will inform Lieutenant General von Stoffeln of the most exalted and most friendly wishes of your majesty so that he henceforth can conform to them."

On March 11 two wishes of the empress were presented to the council: (1) Moldavia and the small part of Wallachia that have not been burned already have been in our hands for several months, but nothing has been decided about their form of government, their taxes and so on. All of those in the divan (ruling council), those serving as governors and others are conducting affairs according to Turkish forms, not ours. Even if this does not violate good order, at the very least it is not fitting. Thus we must deliberate and, in fact, decide how things will be from now on. This I ask of the council. (2) That the commander-in-chief be instructed that the Moldavians and Wallachians not be ruined. They should have the same justice and the same assistance as our subjects here. Generals should be assigned to the provinces to administer them. The council decided that an examination of these matters be postponed until all the provincial deputies could come to St. Petersburg. After they had been heard, orders could be given. Besides, people capable of performing these governmental duties had to be sought in advance.

In requesting the establishment of a Russian administration in the Danubian principalities, Catherine had in mind the regular collection of taxes in any amount which could ease the burden of Russia's military expenses. "I ask you to tell me," she wrote to Rumiantsev, "whether it is possible to use the income from Moldavia and Wallachia to cover extraordinary expenses because it is said that the Turks derive more than three million in revenue from these principalities. Even though I know that it will not be that much now, I still think that, even if it is only one million, that would replace Prince Viazemsky's[7] efforts somewhat."

The reply was an interesting letter from Rumiantsev written on March 25 (from Liatychov). "I always am concerned about collecting and increasing revenue from the principalities of Moldavia and Wallachia to ease the burden on your imperial majesty's treasury of the great number of Turks and Tatars, who were in Moldavia for a long time and who spared nothing, so they have drained off or squeezed out all of its wealth. The people are not merely poor; they are starving. When our forces arrived here they had to fend for themselves. Later the extreme conditions here impelled me to reassure the Moldavians that they would not have to pay the poll tax on cultivators, but only if they gave provisions, forage, horses and oxen. It is impossible to rescind this order.

"General von Stoffeln wrote: 'If taxes are imposed on the inhabitants, this simply will incur more expense. The city of Jassy and other places are still empty. Wallachia also has exhausted its resources to maintain the Turkish army. The lands along the Danube, where grain cultivation predominated, were all burned by the Turks. The inhabitants were taken prisoner or hid in the mountains.' I named members to the divans of Moldavia and Wallachia who were elected by the deputies and vouched for by General von Stoffeln.

"Major General Chernievich has been given supervision in the former and Major General Zamiatin in the latter. Zamiatin certified the receipt of 62,759 leva in taxes for February, out of which 9269 leva were left for the expenses of our forces and salary for volunteers. Officers have been assigned to supervise the collection of taxes because the local treasurers, following their own customs, took special advantage of the present confusion and obviously put profit ahead of any future welfare. Moldavia and Wallachia are not in any position to furnish us provisions, and up to now all the support for the army has come from local supply depots. Even the Polish district has been stripped bare. The sustenance was drained, not by expenditures, but because of disorder. In the last campaign the grass and the grain were destroyed for the most part in the field, and without fodder the horses and cattle perished.

"Advancing into Moldavia, I would have sustenance for three months for sure, but during that time transports from the newly-replenished supply depots should continue. I still can overcome these inconveniences, but I am unable to remedy the subsequent shortages. Hitherto the army has not received the recruits requested to bring the regiments up to full strength. It has yet to be furnished the things it needs to any appreciable extent. My requests have been taken to the proper places, and officers have been sent to receive them, but without success. It cannot escape your sagacity that there is one image and one set of numbers for us on paper and another in practice, both for the men in service and everything else that concerns them. Even in the past war infantry regiments rarely had more than a thousand men under arms, but now they have barely half that number.

"Other armies realized how much more serviceable light cavalry were in general for service and how it was cheaper to arm and maintain them, so they mounted most of their cavalry on small horses. We waged war against the German cavalry on the smallest Russian horses and only used cossacks against them. We decided to imitate them, and so abandoned cossacks in favor of mounting almost all of our cavalry on large horses with heavy and expensive armament, which meant a burden to the service and a loss for the main treasury. Experience has shown clearly how useless they were against the present enemy in the last campaign.

"Where there are more recruits there are, of course, more sick. Other armies have attendants to care for the sick who are not soldiers. But lacking these and with the assignment of military men to the task, only half of them remain under arms, while their weapons are just a burden for the other half. I cannot keep silent but have decided to say the following. You need a commissariat to make all the preparations necessary for your army's welfare. This would be introduced gradually so that everything could be done properly, and in addition supplies would be delivered to the regiments on time. The regiments never would have to fend for themselves for clothing and equipment. In wartime they should be clothed and equipped for summer and winter, because military operations do not wait. Inspectors for the army also are needed to supervise the quality of what the commissariat provides as well to supervise the general order. Your imperial majesty's forces have been reduced significantly as a consequence of new staff establishments for the army,[8] but there has been no saving to the treasuries, either in the commissariat or in the regiments. Both the ordinary [infantry] and cavalry regiments have more adornment, to the point of excess, but this has not improved their fitness for regular service. The colonels have become more concerned about their finery than about its usefulness."

Rumiantsev's letter made a painful impression. The commander-in-chief took a gloomy view of his situation. He would linger, waiting for reinforcements and improvements. If he went into action, this was not the kind of spirit which led to victory. Fabii were needed against Hannibals,[9] but not against the Turkish vizier and the Crimean khan with their disorderly hordes. A bold and swift move was needed against barbarians. That alone could bring victory, and victory was indispensable. It would bring peace, and Russia very much needed peace.

Despite the inadequacies of his army and the need to leave part of his forces in Polish territory to protect the rear and the supply depots from the confederates,[10] Rumiantsev left winter quarters for Khotin on April 23. A bridge was built there to cross the Dniester. Because of heavy rains the Russian army did not reach Khotin until May 12. On May 15 they crossed the Dniester with about thirty-nine thousand men, including the sick, while the Turkish army numbered two hundred thousand. "I am crossing the Dniester with the army," wrote Rumiantsev, "and I am attempting to give the enemy the impression that my forces are greater than they are by marching straight along the near side of the Pruth. I am attempting to use offensive operations to conceal my deficiencies." Roads made impassable by the rain created terrible obstacles, so that Rumiantsev could leave Khotin only on May 25. The march was difficult. "The climate here," wrote Rumiantsev, "burdens us alternately with heavy rains and extraordinarily intense heat. On clear days, which are few, it is extremely hot almost from the moment the sun rises. The soldiers on the march, particularly the new recruits, cannot bear it. On the other hand, the nights are cold, not like those of summer."

The march was hard, and the soldiers could look forward, not to a glorious death on the battlefield, but to death in a hospital from the plague. For this reason Rumiantsev decided to proceed on the near side of the Pruth, where there were few inhabitants, and where there was still no danger of plague. General Stoffeln died from the plague in Jassy at the end of May. His place was taken by Prince Nikita Repnin,[11] already familiar to us. Rumiantsev reported the death of Stoffeln in these terms: "Such an end has troubled me more than I can say. We have lost a sensible commander from among your imperial majesty's servants. He sacrificed himself out of great zeal in your service. He held positions from which I often had ordered him, for his own safety, to retreat. Sometimes I had to tell him, however, to be lenient in responding to the requests of the inhabitants and to encourage them to have confidence in the protection of your imperial majesty."

When he had gone one hundred and thirty-one versts from Khotin, Rumiantsev encountered a new obstacle. The terrain did not correspond to the description made that winter by Quartermaster General Meder. "Apparently a plan of the terrain was drawn in the winter from hearsay, not from eyewitness observation," wrote Rumiantsev, "and now the excuse is being offered that it was impossible to survey the territory exactly because of Tatar attacks then." The commander-in-chief decided to wait until the new quartermaster general, Bauer,[12] on whom he relied completely, could become thoroughly familiar with the terrain and could point out the best roads. "Nature has put so many unusual high and low places here that it is difficult to change direction and there are obstacles on every side."

Rumiantsev also moved too far away from the Second Army, exposing his left flank to the enemy. The commander-in-chief of the Second Army, Count Panin,[13] had halted when faced with the plague. At the beginning of May he sent to St. Petersburg to ask if he should cross the Dniester if Rumiantsev was able to make a stand, not just at the Danube, but even before Jassy, to prevent the Turks from coming to the assistance of Bender. In the event the First Army moved as desired, should he take the Second across the Dniester and begin the siege of Bender before the end of the hot weather, if the plague grew worse.

The council decided to instruct Panin to go to Bender, because rumors about this campaign already were circulating and postponing it would be inglorious. Bolder spirits prevailed in St. Petersburg than on the Dniester, and so the most energetic measures were ordered to achieve peace as quickly as possible. This is evident from the notes of Count Grigory Orlov which he read in the council on May 17. After the capture of Bender, in Orlov's opinion, an infantry corps should be sent to capture Varna. Then it should travel by sea directly to Constantinople to win the quickest and most glorious peace. Less ardent members of the council replied that this undertaking should be delayed for a while. First, information must be gathered about what boats could be obtained on the Dniester and about the Zaporozhian boats called *duby*.[14] How far out in the Black Sea did they go, and could they be brought safely past Ochakov? Besides, before boats were sent to Varna, Rumiantsev had to establish himself firmly on the Danube and set up supply depots there.

But Rumiantsev found that the Russian army had taken too much territory in the previous year and decided to withdraw from Bucharest. "I trust that you will not delay your march," wrote Catherine, informing him of Panin's movements, "nor delay your arrival at a secure base for the effort against Bender. In that case, do not refuse to render all possible aid. I am as confident of your zeal and your fervor in this matter as I am that without fail you will take the most careful precautions to check the epidemic where it has appeared, lest the army suffer any harm. You well know we must overcome the treacherous enemy with our arms. Thus our victory over him would make it easier for me to deal with him in various places and compel him to conclude the desired peace.

"It is unfortunate that you left Bucharest prematurely. I am hopeful, relying on divine assistance and on your military prowess, that you will not fail to achieve the greatest success, and that you will produce results which will bring you glory and demonstrate how great your devotion is to the fatherland and to me. Wherever they had two or three legions, the Romans did not ask how numerous the enemy was, but where he was. They attacked and defeated him, and with a small force were victorious over the numerous hordes opposing them. But we are Russians, and God's grace is with us in this war because our cause is just. I have *you* in command of the army. The army's bravery is well known. Therefore, praying to the Most High for success, I put my hope in His protection."

"I make bold," replied Rumiantsev, "now and henceforth to answer not with words but with deeds. I will always act expeditiously, and I will not fail in the slightest to live up to the expectations for the charge given me. The labors and actions now achieved by the forces of your imperial majesty entrusted to me would furnish the Romans an example, had their era followed ours." The answer in fact was given by deeds.

RUMIANTSEV'S VICTORY ON THE LAGRA

Early in July Rumiantsev encountered a large force of Turks and Tatars where the Lagra river flows into the Pruth. The enemy numbered about eighty thousand. The commander-in-chief nevertheless said: "We cannot bear the disgrace and the indignity of seeing the enemy stand before us without advancing on him." The attack took place on July 7, and the enemy suffered a total defeat. More than a thousand bodies were left on the battlefield, while the Russians suffered only twenty-nine dead and sixty-one wounded. "Doubtless you will have a major place in my century as a wise, skilful and zealous leader," Catherine wrote to Rumiantsev. "I intend to do justice to your achievement, and so as to make my opinion of you and my satisfaction at your successes known to all, I am sending you the order of St. George, first class. I am enclosing with it a list of the villages which soon by order of the senate will be granted to you and to your posterity in perpetuity."

Two grand viziers already had been relieved of duty. Now a third, Khalil Bey, commanded the army. Upon learning how few in number the victors at the Lagra were, Khalil Bey crossed the Danube and advanced on them, fully expecting that his army of fifty thousand would crush the enemy, who had only seventeen thousand. On July 21 they met on the banks of the Kagul river by Trajan's wall. Here there was a repetition of a phenomenon known from ancient history, from the accounts of the struggle between the Greeks and the Persians, of European quality against Asiatic quantity.

For a moment the huge number of janissaries defied the Russian soldiers, but then the voice of the commander-in-chief himself resounded, "Stand, boys!",[15] and those who were fleeing stopped and surrounded their leader, seeing he was in terrible danger. The artillery and the grenadiers' bayonets decided the matter. The Turks fled to the Danube, abandoning artillery and the entire camp as booty for the victors. They lost twenty thousand killed, while the Russians lost only three hundred and fifty-three dead and five hundred and fifty wounded. The Kagul victory gave Rumiantsev the right to remind Catherine about her reprimand in regard to the Romans. "It will be permitted," he wrote Catherine, "to liken the present affair to those of the ancient Romans whom your majesty ordered me to imitate. Your imperial majesty's army would not have gone into action had it asked how great the enemy force was. It only wanted to know where it was."

Catherine's delight was expressed in a letter to the new Roman. "I considered it my primary obligation to convey my gratitude on bended knee to Almighty God for His countless favors and munificences. This was done this morning (August 2) in the Kazan church to the public firing of ordnance, and the whole city greatly rejoiced. Then I returned to the palace and, sitting at table, remembered him who had given us reason for joy. I took delight in his skill, zeal and intelligence. To the accompaniment of cannon salutes, I drank to the health of Field Marshal Count Rumiantsev, and I salute you with the newly-awarded and totally merited title. I must report to you that there were none at my table who did not weep for joy when they saw that I had done justice to their worthy fellow citizen.

"Could anyone regard the successes and the victories of my unimproved army with as much pleasure as I do? It is easier to sense how great my joy is than to write about it. I thank you for having, in fact, accomplished what was said about the Romans, not asking how numerous the enemy was, but where he was. I am certain that you will not fail to name those who distinguished themselves so that I can do justice by them." Those who distinguished themselves were Major General Olitz, Lieutenant General Plemiannikov, Count Bruce, Count Saltykov, Prince Repnin, Quartermaster General Bauer, Major General Prince Dolgoruky,[16] Count Soltykov, Major General of the Artillery Melissino, Glebov, Podgorichany, Potemkin, Brigadier Gudovich and Lieutenant Colonels Count (Semen Romanovich) Vorontsov[17] and Yelchaninov.

VICTORIES AT AKKERMAN, BRAILOV AND BENDER

The defeated vizier fled to the Danube and crossed it in boats to Isaccea, but the rearguard was not able to cross, for General Bauer arrived in time and forced it to lay down its arms. Thus the Russians acquired another one hundred and twenty-seven cannon in addition to the one hundred and forty taken at the Kagul. Ismail, which was still poorly fortified at the time, surrendered to General Potemkin.

Prince Repnin took Kilia. Akkerman surrendered to General [Heinrich Otto] Igelström.

But Brailov held out stubbornly and beat back the assault. On November 3 Rumiantsev wrote to the empress about this setback. "I chose Major General Glebov as the one most capable of conducting the siege because he has served in the artillery. I gave him new instructions every day based on the reports and plans he furnished me. But his actions in this siege contradicted them. The assault, which began early, was carried out in undefended places, so only one side of the city was besieged. This is because it was known that the only route around the enemy camp, which lay between the Danube and the fortress with its suburbs, was on the near side. Undoubtedly the zeal and fervor he [Glebov] surely displayed were an incentive for this courageous effort. Although all the messengers gave conflicting reports, they still agreed unanimously that the entire operation would have been successful if the grenadiers of the Fourth Grenadier Regiment, who did not deserve the rank of the lowest-grade soldier, and whose insubordination and faintheartedness had been noticed repeatedly, had advanced and not held the others back."

Then Rumiantsev made his usual complaint that his army was too small for the territory captured: "It is very difficult to cover all the conquered territory with the small force I now have available. I am concentrating quarters for the army as much as possible in this district, and while I am here I am moving beyond the city of Jassy. Almost all of the generals have left the army because of sickness. The only generals I might be able to persuade to remain are Khrapovitsy and Kheraskov, but they, too, have submitted requests to be discharged. It is impossible to find out what really is in each one's heart. I would note that some retire because they believe that they receive fewer rewards than those with the same seniority. Others retire because they find it dangerous to remain where the army is stationed."

The Turks finally left Brailov at the end of November. Bucharest was taken for the second time. At that time the numerous hordes of Turks in the open country at the Lagra and at the Kagul could not stand their ground against the comparatively small Russian First Army. The Second Army, numbering thirty-four thousand, was held back by the stubborn and desperate Turkish resistance at Bender. The siege of this fortress proceeded, starting at the beginning of July. Count Panin decided to lead his army in an assault in the night of September 15-16. After a battle which continued throughout the night and a fire which destroyed the fortress, the garrison laid down its arms. During the siege and the assault the victors lost more than a fifth of their entire army. Such a loss made an unfavorable impression in St. Petersburg and drastically diminished the significance of the victory won so dearly.

The tone of Panin's report could be considered incongruous and inappropriate. *"L'ours est mort* (the bear is dead)," wrote the commander-in-chief of the Second Army. "He had his den or stronghold at Bender, had almost more claws than there were hunters and was savage and desperate beyond measure. The chasseurs of Great Catherine were sent against him, striving to be true to the dignity of her military reputation. With this inborn loyalty, and zeal for their sovereign, courage and vigilance on the ladders found a way to climb over the walls of his den and shattered his jaws completely. Consequently I would commit an unforgivable sin before my sovereign if I did not say that her hunters whom I led on this chase truly deserved the greatest favor of Great Catherine, before whom I throw myself together with them."

Panin was sent the Military Order, first class, but the decree was short and cold: "This occurrence (the capture of Bender) is all the more important because it corresponds to the glory of our arms and our deeds. As a sign of my pleasure at the service, zeal and steadfastness you have shown to me and to the state in this matter, in conformity to the prescribed statute [I grant you] the Military Order," and so on. With the capture of Bender the activity of the Second Army had to be restricted for a time.

POLICY TOWARDS THE TATARS

We have noted how Count Panin had been ordered to try to wean the Tatars away from the Turks.[18] On March 4 Panin informed the empress that success could be predicted. He included a report from Second Major Bastevik,[19] who had been used to make the first contacts. The council deliberated on the matter on March 15 and concluded that "The Crimean and other Tatars allied with them, because of their nature and disposition, never will be useful subjects of her imperial majesty. No reasonable amount of taxes will be collected from them, nor can they be used to defend the Russian frontier, for they alone attack these frontiers. Finally, by taking them under its direct rule, Russia would stir up universal and deep-rooted envy against itself and would awaken the suspicion that it was trying to increase its domains without limit. Good sense demands that you be careful about awakening such feelings, especially when there is nothing definite or significant to be gained. The Tatar people think that citizenship means the right to demand everything for their own benefit. They consider that service and benefit to others merely means living peacefully and not engaging in brigandage. There is little for Russia to gain from ruling the Crimea and the other Tatar hordes which belong to it.

"On the other hand Russia could increase its power markedly if it separated the Tatars from Turkey and established a new dependent power. The Porte thereby would cease to be of concern for Russia and its neighbors, because it would have no way to disturb the Russian frontiers. It even would be difficult for it to lead its forces across the Danube, because the independent Tatars would be on its right flank. In order to gain this benefit from the present war, we have to redirect what has been our constant aim, freedom of navigation on the Black Sea, towards encouraging and assisting the Tatars. Therefore first of all we must make a firm decision not to stop fighting, even if it costs us an extra campaign, until the Porte formally recognizes the independence of the Crimea and the hordes belonging to it.

"Therefore we must conduct negotiations with the Tatars in such a way that Count Panin influences them, not towards acceptance of our rule, but towards independence from Turkey. He should promise our guarantee, our patronage and our protection. He should give the firm assurance that, if they sign a treaty for secession from Turkey now, we will not conclude a peace with the latter that does not confirm by treaty the independence of the Crimean territory.

"Finally Count Panin should demand from the Tatars in return that they furnish us with the means to defend them against Turks. They should accept our garrison and some of our fortresses and give us one harbor on the Crimean coast where our fleet could prevent a Turkish landing." (Next to these words in the protocol Catherine noted, "We must have the passage from the Sea of Azov to the Black Sea in our hands, and we should look to achieve this.") Naturally such an agreement should include a proviso for freedom of trade on land and by sea. If these important negotiations are to be concluded to our advantage during the present campaign, there is no time to be lost. Our Azov flotilla must occupy the stipulated port on the Crimean coast, so that at the outset of peace and negotiations with the Turks the preliminary points already will be decided. We should control the passage by bringing some of our ships from the Mediterranean into the Black Sea, in fact, into that harbor which already will be ours. In this way we can secure a solid basis for our fleet and, consequently, complete freedom of navigation on the Black Sea."[20]

The empress confirmed the council's decision, and Panin was sent the corresponding rescript which, with Catherine's additons, already specified which places should be demanded from the Crimeans to secure the passage from the sea of Azov to the Black Sea. These were Yenikale on the Crimean coast and Taman on the Kuban coast. Understandably these demands to cede territories could not be raised at the outset of negotiations. It was a difficult matter anyway. The words "freedom and independence" easily could stir up peoples for whom independence was difficult, for whom for centuries independence had been just a dream, and who impatiently awaited the first opportunity to make this dream a reality.

But this was not the case for the Crimean Tatars. They scarcely were aware of their dependence on the Porte, a dependence firmly grounded in their common faith. Dependence on Turkey easily was very advantageous for the Tatars. First of all, they could practice brigandage with impunity under the Porte's protection. Strengthening Russia's power would make this impossible. They no longer would receive gifts [pominki] or tribute from Moscow, but this only would intensify their hatred and fear of Russia. Conversely it would increase their sympathy for Turkey, who shared their faith, and increase their need for Turkish protection.

The Tatar relations to the khans and to the numerous Girey family were very loose, which is often the case in governmental relations of backward peoples to great ruling families. They overthrew the khan at the first sign of displeasure and were not afraid that the Porte might prevent this. For their part the Gireys[21] clung to the Porte, and when they were overthrown in the Crimea they found refuge at Constantinople. They had domains in Rumelia[22] and, according to a legend which flattered their ambitions, if the Turkish dynasty ceased to exist, the title of padishah[23] would pass to them. They were offered independence, but that clearly was a mistake. Deciding this in St. Petersburg did not mean securing Crimean independence, because here only one perspective was seen, the one advantageous to Russia, nor was there any detailed examination of the difficulties resulting from not defining the goal precisely. If the Tatars became completely independent, naturally they should receive the right to conduct their own relations freely with other powers, to enter into alliances with one or the other of them as they saw fit and, in case of war between Russia and Turkey, to make an alliance with the latter against the former. Taking independence in this exact sense, it would be impossible to argue that the independence of the Crimea would make the Porte a virtual nonentity in regard to Russia. Independence merely would make it impossible for the Porte to conduct major operations against the Russian frontiers. It also would be difficult for the Porte to lead its armies across the Danube, since the independent Tatars then would be on their right flank.

To gain the proposed advantages, this independence must be restricted; that is, bind the Tatars to a firm and permanent alliance with Russia and compel them to renounce Turkey forever. Of course such alliance should not be specified in the treaty. The alliance should guarantee the garrisons in the fortresses, the harbor on the Black Sea and the acquisition of localities to protect the entrance to the strait between the Sea of Azov and the Black Sea. In these relations a new term, *protection*, naturally and necessarily makes its appearance. Russia would be the protector of the Tatars, and Tatar relations with the Turks would be conducted solely by the Russians. It was believed that foreign powers would not see a lust for power. They would be content and not realize that Turkey's role on the northern shore of the Black Sea had passed to Russia.

The Tatars would understand very well that what they were being offered was exchanging dependence on Turkey for dependence on

Russia. It would be sinful for them, however, to break with their coreligionists and put themselves under the protection of a Christian power. As an extreme measure they were prepared to do this, but only as an extreme measure and only to gain time, to escape a very difficult situation and to avoid destruction. As soon as circumstances changed, they would turn again to Turkey and free themselves from "freedom." The Christian peoples had suffered terribly under the Turkish yoke and had endured all the consequences of Muslim fanaticism and contempt for the infidels. They had longed for freedom, whereas the Tatars were in the opposite situation, and linking them with the Christians in one act of liberation from Turkish yoke would be a mistake.

In the spring of 1770 the Tatars were not yet in dire straits. Khan Kaplan Girey, the successor to the late Khan Kirim Girey, replied to Panin on March 15: "You declare that your queen wants to grant the previous Tatar liberties, but you do not need to put such words in writing. We ourselves already know. We are completely content with the Porte and we are enjoying prosperity. In former times, when we still were independent from the Ottoman Porte, there was a great deal of civil strife in the Crimean territory, creating disorder. All this was manifest to the world. Why do you recommend that we change our former customs for the better? There is nothing in your intention except empty words and foolhardiness." Panin undertook the hopeless task of responding to the khan. The responses Rumiantsev had made at the Lagra and at the Kagul had made a stronger and more powerful impression. The Tatars were shaken, and their disagreements advanced the cause of St. Petersburg.

The Tatars under discussion were divided into the Crimeans proper, the Osedly[24] and the Nogay, who under different names roamed the then deserted shores of the Sea of Azov and the Black Sea from the Kuban to the Dniester. The Nogay did not have the same incentive, or at least had it to a lesser degree, as the Crimean Tatars to stay with Turkey. As was generally the case among the Central Asiatics, they did not have a strong Muslim consciousness. Petty private interests predominated because of the backward and extremely narrow sphere in which they lived.

The Tatars are well known from the Russian history of the sixteenth century. Then they ruled the lower Volga, serving as a link for the Muslim world between Kazan, Astrakhan and the Crimea. Their duty was to protect the heathen encampments from the pressure of the European Christian world as represented by Russia. Because of their civil wars and greedy aspirations, they handed Kazan and Astrakhan over to the white tsar.[25] When one of their princes, an adherent both of the Crimea and of Turkey, fell out with Moscow, another said to him: "Your people go to Bukhara to trade, but mine go to Moscow. As soon as I go to war against Moscow, I go stark naked and there will not be shrouds sewn for the dead." As a result he invited Ivan IV to rule Astrakhan. [26]

During the period described the Tatars and Kirim Girey attacked Russia, drawn by the hope of easy gain. They had trouble at Khotin, however, and had to retreat to the Pruth. Conditions there were unfamiliar, and they longed for their own steppes. The proposals which began to reach them from Panin's agents made a strong impression. Independence, Russian or Turkish protection made little difference to them. Why not therefore accept the Russian proposals if the Russian army would let them return to their native steppes? Their ancestors had been friendly with Russia. They had made their living from the herds of horses they had sent to sell in Moscow! But still they did not move, because they were afraid of the khan and the Turks.

After Lagra and Kagul it was impossible to delay. On July 25, the same day that Panin at Bender received the news of the victory at Kagul, a letter came to him from four nobles from Yedisan and one from Belgorod (Akkerman) requesting permission to go to the Crimean coast. Panin answered that to receive this permission the Tatars should put themselves under Russian protection, renounce Turkish citizenship and send hostages. On August 9 Panin reported to St. Petersburg that the Yedisan, Budjak and Belgorod hordes had given up Turkish citizenship, and as a result had crossed over to the steppe between the Dniester, the Bug and the Siniukha rivers. Following this the Crimean nobles began negotiations with Panin, but with no results. The khan was able to force his way into the Crimea. There the Nogay, Yedichkuly and Dzhambuluky, who had remained there, decided to follow the example of the related Yedisantsy. Many of them, despite the khan's order, broke out of the Crimea to join their own kind.

At the beginning of October Chancellery Councillor Veselitsky was sent to make the final arrangements with Yedisan Horde, whose leaders were at the Berezan river. The chief noble of the Yedisantsy, Dzhan Mambet Bey, informed Veselitsky that the Yedichkuly and the Dzambuluky had agreed to put themselves under the protection of the Russian empress and already had sent leading nobles with letters to Panin. "We," said Dzhan Mambet Bey, "together with the Yedichkuly and the Dzhambuluky, now have fulfilled our word and our guarantee. We would not have been entrusted with this had we not been confident that our kinship with these hordes would ensure their agreement. As far as the Crimeans are concerned it would not be a bad thing if your excellency (Panin) saw to it that, should the Crimean nobles receive your letter rather coldly and order it to be answered in like manner, they instead write their letter to conform to the requests already made of them and to what the Nogay have stated in their sworn letter. Otherwise they should be treated as enemies, without mercy. They should be threatened with fire and the sword because when the Yedichkuly and the Dzhambuluky agree to join the Yedisan and Budjak Tatars, the Crimeans will agree to all of the demands, and consequently Khan Kaplan Girey will not be respected."

The interpreter Kutlubitsky, who was sent to the Crimea at the end of the year, conveyed similar information. When he arrived at Bakchisaray,[27] Kutlubitsky went to Temir Sultan, the Yedisan noble living there. Temir Sultan was of one mind with his people, and when Kutlubitsky asked whether the Crimeans were hostile to Russia, the nobles answered: "Could the Crimeans contemplate any hostility to Russia, when they are so weak since the Yedichkuly and Dzhamduluky Hordes left the Crimea? I am living in Bakchisaray merely to persuade the Crimeans to accept the same conditions the other hordes accepted who have entered into friendship and alliance with Russia." Temir Sultan's efforts were in vain. The Porte and the Crimeans loyal to it took their own measures. Not expecting Khan Kaplan Girey to have the necessary energy for such dangerous circumstances, the sultan removed him and sent Selim Girey in his place. Russia had to use force to compel the Crimeans to do that to which the Nogay so easily and freely had agreed.

THE FLEET ARRIVES IN THE MEDITERRANEAN

Just as Rumiantsev's victories created the schism among the Tatars and forced the khan to evacuate the main theater of military operations and hasten to the Crimea, news arrived of the brilliant successes of the Russian fleet which had been sent to help the revolt of the Turkish Christians. We saw how many difficulties attended the voyage of Spiridov's squadron.[28] Of the seven ships and eight other vessels which left Kronstadt on July 26, only three ships and four small vessels assembled at Minorca at the end of December 1769. Sickness continued to rage and carried off a sizable number of the men. Count Alexis Orlov[29] waited impatiently at Leghorn for the arrival of the squadron and sent his brother Fedor[30] to meet it at Port Mahon [in the Balearics].

It was not until the beginning of February 1770 that one ship, one frigate and one packet appeared at Leghorn. They had been delayed by a bad storm. Of these vessels, the packet *Postillion* went aground on a shoal. Count Orlov reported this to the empress: "The *Postillion* has gone aground on a shoal, and, even using every means possible, because of dry weather, we will not be able to refloat it for two weeks. As I observed how many hardships there are in that service, I must attest honestly to the great negligence, ignorance and carelessness on the part of the officers. All the sailors are lazy and slovenly. One's hair stands on end and one's heart is heavy. The commanders are not ashamed to conceal deficiencies and to paint over the rot with bright colors. Things have reached such a point that they have neither provisions nor money nor anything else. It must be admitted that if all the services were in such disorder and ignorance as the navy, then our fatherland would be impoverished indeed. But I will say also that we now are confident that all these evils have been overcome, and that everything now will proceed.

"Our vessels are in such a state that if we did not have to deal with the Turks, we could easily give all of them up. If we did not have to engage the Turks much in combat, but only pursue them, they would not leave their harbors because of the ignorance of the officers. I questioned the officers whether they had had occasion to encounter the barbarians anywhere. They answered with a sigh that they thanked God that they did not venture out in such weather! I laughed heartily and discussed everything frankly with them. I added that they should be ashamed, and that such base thinking did not befit Russian officers and men. There is a great shortage of doctors and sickbay attendants, whom I am trying to find. I am determined to bend every effort to remedy the naval shortcomings."

Since setbacks and difficulties did not make the principal figures despair, success was possible. "We now are confident that all these evils already have been overcome, and that everything now will proceed," wrote Orlov. Catherine's answer expressed the same confidence that "everything will proceed." "Whatever is to be done," she wrote, "will be done more intelligently. This voyage will be the best thing in the world for our fleet. Whatever is stagnant and rotten will come to light and in time will be honed to perfection." In addition to the squadrons sent out in the fall of 1769 under the command of Rear Admiral Elphinstone,[31] consisting of three ships, two frigates, and three other vessels, Catherine wrote Orlov in January 1770 that she was getting several other vessels ready for the spring. "In a word, I will do what I can. I now can help with ships and men more easily because the weapons of our towheaded neighbors (the Swedes) have misfired."

Nor was Catherine upset by Prince Dolgoruky's lack of success in Montenegro. "What has happened in Montenegro with our Major General Dolgoruky does not deserve much attention, because we had high expectations for the exertions of the Christian subjects of our treacherous enemy. Let the Greeks there who have been corrupted by centuries of slavery and perfidy take matters into their own hands. All that is needed is our naval diversion to reinforce the Maina ports or some other safe refuge for the navy to shock and terrify all the Turks in Europe and thus to increase the glory of and respect for the power and strength of our empire." Catherine fulfilled her promise. In July a squadron set sail from Reval under the command of Rear Admiral Harf,[32] who had been recruited from the Danish service "because of his outstanding skill and experience in naval warfare." More than twenty-five hundred infantry were with this squadron, including five hundred men of the Preobrazhensky Guards Regiment. No expense was spared, for the expedition to the archipelago in 1769 and 1770 cost about nineteen hundred thousand rubles.

OPERATIONS IN GREECE

The Russian ships arrived at Morea at the middle of February and anchored at the port of Vitula on the Maina peninsula.[33] The inhabitants there long had awaited their arrival impatiently and greeted them in their own fashion by firing rifles and pistols all day. The plan was to form two detachments, or legions, from the inhabitants of Morea, an eastern and a western. Captain Barkov was supposed to assemble and command the former and Major Prince Peter Dolgoruky the latter. Barkov quickly assembled a thousand men of Maina and moved to Mistra (Sparta) and defeated a three-thousand-man Turkish force before its walls. On March 8 Mistra surrendered under the condition that its garrison could leave freely. But as soon as the Turks surrendered their weapons, the men of Maina fell on them and slaughtered more than a thousand. Barkov saved the rest at the risk of his own life. This success increased the size of Barkov's detachment to eight thousand men. He went to Tripolis, but when his force advanced on the city suburbs a large number of Turks attacked them from all sides. The Greeks did not hold their ground but threw down their weapons and fled, deserting the small number of Russians. The handful of brave soldiers began to retreat, defending themselves as they went, and most of them perished. Only four men were saved, carrying the sorely-wounded Barkov to Mistra. The banner also was saved because Barkov ordered it taken off the staff, and wrapped himself in it.

Meanwhile Prince Dolgoruky conquered all of Arcadia and then went to Navarino, which was under siege by a Russian unit brought there by two ships and a frigate. This unit was commanded by Brigadier Hannibal. Navarino surrendered on April 10, and the whole Russian fleet gathered in its harbor as best it could. Almost all the available Russian infantry forces with the chief commander of the Russian expedition [Alexis Orlov] assembled here also.

"I think that you should try," Catherine wrote to him, "to obtain a port on an island or on the mainland and hold it to the extent possible. Having said this, I admit that I have two things in mind. One is that until your little force has increased appreciably, run no risk with your small numbers. The second is that, if we do nothing else, we would lay a good basis for the future if Russia could obtain a port on that sea which we would try to hold when peace was concluded. In peacetime it always would be a commercial link with the requisite peoples, and of course our power would not decrease in that area. If things turn out so that you can pursue this plan, you always will find this port an advantage and not a detriment. Perhaps an island would be more suitable than the mainland, even if it were not the biggest island; but a port on the mainland also has its advantages."

Now Orlov realized that Navarino was just such a port on the mainland with its special advantages. He could not help seeing the wisdom of the empress's warning: "A port is needed, so that until your little force has increased appreciably, run no risks with your small numbers." One detachment already had risked danger and almost had been wiped out because it had not gained a firm base on the coast and had not awaited "an appreciable increase of its small force." They had sent an insignificant detachment into the interior, relying on the local inhabitants. News of the fate of Barkov's detachment, of the conduct of the Greeks at Mistra in Tripolis, of their treacherous savagery in the one place and their shameful cowardice and dishonorable behavior towards the Russians in the other appears to have made Orlov terribly exasperated with the Greeks. "All Morea is free from the Turks except the fortresses and the large cities—Tripolis, Corinth and Patras," he wrote. "Our forces are so weak, however, that not only have I given up hope of conquering all of it, but also of holding the places already captured. The timidity of the Greeks and of the men of Maina makes me despair. The disorder caused by foolish talk discourages me even more. The best thing I could do would be to secure myself by land and by sea, to burn everything in Morea, to cut off all transport of provisions to Constantinople and to attack with naval forces.

"It will be hard to accomplish this if Elphinstone does not come soon. The people here are flatterers and deceivers, inconstant, impertinent, cowardly and partial to money and booty. Nothing can stop them from striving for this. Not the least of the traits of our coreligionists is that they are gullible, unstable, and tremble at the name of the Turks. They only profess their faith with their mouths, and there is not the slightest trace of Christian virtues in their hearts. They are accustomed to spend their lives in dissipation, hating any kind of order and not knowing how to obtain it. They live in a state of spiritual disarray. They are ruled by the slavery and the bonds of Turkish rule into which they are born and in which they grow up, and by gross ignorance as well. Therefore it is hopeless to do anything tangible for their welfare."

All the blame was laid to the Greeks, but the historian must separate it and assign a certain amount to their accusers. A mistake had been made in St. Petersburg, albeit a very natural one. The daring enterprise had been conceived of inciting the Christian population of Turkey to revolt against the Porte, diverting the Turkish forces, dealing a powerful and shattering blow to the enemy, securing themselves against him for the future, and gaining for the Russians the glory of liberating the Christians and the descendants of the heroes whose names were on the tongue of every educated man. This enterprise was conceived with some basis for hoping that it would succeed. Karazin[34] and his comrades were right when they spoke of the readiness of the Christians to throw off the heavy and hateful yoke. But the moral and material resources of the Christians had to be studied more exactly and more precisely. As often happens when a matter is considered from a distance, the details disappeared and merged, and only the prominent and general features were visible; that is, the impetus throw off the heavy barbaric yoke, the common faith and so on. Consequently these general features were idealized and were seen through rose-colored glasses. It was only necessary to appear on the scene, and the people would welcome the liberators as brothers with open arms, would be wonderfully courageous, and would endure every kind of sacrifice to liberate the fatherland.

Thus sight was lost of the petty detail and the minor question of how these brothers in faith would understand each other. Catherine had advised Orlov to proceed cautiously, not to risk his insignificant infantry forces until he had assembled a sizeable local militia. Catherine had wanted a general and concerted effort and had forbidden him to take action with small groups or on his own initiative. But it had to be ascertained in advance whether the Greeks were capable of taking common action. Greece was divided by nature into small districts, cut off from each other and unable to supply themselves. Therefore people had to look outward and seek their livelihood at sea. The ancient history of Greece had been determined by these natural conditions, and its modern history was determined by them as well. On land they were weak and scattered. Each district was distinct, and there were no common interests. They were unable to establish a firm central government, and their political perspectives were narrow.

The strength of the people lay in the "wooden walls" of the oracle which had saved ancient Athens in the struggle with the Persians.[35] Their strength lay in their ships, in naval action which impelled the Greeks to hold on to a narrow strip of territory on the coast. It is extraordinarily difficult to help any nation in distress and to help them win independence. Disparity in levels of development and levels of power leads to inevitable conflict. The nation which is offering help is more developed, more powerful, and naturally assumes the role of leader and protector. It requires its weaker follower to submit to its "way of thinking." But the less developed nation does not comprehend this way of thinking, for it has its own ideas and its own views. These are very narrow and sometimes troublesome, but what can be done?

The Greeks put their hopes in Russian aid and quickly joined the insignificant Russian units. But when the Turks began to attack with superior forces, the Greeks fled because they lacked the usual sense of military honor, and rather believed that the Russians were bound to help them while they themselves did not have to submit to being slaughtered by the Turks, which they could do without the Russians. Most damaging was the misunderstanding of what mutual aid between the stronger and the weaker partner meant, because each one demanded more of the other than either could or wanted to give. The Greeks with whom Orlov was dealing were not cowards but, given the conditions under which they lived, they were capable neither of offensive action nor of doing battle in open combat. They were brave and invincible in waging a defensive war to protect the fortresses they had built or were provided by nature. This important circumstance was not taken into consideration.

Orlov wrote that Turkish slavery had unfortunate consequences for the Greek character. It was not necessary to go to Morea to confirm this, for the cause and the effect also were to be seen in Leghorn and in St. Petersburg. The Greeks had given the Russians an unpleasant surprise by hastening to slaughter the Turks who had surrendered. But given the general Turkish opinion of Christians and Christian opinion of Turks, how could the same relations and rules of conduct be established between them as those that civilized Christian nations had established among themselves? When they saw the cursed enemy, the oppressor, the Greeks forgot everything. The principal difficulty between the Greeks and the Russians was not that they did not understand each other's language, but that they did not understand each other's "way of thinking." Rendering aid, given such a difference between the peoples, was extraordinarily difficult. It was necessary to be prepared for any eventuality and to be equipped with the patience and calm of a schoolteacher. This did not mean shrinking from the hard tasks which the greater national interest required. It only meant that before they were resolved the present and the previous situation had to be studied in depth so there would be no confusion. But we will not be too harsh in judging the Russians of the eighteenth century. They took the first step.

THE BATTLE OF CHESME

Orlov wanted to strengthen his position at Navarino, but in order to do this he felt he had to capture the fortress of Modon. Prince Yury Dolgoruky, whom we already know from his adventures in Montenegro,[36] went there with a small force. Dolgoruky attacked a Turkish force which had come to the aid of the besieged fortress. His inferior forces were defeated, and he lost his artillery. "This unfortunate day," Orlov wrote to the empress, "has turned everything upside down and ended any hope of success on land." Naval operations now began because Elphinstone's squadron, which had suffered all the troubles and delays that Spiridov's squadron had experienced, finally appeared, proving that it made no difference whether the commander had a Russian or an English name. Operations in May were limited to the pursuit of the Turkish fleet. Some vessels stopped at Navarino with Prince Alexis Orlov, who found it impossible to remain there any longer, and sailed to join the two squadrons after he had blown up the Navarino fortress. On July 11 Orlov joined the squadrons and found that "the commanders are quarrelling, while their subordinates are despondent and dissatisfied." There were more than five hundred men sick in both squadrons. Although Orlov was not a sailor, he took command of the fleet as the empress's plenipotentiary agent and stopped the quarreling between the commanders caused by Elphinstone's unwillingness to submit to Spiridov's authority. He took the fleet to the island of Paros to drive out the Turkish fleet and destroy it. That was the only way to negate the impression created by the failure in Morea.

"If it is God's will that the enemy fleet be crushed," Orlov wrote to the empress, "we shall try and make use of every opportunity for joint action with the peoples subject to Turkish authority in whatever theater will be more advantageous.... If the fleet is victorious we will not need money, because we will be the masters of the entire archipelago, and we will attempt to starve out Constantinople itself.... If we lose a naval battle, or the Turkish fleet is in a favorable position in these waters, there is no hope of wintering in the archipelago, and I think that I will be forced to return to the Mediterranean."

Catherine approved all of Orlov's decisions. There is no trace in any of her letters of dissatisfaction with the failure of the naval expedition. "Although we now see," she wrote, "that the results of the Morea expedition did not correspond to the courageous start of your enterprise, this was because of the cowardice, thoughtlessness and treachery of the Greeks who especially at Modon played such dirty tricks. We have been gratified particularly to hear from you that under your leadership all ranks, from the lowest to the highest, fulfilled their duty as true sons of the fatherland bravely, zealously and with the greatest enthusiasm. We shall regard them henceforth with special attention. The Greeks of Morea presented a poor example of bravery, courage and steadfastness, qualities which you had in great measure. They did not want to free themselves from the yoke of slavery which their own spirit of timidity, infidelity and deceit imposed on them. You have acted wisely and intelligently by leaving them to their fate and by directing our combined naval forces in pursuit of the enemy by sea. We say to Prince Yury Dolgoruky that, although it was an unfortunate day at Modon, nevertheless skill and bravery accomplished everything possible, and so that day has won him glory."

These letters were sent at the beginning of September when the fleet already had revived the glory of Russian arms, tarnished by the failures at Morea. At dawn on July 24 the Russian fleet saw the Turkish fleet at anchor at the entrance to the Chios strait on the Anatolian coast near the small fortress of Chesme.[37] Orlov hurried to overtake the enemy fleet to prevent it from joining the squadron coming from Constantinople. The juncture already had been effected,

Count Alexis Gregorevich Orlov

however, so the Russians were faced with sixteen ships of the line (six had between eighty and ninety guns, and the rest between sixty and seventy), six frigates and many assorted small vessels. Orlov openly admitted in his report to the empress that he was afraid when he first caught sight of such a sizable force. "When I saw this armament, I was terrified and did not know what I should do. But the bravery of your imperial majesty's armed forces and the zeal of all to be loyal slaves of Great Catherine forced me to make a decision and, disregarding the superior forces, to attack, to perish or to destroy the enemy."

The battle began at eleven o'clock in the morning and lasted for more than four hours, but still hung in the balance. Spiridov and Count Fedor Orlov were on the Russian ship *Eustatius,* which grappled with the Turkish admiral's ship and began a desperate hand-to-hand combat. Finally the Turkish ship caught fire, and Spiridov and Fedor Orlov were able to escape their own ship, which was in great danger. In fact the burning mainmast of the Turkish ship fell on the Russian ship, and the sparks which flew from it ignited the powder. The *Eustatius* exploded, and the Turkish ship exploded after it. Then all the other enemy ships fled to the bay of Chesme. The victory cost the Russians a ship on which there had been six hundred and twenty-eight men, among them thirty officers. But the victory had to be won completely. In the evening the flag and other officers met with Alexis Orlov and decided to burn the enemy fleet in the bay of Chesme. "We must decide the matter," Orlov's orders stated. "The other fleet must be conquered and destroyed without losing time. Unless this is done here, in the archipelago, we will not be able to win more victories." On June 25 fire ships were prepared and the designated ships moved out on the still, moonlit night of June 25-26. At the outset, at two o'clock, first one Turkish ship then another were set on fire from the Russian ships. Now a "hurrah" resounded from the Russian ships, and three rockets soared up. This was the signal to send the fire ships into action. Despite a difficult beginning the operation proceeded successfully, thanks to the daring and cunning of Lieutenant Ilin. He made fast to a large Turkish ship, ignited the fire ship and left on a sloop, but stayed to observe what would happen. There were deafening explosions, and the widespread glow revealed a terrible scene. All that could be seen were corpses and ships' wreckage. The water was covered with ashes and blood. By dawn the Turkish fleet no longer existed. Fifteen ships, six frigates and up to fifty smaller vessels had been burned. The Russians were able to capture only one ship and six galleys.

Spiridov wrote to Count Ivan Chernyshev[38] under these first impressions. "We attacked, defeated, destroyed and burned the

Turkish fleet. We blew it up, turned it into ashes and left only a terrible disgrace on the site. We have become the masters of the entire archipelago." Orlov informed the empress about the great event quietly and calmly, not trying at all to magnify his own role: "I regret," he wrote, "that I cannot hope to greet your majesty with a land victory equal to that at sea. Were I that fortunate, my wishes would be completely fulfilled, and I could hope to earn your favor. The only thing left for me to do now is to try to interdict supplies to Tsargrad [Constantinople], and to attempt if possible to recover for the state the expenditures of this expedition."

This news made an extraordinary impression in St. Petersburg. The dismal condition of the Russian fleet had caused great chagrin and humiliation, and consequently there was less expectation of great deeds. There had been great chagrin at reports of the failure of the expedition to Morea, for which the fleet was supposed to render assistance. Consequently news of the unexpected victory of this same fleet, of the destruction of the enemy fleet and of the unprecedented triumph, which had demonstrated a new aspect of Russian power, caused even greater joy.

Catherine's delight easily can be imagined, because in her reign had been accomplished what even the great founder of the Russian fleet [Peter the Great] had not imagined. This had been achieved after long years of naval decline in Russia and by a man from a family which Catherine had raised to power, something for which she had been reproached continually. "Nothing more significant than this can be expected from your quarter," Catherine wrote to Rumiantsev. "God is marvellous in His wonders! Almost never has the world heard the like. We paid reverence to God on the 14th of this month (September), and on the second day a solemn requiem was held for Peter the Great, the founder of the fleet, he who was responsible for Russia's new glory. We are benefitting from the fruits of his labor. Our fleet is like Isaac who was married for seventy years and left a posterity whose fame has reached even to the present. Our fleet has been covered also with glory seventy years after its founding, and may God grant that this glory last longer than the posterity of Isaac."[39]

The rescript to Orlov stated that "such rare occurrences are a new proof that victories are won not by numbers but only by courage and bravery. Obvious examples, manifest by the Russian forces, now can be seen. On July 21 our field marshal Count Rumiantsev with seventeen thousand men defeated one hundred and fifty thousand Turkish swine and sent them fleeing beyond the banks of the Danube. Our victory with nine ships over a large number of the enemy at Chesme on June 24 inspired a similar dread of the Russian naval forces, hitherto held back from punishing the enemies of the empire. But our fleet now shines in the world with unimaginable splendor. Under your wise and daring leadership it now has dealt a massive blow to Turkish pride. The whole world acknowledges that you have won great honor and glory. You are crowned with laurels, and also your entire squadron." Orlov was awarded the Military Order, first class, and the right to retain the imperial emblem for life and to include it in his coat of arms. Spiridov was awarded the Order of St. Andrew with villages. Count Fedor Orlov and Rear Admiral Grieg,[40] whom Count Alexis Orlov particularly had commended, were awarded the Military Order, second class.

CONSEQUENCES OF THE VICTORY AT CHESME
The famous French agent Baron Tott,[41] who like Valcroissant was sent to Turkey to render all possible to the Turks and do all possible harm to the Russians, painted a very negative picture of the Dardanelles fortifications in his memoirs. Thus it is natural to regret that because of his ignorance of the situation, the victor of Chesme did not decide to slip through the Dardanelles and, by appearing before Constantinople, force the sultan to conclude the peace which Russia so desired. But it should be determined whether Tott's testimony indeed was correct. He had been charged with fortifying the Dardanelles, and it would have been to his advantage to present the previous defenses in the most wretched light possible.

The battle of Chesme struck terror above all into the rich commercial city of Smyrna. Russians heard there for the first time about *European interests* which they would encounter and have to deal with continually from now on in the East. Orlov received a letter dated July 21 from the European consuls in Smyrna. It stated that the populace and the armed forces in Smyrna, driven to fury and despair by news of the events at Chesme, had hurled themselves on the Greeks and killed a large number of them. Two Europeans also had been killed. This upheaval had terrified all the Europeans.

Most of the Franks[42] had sought refuge on ships, and others had locked themselves in their houses. Trade had come a halt. After several days calm apparently was restored, and trade began to pick up. Fear at the approach of the Russian fleet had alarmed the Europeans greatly because this dreadful hour would initiate the slaughter and pillage of the subjects of the European sovereigns and naturally would destroy their commerce.

"This dire extremity," wrote the consuls, "has prompted us to send plenipotentiaries to your excellency to explain our perilous situation and to request that you not turn the victorious arms of her imperial majesty against this commercial city. It should not be seen as an enemy location, but more as a colony founded by various neutral states. The Russian empress certainly does not wish to destroy their commerce and sacrifice their subjects. The city administration awaits the liberation of those prisoners whom your excellency still holds. If your excellency crowns this magnanimity with the liberation of these prisoners, this new ray of mercy will bring you as much honor as a victory. The Turks will be indebted to us, and this will guarantee our security." Orlov answered: "In accord with the grace of the Most High, I will carry out the obligation, one I never have violated, to render all possible assistance to neutral peoples and not just to our allies. This is and always will be my constant standard of conduct. As soon as I heard of the disturbances in Smyrna I abandoned my plan to go to that city, only because the approach of our fleet might spread still more debauchery and disorder. To that end I immediately freed the master of the janissaries and many other Turks and ordered them to tell your city administration to stop the willful slaughter there as soon as possible and in particular to assure the safety of your persons.

"I also would be very glad to agree to everything else you ask of me, if various reasons did not prevent this. Lacking any negotiated agreement with the other side, could I answer for something which unforseen circumstances might impel me to do in the future? You want to assure me, contrary to what is generally accepted, that the city of Smyrna be regarded as a settlement founded by various European peoples rather than as an enemy location. This I find incomprehensible. According to your standard Constantinople itself should be regarded in the same way, as well

as all the other cities on the coast under Turkish rule in which there
are some European inhabitants.

"As far as commerce is concerned you can rest assured
completely. As long as the flag of her imperial majesty rules these
seas, you can rely fully on her protection. Already you have clear
proof of this. This is provided that nothing in commercial activity
violates the laws of war. If my approach to your city were to be the
cause of some disturbance, I would be as guilty here as I was of
the final destruction of the Ottoman fleet. Freeing some prisoners
and treating those remaining with me leniently would not incline
the hearts of the Turks to admit what I should expect of them after
such a step. But in consideration of your request, I will free some
more of them for the sole reason of satisfying you and insuring your
safety."

Catherine was very pleased with this answer which, according
to her, "radiated magnanimity and love of mankind." "Here you have
depicted your soul," she wrote Orlov. "We long have been acquainted with it, but now the whole world sees and recognizes it."

Within a short time rumors circulated in St. Petersburg about new
successes of the Russian fleet. "Some say," Catherine wrote to
Panin, "that the Dardanelles have been taken, while others say that
the Turkish fleet has been burned again. But if I had to choose, I
rather would take the Dardanelles, because that would bring us
closer to a *peace congress* in the near future."[43] But these expectations were not realized. An attempt to capture Lemnos, the island
closest to the Dardanelles, failed. Moreover the ship *Sviatoslav* was
destroyed. The island of Paros was chosen for winter quarters for
the fleet, and in November both Alexis and Fedor Orlov left for
Italy. Spiridov was left in sole command of the fleet, since Elphinstone had been forced into retirement. Orlov had written to the
empress in the report of the battle of Chesme: "I ask your pardon
in advance. If Rear Admiral Elphinstone does not change his ways,
I will be forced to remove him from command for the good of your
majesty's service and to entrust that fleet to Brigadier Captain Grieg,
whose virtue, loyalty, zeal, diligence and prudence convinced me
that matters will proceed much more successfully under his
leadership."

Later Elphinstone was found guilty by a naval court-martial for the loss of the *Sviatoslav*. Elphinstone wrote a memorandum to justify himself. Catherine's remarks on the matter have been preserved: "Nothing would be easier than to refute this memorandum, especially the section about the battle of Chesme and about his stay at Lemnos, to which he had not been summoned. He also was guilty of abandoning his post before the Dardanelles. Finally he forced the captain to proceed on the same course on which the *Sviatoslav* was lost. It can be said only that Elphinstone is one of those crazy people who are carried away by the first impulse and pay no heed whatever to the consequences. I do not know if he can clear himself of the suspicion of wrongdoing if he were forced to give an accounting of the extraordinary expenditures of the sums entrusted to him. He gave only three thousand ducats of this amount to Admiral Spiridov. In truth it would be better to waste five thousand rubles on this affair than to put him on display before Europe and occasion the displeasure of the English court which sent him to us as a favor and rendered us every assistance, which has been very useful for us. Making all of this public would stir up dissatisfaction against the English government at home and could have unpleasant consequences for English commerce in the Levant."[44]

OPERATIONS IN THE CAUCASUS

The expedition to Morea and the uprising of the Christian population of European Turkey had failed through the fault of that population, as Orlov confirmed in his reports. There was a similar lack of success in Transcaucasia, also the fault of its Christian population, as confirmed by Count Todtleben,[45] who was the commander of the Russian forces there. Todtleben's advance with Tsar Heraclius on Akhaltsikhe did not reach its objective, and they had to return to Tiflis. According to Todtleben's report this was because the Georgians gave no help at all, but merely stood by quietly, doing nothing but pillage during the battle between the Russians and the Turks. Tsar Solomon told Todtleben that he did not allow his soldiers to eat Turkish grain because it was poisoned, but the Georgians seized this same grain, ate some of it themselves and sold the rest to the Russians at a high price. Finally the Russians were left with no grain at all, so that on the way back the Russians had to eat horse meat. Todtleben complained that Solomon changed his proposals, promises and demands every day, and that he himself did not know what to do. Solomon complained that Todtleben ignored his frequent appeals, while he, Solomon, was operating successfully and had beaten a Turkish army, destroying the fortress of Duki, which had been in Turkish hands.[46]

THE CHOGLOKOV AFFAIR

Todtleben requested that all officers of Georgian descent in his army be recalled because their reports and opinions were totally unreliable. Soon he had to complain about a Russian officer, Lieutenant Colonel Naum Choglokov, son of the well-known Choglokovs who played such a role in the history of the younger court at the time of Empress Elizabeth.[47] Choglokov had gone to the Caucasian Army as a volunteer. Lieutenant Lvov, who also had gone as a volunteer, caught up with him in Mozdok and was struck that Choglokov had such a sizable staff and train. Choglokov explained that this was necessary because he was a close relative of the sovereign (his mother, née Gendrikova, was a cousin of Empress Elizabeth). Once he opened a small chest filled with more than fifty gold snuff boxes and watches worth seven thousand rubles. When Lvov asked him why he had such things in Georgia Choglokov answered: "I recently ordered a village sold in Russia, and I expect the money very soon." From this Lvov noticed that he was very upset. "Either I will die on the scaffold or become tsar," he said.

When they arrived in Georgia, Tsar Heraclius and the whole court received Choglokov as the empress's cousin and the next in line to the throne after the grand duke. Todtleben told him not to travel to the Georgian camp, but Choglokov did not listen and shouted: "I am a free man here and am under no obligation to Todtleben. Perhaps I have orders of my own, and perhaps I have been sent with a special commission, and not to Todtleben!" When the latter heard about this he spoke to Choglokov: "I was sent an order that you would be a volunteer under my command. Count Nikita Ivanovich (Panin's) recommendation is as follows: Leave off fraternizing with the Georgians. I am well acquainted with them. I know all of their factions opposed to Tsar Heraclius and how glad they were that he was taken under Russian protection." Lvov wrote to St. Petersburg that there were even more factions in Georgia than in old Russia. Practically no three families could reach agreement. The main reason was that there were many pretenders to the Georgian throne with better claim to it than Heraclius, and thus most of the prominent men could not abide him.

On the evening of Holy Saturday Choglokov began to talk to Lvov, with whom he shared a room: "Do you know that I soon will be tsar's *serdar*, that is, military commander? Your count will be arrested today, and so I will have seniority here. I already have reached agreement with Major Remennikov and several other officers." When Lvov reported this Todtleben answered that he knew everything. That night he ordered Remennikov and Choglokov arrested, whereupon the latter challenged him to a duel. Todtleben went to Tsar Heraclius the next day to give him Easter greetings and told him about the arrests. The tsar said: "Choglokov is a strange man! He has told me many times that he has orders from the sovereign to go into Armenia. He asked me for three thousand Georgians and affirmed that he could do anything he wanted in Armenia."

Heraclius himself soon came out against Todtleben in the case of Colonel Ratiev (of Georgian origin). Ratiev, who was supposed to convey the artillery to the Caucasian Corps, delayed in Mozdok and paid no attention to any of Todtleben's orders. The latter, seeing an evil motive, sent to have him arrested. Ratiev arrested those who were sent, however, and went himself to Tsar Heraclius in Tiflis. Choglokov also took refuge with him after escaping arrest. When Todtleben sent a request to Heraclius to hand over Ratiev and Choglokov, his envoys were detained in Tiflis. Todtleben then realized that all the couriers sent to him were being intercepted and taken off to Tiflis. They did not want the Tomsk Regiment, which was on its way, to reach him and cut off communication with Mozdok. Then he decided to forestall his enemies, left his camp and arrived at the city of Diushet after a quick march of two days. He took the city and also captured the fortress of Ananury.

On May 12 Todtleben wrote that when he joined the Tomsk Regiment he intended to proceed directly to Tiflis, to take vengeance on his opponents, recover the artillery, the forces and the supplies that Ratiev had carried off, subject all of Georgia to Russian rule, strip Heraclius of the Order of St. Andrew that he had been awarded previously and either send him to St. Petersburg or throw him into the Black Sea. Chogolokov, on the other hand, wrote to Tiflis that Todtleben hated him because Tsar Heraclius had shown him preference. According to Chogolokov's observations Todtleben either had gone insane or was plotting some kind of treachery and was acting totally contrary to the interests of the Russian court. He had caused quarrels among the tsars there, and he had dealt roughly with the princes, beating many of them and keeping others in chains. He had destroyed villages and taken cattle and grain needlessly. He had been in correspondence with the pasha of Akhaltsikhe. He had ordered twelve of the best Russian officers sent back to Russia, and all he had left behind were Germans and the most unfit Russians.

After the empress read Todtleben's report she wrote to Panin: "I only glanced through Todtleben's letters, in which I noticed Choglokov's insubordination and the abusiveness of this unbridled and brainless youth. Therefore I place no value in his unprecedented suspicions of Todtleben. I think he would be more apt to spoil our affairs in Georgia than to bring them to successful fruition. They should be entrusted to someone else." Guards Captain Yazykov was sent to Georgia to make a more exact evaluation of the matter and to put an end to the disputes.

PREPARATIONS FOR PEACE NEGOTIATIONS

These disputes in the distant Transcaucasia could not make a strong impression. Little was known about them in Russia and nothing at all in Western Europe where, on the other hand, people were well aware of the battles of Kagul and Chesme. Catherine was quick to make use of these successes to conclude peace as soon as possible. On August 12 Count Grigory Orlov at the empress's behest proposed to the council that it seemed necessary to send someone to the army to assess carefully the possibilities of opening peace negotiations. He could approach the vizier or someone else with a declaration that our side wanted peace, or could make it known that someone with plenipotentiary powers was with the Russian army.

In considering the expenses already incurred by the state, even one not well informed could see that these were large and had to be even greater in the future. Although God had blessed our arms, the enormous distance of our active forces, the difficulty of supplying them with necessities and the armed conflicts in different parts of the world all meant a terrible burden for the state. For these reasons peace had to be sought and as quickly as possible. If it were not achieved, at least we would know how to prepare for the next campaign and how to act to achieve peace. If thus we succeeded in beginning peace negotiations we would avoid the obstacles attendant on peace negotiations through the mediation of neighboring powers. The Porte henceforth would be brought to the inescapable conclusion that it was not some sort of machination which made Russia wish for peace but rather the true greatness of its peaceloving character.

Acting with moderation in our present favorable situation will demonstrate further our disinterested desire for peace. The council has found it necessary to send a capable man to the army for peace negotiations with the Turks. It also has decided, however, that Count Rumiantsev be ordered to respond in a letter to the conquered vizier that if the Porte desires peace, it must free the Russian minister Obrezkov[48] from captivity and send plenipotentiaries to a designated place. Furthermore his great autocrat [Catherine] has spared human life in all the victories God has given her and ardently wishes to order peace negotiations begun and her plenipotentiaries sent. Count Rumiantsev should not make this response before Bender is captured. The council also decided that, even if peace negotiations began, every effort must be made to prepare for a third campaign and to insure that the army be supplied to prevent shortages.

The thought of a third campaign weighed heavily on Catherine, and her handwritten memorandum was presented to the council on September 9: "(1) Since Count Rumiantsev now holds the fortress of Kilia and the city of Ismail, both on the Danube, it seems the time has come to write to him to make all possible preparations. At the first opportunity he should transport a corps on the Danube, either to Varna or beyond the Danube by sea, to strike terror and fear into the heart of the Ottoman empire. This will hasten the conclusion of peace. Meanwhile everything will be prepared. (2) Send the rescript as soon as possible to Count Rumiantsev with suggestions for direct peace negotiations between the vizier and our plenipotentiaries. (3) Count Rumiantsev should inform us about the exact condition of Count Siniavin's[49] flotilla. He should be ordered to act in conjunction with Count Rumiantsev. (4) Count Peter Panin should be advised again to attempt as far as possible to begin negotiations with the Crimean Tatars of Kerch and Taman so as to facilitate Siniavin's voyage." But friends made it impossible to move speedily to peace negotiations.

PRUSSIA AND THE PROSPECT OF POLISH PARTITION

Frederick II[50] continued his policy of using Austria to frighten Russia. In the spring of 1770 he referred to the strengthening of the Austro-French alliance by the marriage of the French dauphin to Maria Theresa's daughter[51] Marie Antoinette. Frederick suggested that Choiseul[52] was inciting the Viennese court to war and also suggested that if the Russians intended to become neighbors of the Austrians in Moldavia and Wallachia, that would lead immediately to war. At the same time Frederick reported that the Porte had requested his mediation, and therefore he wanted to know under what conditions the empress wanted to conclude peace. He especially wanted to know what had been decided concerning Moldavia and Wallachia. The response was courteous and compliant. The empress would be very glad if the king would influence the Porte to open negotiations. As a first indispensable condition Obrezkov had to be freed. The empress was not seeking acquisitions, nor had she begun the war to extend her borders. Honor and duty had forced her to stand up for those who took her side in the conflict. In particular she could not sacrifice the Greeks to Turkish vengeance. Their safety had to be guaranteed. This was the situation when Frederick met with Joseph II [of Austria] for the second time.

We observed the purpose of the rapprochement between Austria and Prussia which became evident at the first meeting between Joseph II and Frederick II the previous year.[53] Frederick described this meeting in his memoirs: "It would be an unforgivable mistake in politics to rely blindly on Austrian conscientiousness. Under those circumstances when Russian preponderance became too marked, and when it was impossible to predict what limits Russia would set to its conquests, it was a very opportune moment to seek rapprochement with the Viennese court. Prussia had not forgotten the blows which Russia had dealt it in the previous war. It was not at all in the king's interest to contribute to the strengthening of such a terrible and dangerous power. The choice was posed either to leave Russia in possession of its vast conquests or, what was the wiser course, attempt by cunning to turn Russia's successes to our advantage."

The king did not neglect to do this. He sent a political project he attributed to Count Lynar,[54] who had arranged the Convention of Kloster-Zeven between the Hanoverians and the French in the last war.[55] (The project was that Austria and Prussia take part in the war between Russia and Turkey. For this Austria would get the Polish district of Zips and the city of Lemberg[56] and its district. Frederick would get Polish Prussia with Warmia and a protectorate over the city of Danzig. As a reward for its military expenditures, Russia would take whatever part of Poland it found suitable. "The great Russian successes in Moldavia and Wallachia," continued Frederick, "and the victories won by the fleet in the archipelago had so blinded the court of St. Petersburg that no attention was being paid to the pretended memoir of Count Lynar. After this failure the king felt compelled to use other means."

Concerning the details of this affair it is known that the king sent Lynar's project to Solms[57] in strict confidence at the beginning of 1769. The king described the project as brilliant rather than solid and left it up to the ambassador whether to show the project to Count Panin. Solms answered that he considered it better not to show the project to Panin since it was doubtful that it was to his taste. Supporters of the present system in Russia wanted no ties with Austria but instead proposed a system of mutual trust. It was feared that Austria would use the proposal for harmful ends. Previous measures for Poland would be revived, and revived to the extent that their aim apparently was the thorough pillaging of Poland. The Russians did not count on the continuation of the Turkish war. They hoped that Poland would be quiet, and they supposed that Prussia would restrain Austria. In addition they wanted to demonstrate their impartiality and increase confidence in their statements. Panin really wanted to preserve Poland only to use it later against the Turks. The king answered that he considered Lynar's project chimerical and left the ambassador free to make use of it or not. Persistent cunning under the guise of complete indifference and even disdain!

Solms told Panin about the project, concealing the fact it had been sent to the king. Panin answered that perhaps Zips could be ceded to the Austrians, but not Lemberg, which lay in the middle of Poland far from the Austrian border. Was it worth the effort, continued Panin, to ally these three great powers just to hurl the Turks beyond the Dniester? If they were to join in order to expel the Turks from Europe, that would be easy to do. In any event an alliance of the three courts was the best way to assure the tranquillity of Christendom. The only obstacle was the rivalry between Austria and Prussia. Austria ought to cooperate with Russia against Turkey and would find full compensation for Silesia. Thereby Prussia would gain security and might add Polish Prussia and Warmia to its domains. Then it would be easy to end Turkish dominion in Europe. It might be possible to turn Constantinople and the districts retained by the Ottomans into a republic.

"But what would Russia take for itself?," asked Solms. "Even without this Russia already has so much land that it is hard to manage." "We need only a few border districts," answered Panin. It seemed that Panin's plan only could irritate Frederick. He should be shown some new fantasy of the type of the Northern System.[58] The Prussian king's main goal was to acquire new domains without war. In a political testament written at the end of 1768[59] Frederick said that it was better to acquire Polish Prussia privately through negotiations rather than by right of conquest. In case Russia felt a strong need for Russian aid it might be possible to stipulate Thorn and Elbing and their surroundings.[60]

It should not be forgotten that Frederick now was a different man. Whereas before the Seven Years War he had been daring, enterprising and always ready to act to forestall his opponent, after the war he became extraordinarily cautious and began to be very afraid of war. We saw the impression that news of the war between Russia and Turkey had produced on him.[61] Later he did not want to hear about war at all. Therein he became totally like both his predecessors in that his main goal was the expansion of Prussia without war and without any risk. We cited the passage from Frederick's *Political Testament* stating that it was better to make acquisitions through negotiations.[62] In this connection we should not forget the words of his father Frederick William[63] concerning the acquisition of German territory: "I was the first to plant my foot in Berg, my son will acquire other places and my grandson will go to Düsseldorf and beyond."

All this completely explained Frederick's intentions and methods as well as his important role in the resolution of the Polish question through the so-called First Partition. But it does not follow that Frederick was the first to devise this method of resolving the question, because this method, so to say, had been in the air for a long time. For a long time Poland had been suffering, had become a nonentity, and thus had been despoiled by all as a result of its own weakness, and its soil became the scene of inevitable conflicts among the great powers. Proposals that a few partition Poland and alienate a part of its territory for the benefit of one of its neighbors, especially Prussia, had been made for a long time and had become commonplace. No one was surprised, and everyone considered them part of the natural order of things. Each time the Polish question was raised the idea of partition or of alienating a part of Polish territory came into everyone's mind. If partition had not yet occurred it was only because not all of Poland's powerful neighbors agreed that this would be beneficial or necessary for all of them.

PREVIOUS PLANS TO PARTITION POLAND

We have watched the efforts among the eastern German states to extend their territory at the expense of the neighboring Slavic lands. Saxony and Prussia followed Austria's example by striving to increase their power at Poland's expense, and they became rivals in the process. This rivalry naturally created the impetus for the partition of Poland. When Elector Augustus of Saxony succeeded in becoming king of Poland[64] he did not intend to limit himself to this empty title. Elector Frederick of Brandenburg also became king at Poland's expense by taking East Prussia.[65] This did not satisfy him, so he proposed the partition of Poland among the neighboring states at every opportunity. His primary goal was the acquisition of the other, so-called Royal or Polish (West) Prussia.

Frederick I had proposed the partition of Poland to Charles XII of Sweden.[66] Patkul[67] on the other hand offered Frederick compensation in Polish Prussia, Courland or wherever else he wished if Prussia would join an alliance with Russia. After Poltava[68] the Polish king, Augustus II, dethroned by Charles XII, sent to Berlin to ask if Prussia were inclined to make him king of Poland again. Frederick showed the ambassador a plan to partition Poland and Sweden. Livonia would be given to Stanislaw Leszczynski,[69] while Polish Prussia and Warmia would go to Prussia, which also would acquire a protectorate over Courland. The part of Poland around Warsaw, as well as Lithuania, would fall to Augustus II. Of the Swedish districts, Scania would go to Denmark and Verden to Hanover. St. Petersburg would remain under the tsar. But the Russian emperor made it known that he wanted to meet with Frederick and conclude an alliance. Frederick proposed a plan of partition to him, but Peter I found it unfeasible (*nicht practibel*). He promised Prussia only Elbing and the surrounding area, if Frederick would prevent the Swedes from entering Poland from Pomerania.

On another occasion Frederick and Augustus presented to the tsar a more advantageous plan for the partition of Poland. In addition to Swedish Livonia, Russia would get a part of Lithuania. Prussia would get Polish Prussia, Samogitia and Courland. The remaining Polish territory would be left to Augustus as an hereditary domain. Russia's answer was negative this time as well. "If this is to be done," said Peter, "a completely different plan of partition has to be drawn up. As a first condition Prussia should join me in an offensive alliance against Sweden and move its forces into Pomerania."

But Frederick I feared war throughout his life just as Frederick II did after the Seven Years War. During the reign of Frederick William I the partition of Poland was brought up again by the Polish king, Augustus II. He had become more and more convinced that it was much better to rule over part of Poland as an absolute hereditary monarch than over the whole country under the conditions to which the king of the Polish Commonwealth was subjected. According to his new plan Prussia would get Polish Prussia and

Warmia, Austria would get the Polish territory bordering on Silesia and Hungary, while Russia would get all of Lithuania. The plan failed because Peter the Great opposed it.[70]

At the death of Augustus II the question was raised again of who should be king of Poland, the son of the deceased, the elector of Saxony,[71] or Stanislaw Leszczynski. Russia and Austria agreed on the former, but Prussia was opposed because of its rivalry with Saxony in efforts to gain ascendency, namely at Poland's expense. A proposal then was made to Prussia from both sides to take part of the Polish domains for its share.[72]

When Augustus III died the partition of Poland once again became a matter of general discussion. The French government, aware of its weakness and of the impossibility of fighting Prussia in Poland, consoled itself with the hope that hitherto partition had been impossible because of the rivalry among Poland's neighbors. "Partition," it was said in the royal council, "should occur only as a consequence of special circumstances. Finally, it is most unlikely that these four powers (Austria, Prussia, Russia, and *Turkey*) should agree to partition Poland, or that one of them, as a result of some extraordinary circumstances, should seize some Polish district. Even assuming this possibility it still is doubtful whether this occurrence could be of interest to France."[73] Beranger, the French *chargé d'affaires* at St. Petersburg, informed his court at the very end of 1763 that there *no longer* was any question of the partition of Poland. He had spoken with the vice chancellor,[74] who had informed him that Russia's interests required maintaining the complete integrity of the Polish domains. He also said that it was possible that the Prussian king would take a more active interest, but that Russia would oppose him as soon as this interest was expressed. "There *no longer* is any question of partition." Probably word had come to Beranger about [Zakhar] Chernyshev's[75] proposal which had been dismissed courteously in a conference as unworkable.[76]

ATTITUDES TOWARDS PARTITION

Partition also was discussed in Vienna at the death of Augustus III, but it generally was regarded as not in Austria's interest. It was suspected that the Prussian king, together with Russia and Austria, intended to acquire part of the Polish domains, but it was considered unprofitable for Austria to go beyond its natural frontiers, the Carpathian Mountains. It would be another matter if Prussia agreed to cede Silesia to Austria. In that case one could take what one wished, but it was hard to imagine that Frederick would agree to the cession of Silesia.[77] The current thinking in Dresden still echoed that of Augustus II. If Poland's more powerful neighbors agreed on partition, one part, as well as the royal title, would be left to the elector of Saxony and his successors. The wife of the elector of Saxony, Maria Antonia, wrote to Empress Maria Theresa: "It is true that there is an agreement between Russia and Prussia concerning the partition of Poland. England not only will offer no objection, but also hopes to persuade your majesty to participate in it. In this event a small piece should be ceded to us as an hereditary possession, carrying with it the royal title."[78] Maria Theresa responded unfavorably concerning partition and advised the wife of the elector to strive to maintain Poland's integrity.

The election of Stanislaw Poniatowski[79] did not put a stop to the widespread rumors of partition or of the alienation of Polish territory for the benefit of one of Poland's neighbors. France offered Frederick II a part of the Polish domains. The French ambassador in Berlin reported to his government that Frederick was busy with another plan for Poland besides the French proposal, something confirmed by the king's own statement in his memoirs. On the other hand Kaunitz[80] drew up a plan for the return of Silesia, for which Prussia was to be compensated with Polish territory! Finally, the Russo-Turkish War brought Austria and Prussia closer, and the beginning of that rapprochement was apparent in the meeting between Joseph II and Frederick II at Neisse. This was just an initial contact which was to be continued. After the meeting at Neisse, Frederick wrote to his brother Prince Henry[81] that a second meeting had been proposed. These meetings were the precondition for closer alliance for which ambitious Russian intentions would provide the impetus.

Frederick had written to his brother even earlier: "Russia is a terrifying power before whom all of Europe will tremble for half a century. Descended from those Huns and Gepids who destroyed the Eastern empire, the Russians very quickly can fall upon the

West, making the Austrians suffer and repent because they summoned this barbaric people into Germany by their false policies and taught them their military art. But the Austrians have been blinded by passion, that venomous hatred they feel towards us, and their eyes are dimmed towards the results of their actions. Now I see the only way to protect myself from this dangerous flood in an alliance among powerful rulers."

"To embark on this project in agreement with the emperor would be a great, useful and beneficial deed," answered Henry. "Two such powers as Prussia and Austria will be able to see the entire undertaking through only if they can reach a mutually beneficial agreement. This unity will be true and genuine if there is enough confidence that you and the emperor can divide the realm as Octavian and Antony did."[82]

Frederick checked his brother's delight, pointing out that it was a difficult matter, requiring considerable time, while he, Frederick, already was staring into the grave: "Maria Theresa should break the habit of hating me, which she has been accustomed to doing for thirty years. Other considerations must be weighed here. Would not our alliance with Russia provide the only impetus for Austria's rapprochement with us? Until that exists, Austria can undertake nothing."

Henry did not stop thinking about the utility and the possibility of rapprochement between Prussia and Austria in the near future. "There are no powers," he wrote, "who would not become friends when an agreement is concluded whose goal was the enhancement of both. The objection could be made that Austria's strength, increased by its new domains, would become still more dangerous. The response could be made that when the agreement was made there would be a balance of power, but in case of a rupture the envy of the other powers would turn them against the stronger one. You could expect to have more allies than Austria. If there must be an agreement between you and Empress Maria Theresa, I should hope it would happen when the Russians and the Turks were at war and when France and England were occupied with their financial difficulties and domestic quarrels."[83] Henry's words did in fact to refer to the partition of Poland: "There are no powers who would not become friends when an agreement is concluded whose goal was the enhancement of both."

But Choiseul had known about the first meeting at Neisse even before it happened, and feared its consequences for the Franco-Austrian alliance. He guessed that the Polish question would come up between Frederick and Joseph, and he wanted to forestall it with his own good intentions, or at least find out what Austria's intentions were. He began to talk to the Austrian ambassador at the French court, Mercy d'Argenteau:[84] "For some time I have been pondering important political considerations in connection with the kingdom of Poland. They consist principally in the fact that possibly it would be more conducive to the common good if the Austrian court took advantage of the present disorder in the kingdom and took over the best part of it."[85]

PARTITION IS CONSIDERED

We saw that the possibility of partitioning Poland among its four neighbors, Russia, Prussia, Austria and Turkey was being considered. The latter had not hesitated to declare its readiness to participate in a partition together with its good ally Austria. In March, 1770 the Austrian minister in Constantinople, the later famous Thugut,[86] reported to his court that the chancellor [reis Efendi] asked him if Austria and the Porte could unite against Russia. Then he told them that before the present war began Russia together with Prussia had used a large sum of money to persuade the Porte to turn its arms against Austria. The Porte, said the chancellor, was prepared to accept any stipulations for an alliance. With this alliance rules could be laid down for all powers. When the Russians were driven out of Poland, it would depend on Austria whether Poland would be given a new king or be divided between Austria and the Porte.[87]

Austria was prepared to act on everything with everyone. One did not need the perspicacity of Frederick II to notice the young Emperor Joseph's terrible ambition, his striving to take the lead at any cost, to expand his state and to recoup the losses suffered in previous wars. Joseph did not come by this ambition on his own, for he had been incited by the example of Frederick II. The achievement of the Prussian king, who had succeeded in gaining such a great reputation, and who had not been fastidious in the means he used to strengthen his state, had caused Joseph sleepless nights. It was hard to say who was the more ambitious, the young emperor or the old chancellor, Kaunitz. The latter also thought only about one thing; that is, that Austria should exploit favorable circumstances to get compensation for the concessions extorted at the conclusion of the previous peace. This was the case despite the chancellor's brilliant achievement in changing the age-old political system of Europe[88] and despite the alliance between Austria and France. Silesia had been lost, and young states, Russia and Prussia, had gained the upper hand, while the alliance of the old states, Austria, France and Spain, barely was able to oppose them. What was needed was not despair, but waiting for favorable circumstances and using them to enhance Austria and to restore its standing to its former level. Thus it would not be said that the era of Kaunitz was an unhappy and inglorious one for Austria, an era of territorial losses and of the infamous loss of Silesia. Might it be possible to recover Silesia, not by war, but through diplomatic agreements? If Silesia could not be recovered, perhaps some equivalent territory could be acquired.

What to choose, what to take? The prospects were varied. Easiest of all would be to partition Poland. The Prussian king immediately would fish in troubled waters, but would have to share, not take everything himself. On the other hand there was Turkey. The last peace had been a shameful one, and important territorial concessions had been made to the Porte. Advantage had to be taken of the favorable circumstances offered by the troubled waters and to recover what had been lost. Would it be Poland or Turkey? The choice was a difficult one, for one was no better than the other. The Prussian king now deliberately inflamed this covetousness, presenting all kinds of enticements so that Austria would jump for them eagerly.

At the farewell audience for the Austrian ambassador Nugent,[89] Frederick referred to Bavaria, which could round off Austria nicely; referred to Lorraine and Alsace, which could be captured from France in two campaigns; and referred to a very suitable rounding off of Austria in Italy using, among others, the Venetian domains. The implication was that taking territory from these decrepit entities was the most natural thing in the world.

One good turn deserved another. If a man of good will gave all this so altruistically to Austria, courtesy required that Austria offer something in return. Nugent told Frederick that it would not be hard for him to round out his domains by drawing a line from the Prussian border through Graudenz, Thorn and Poznan to Glogau. "Everything between this line and the sea will be quite suitable for your majesty. If you take the bishopric of Warmia in addition, the rounding-out will be complete." The king said nothing, but pondered the matter. Nugent had gone too far. His proposal was so extreme that it could not be subject of a simple conversation.

MARIA THERESA AND THE PARTITION OF POLAND

There were two who were lusting for acquisitions, one a feverish and restless youth, the other a cautious, quiet and pedantic old man. Then there was Maria Theresa, the famous queen-empress, who had taken her son, the German emperor Joseph II, as her co-ruler for the hereditary Austrian lands. She had kept the old chancellor Prince Kaunitz, whose personal experience and practical wisdom were supposed to restrain the hot-headed Joseph. He was to guide him in accordance with her views, since Kaunitz agreed with her completely! This was not the same Maria Theresa of old who had inspired the Hungarians to shout: "We shall die for our king, Maria Theresa!"[90] The latter part of her reign had been marked by serious struggles, when enemies had to be warded off from all sides and when strenuous efforts were needed to save her ancestral heritage from rude predators. It was this kind of reign that had worn Maria Theresa out. "I am horrified at the thought of how much blood has been spilled during my reign," she said. "Only dire necessity could make me guilty of spilling even one capful of it."

In addition Maria Theresa was a pious and conscientious old woman. She did not want to hear of taking Turkey's side and going to war against Russia. In the first place that would mean fighting against Christians on behalf of infidels. Secondly, Russia had waged a just war. It had not wanted war, while the Turks had been the instigators. Of equal weight was the fact that Maria Theresa did not want to go to war against the Turks and take territory from them. She considered herself indebted to the Porte because it had not threatened Austria at any time during the latter's desperate struggle with its enemies. Even less did the empress-queen want to partition Poland and harm a land that was in no way hostile, was Christian and, most important, Catholic. Despite all her aversion to war on grounds of religion and conscience Maria Theresa ultimately gave in. She responded to each plan which went against her views and wishes with disgust, with protest and with wailing. She dragged out the matter with her indecisiveness, which made her passionate son lose his patience. She finally gave in, but did not cease to protest and complain.[91]

Catherine, who had no love for Maria Theresa, wrote about her: "When I read that Maria Theresa entered a convent after her husband died, I concluded that she had intended to take the veil, but after twenty-four hours she came out again. Betskoy[92] says he knew she conferred with Kaunitz, but it seems to me that we have many noblewomen like her in Moscow." With regard to political inconsistency, Maria Theresa's conduct should not be judged too harshly. Her reign up to the end of the Seven Years War, regardless of the difficulties it presented, had one simple distinguishing task. Maria Theresa was in the habit of considering herself aggrieved and robbed, victim of the greatest injustice. The goal of all her actions was to recover what had been stolen and to preserve the heritage of her forefathers from further depredations. The struggle was over and, weary of it, Maria Theresa wished to spend the rest of her life preserving the glory of her honorable and irreproachable actions.

But now from one side her son and co-ruler and from the other side her chancellor constantly reiterated that it was impossible to maintain a calm and passive position. Russia was growing stronger, Prussia was growing stronger, and if Austria did not want to be overwhelmed by them it also must grow stronger. It should take what fell into its hands. The integrity of the monarchy and the welfare of its subjects were at stake. What would happen to them if Austria became weaker than its neighbors? Thus Maria Theresa, with bitter complaints, agreed to measures which she considered unlawful and which detracted from her reputation for honesty.

At first Maria Theresa did not want to hear about Joseph's proposed encounter with her sworn enemy Frederick II, but then agreed to the first meeting. She then agreed to the second meeting, at which Kaunitz himself was supposed to be present. It was no longer just a question of an initial contact or of an exchange of mutual compliments and assurances that the old enmity was forgotten and that they were prepared to live in friendship. Now Russia had won brilliant victories over the Turks both on land and sea. Now joint measures must be taken to put a stop to these successes and to prevent Russian from gaining too favorable a peace or a decisive predominance in Eastern Europe. Turkey, which had not wanted peace at the beginning of the year, now invited Austria to expel the Russians from Poland and to partition Poland. Now Turkey, alarmed by Kagul and Chesme, turned to Austria, asking for mediation and asked the same of Prussia. "In that case," Kaunitz wrote to Joseph, "good will come of misfortune. The Turks finally want peace and want our mediation. Now Russia must be made to want the same. This is what is to be done *(hoc opus hic labor)*. This is not easy in the present enthusiasm. I think that perhaps the Prussian king truly is in favor, but only if it be to his advantage."[93]

FREDERICK II, JOSEPH II AND KAUNITZ MEET IN NEUSTADT

The second meeting of Joseph and Kaunitz with Frederick took place in Neustadt in Moravia at the beginning of September (New Style). "I found neither everything good nor everything bad of what I had been told about the Prussian king ," wrote Kaunitz to Maria Theresa. "Frederick began the conversation with me by stating that he ardently desired the conclusion of peace between Russia and the Porte as soon as possible. He wanted to assure me that this was much more to our benefit than to his since the unexpected successes of Russian arms had enabled them to cross the Danube, which we could not allow. We thus would be drawn into open war with the Russians, which gradually could lead to a general war. This had to be prevented in the interest of mankind, of Prussia and of Austria. In his opinion the conclusion of peace could not pose great difficulties because the Russians probably would be satisfied with Azov. They would be satisfied if the rulers of Moldavia and Wallachia were independent of the Porte. The Turks because of their dismal situation would not reject such reasonable conditions. An attempt should be made to conclude peace this winter.

"After I had listened to these rash ideas," Kaunitz continued, "I answered that it was not easy to conclude peace under such circumstances. The Turks could continue the war longer than Russia, and a change in the fortunes of war was not impossible. Besides the Russian army was suffering from the plague, which quickly could wreak such havoc in the Russian empire that the greatest military successes would not make up for it. Russia could not have chimerical ideas of destroying the Ottoman empire or of seizing some of its important territories since Russia knows that we, Austria and Prussia, could not permit it. The king objected that I was mistaken concerning Russia's potential for continuing the war. The war on land had cost very little, two hundred thousand rubles up to now. The war at sea had been somewhat more expensive, but Russia had obtained a foreign loan of seven million florins. Since her accession to the throne the Russian empress had increased her income significantly. She had the means for war, and therefore we should make every effort to persuade Russia and the Porte to conclude peace. I answered that we were prepared to hasten the conclusion of peace, but without peace all our efforts would be in vain, especially in regard to Russia."

In the second conversation with Kaunitz Frederick, according to the Austrian chancellor, changed the proposed peace conditions. "We will conclude peace as quickly as possible," he said. "The Russians probably will demand Azov and the Crimea, but I hope they drop their pretensions to Moldavia and Wallachia. Perhaps they will continue to insist that these principalities have rulers independent of the Porte."

Kaunitz repeated that hastening the conclusion of peace depended on Frederick, who ought to use all his influence on the Russian empress. "You do not know the Russian empress," answered the king, "she is very arrogant, very ambitious, very vain and therefore it is hard to deal with her. Since she is a woman, one cannot talk with her as with a minister. One must approach her carefully so as not to irritate her. Moreover I will follow your advice, but only give me ammunition so I can frighten her. Could you not write to Rumiantsev that you hope he will not cross the Danube? Or could you not persuade France to declare to you that, if the Russians cross the Danube, and consequently you declare war on Russia, it will send an army of one hundred thousand to help you? If you send this information to me I will make use of it."

Kaunitz wrote Maria Theresa that he was astounded to hear such childish ideas from such a wise sovereign and hastened to reply that both proposals were unsatisfactory. The first was inadequate because one should not threaten without previously deciding how to carry out the threat, and because the Russian army's crossing of the Danube by itself could not be sufficient cause for a breach between Austria and Russia. The second was lacking because Russia would regard such a threat by France as a joke and would pay no attention to it. The Austrian chancellor's haste to label Frederick II's ideas childish was to no avail. The Prussian king attained his goal. He had to know to what extent Austria and France could block his own plans by joint intervention in Russo-Turkish relations. Kaunitz had revealed that Austria had not decided on war and certainly would not so decide. Austria would not threaten, lacking the means to carry out a threat. Moreover Rumiantsev's crossing of the Danube would not upset Austria. Finally the alliance between Austria and France, apparently so imposing, in reality was not that firm. Frederick saw that he had control of the situation, that Austria would not move without him and would serve as his tool.

It was decided at Neustadt that Frederick would transmit to St. Petersburg the Porte's desire to begin peace negotiations with Austria and Prussia as mediators. Moreover conditions were agreed upon in the form of a letter rather than a treaty for future relations between Prussia and Austria. This document was entitled a "Political Catechism." For us the following articles are worthy of note: "Neither of the two courts, unless it is directly contrary to its own interests, will oppose the advantage of the other, unless the question is of extraordinary importance. If it is a question of significant or very important acquisitions, then they will give prior notice to each other in friendly fashion and make arrangements in advance for their mutual and proportional advantage. Each of the two not only should consent to this, but in acquiring it also should assist the other consciously if necessary."[94]

These articles are important for us in connection with the Austrian seizure of the Polish districts of Zips, Nowy Targ, Chorstyn and the localities of Wieliczka and Bochnia, with their extensive salt mines, under the pretext that these territories belonged to Hungary until 1412, mortgaged at that time to Poland. The military occupation of these lands occurred before the Neustadt meeting. Austria's declaration remembering what had been forgotten since 1412, and reclaiming for Hungary territory that had belonged to it then, came long after the meeting, at the beginning of November 1770 to be exact.[95] We cannot be certain that the agreement at Neustadt came as a result of this seizure, or that there was a general discussion of the partition of Poland.

It is obvious that the "Political Catechism" was proposed to explain the seizure of specific Polish districts, which were included in the first part of the Catechism as acquisitions of a lesser importance. When Frederick accepted the Catechism the Viennese court explained that it was keeping the occupied territories as formerly belonging to Hungary. Understandably, if Austria were the first to take advantage of the Catechism, naturally Frederick also would take advantage of it. Returning from Neustadt, Joseph and Kaunitz, one more forcefully than the other, suggested to Maria Theresa that success would come in cooperation with the Prussian king. Nothing could be done without him, and Kaunitz said directly that Frederick should be rewarded with Courland and Semigalia for going to war against Russia. "Of course," Kaunitz remarked, "the king much rather would have Polish Prussia and the bishopric of Warmia, but such acquisitions would be very significant, and Austria could not agree to them without a corresponding expansion of its own domains. Such expansion should result from acquiring land from Poland and from Turkey in agreement with both powers." "The plan of partition," answered Maria Theresa, "is broadly conceived, but it surpasses my understanding." His mother's remarks did not deter Joseph. After the meeting with Frederick the policy of seizure gained ascendancy in Vienna, and further Russian successes in the war with the Turks no longer were feared. In Joseph's opinion Thugut should persuade the Porte not to conclude too unfavorable a peace with Russia, giving assurances that Austria ardently desired the preservation and the welfare of Turkey and would extend sizable aid at the proper time as circumstances dictated.

CONSEQUENCES OF NEUSTADT FOR RUSSIA

"Our course of action is set," Joseph wrote to his brother Leopold.[96] "It consists of presenting all the dangers of a strengthened Russia to the Prussian king and proposing that he work in concert to prevent this by all possible means. If he makes no proposals, at least we will prevent a possible hasty and shameful peace concluded by the Porte. A second campaign would weaken both combatants and either could reduce Russia's gains or increase them to the point that we would have to act. This could happen in two ways: (1) If the Russians break through the Danube and reach Adrianople, that would be the time for us to move forces to the Danube to cut off their retreat. This would force them into a hasty withdrawal, during which their army could be annihilated and the Turks, saved from ruin, easily would agree to compensation for our expenses; that is, to cede that part of Wallachia handed over in the Treaty of Belgrade lying between the Banat, Transylvania, the Danube and the Olta river.[97] (2) If the Russians, having forced the Dardanelles, threaten Constantinople and the entire empire with an assault by sea, it would be absolutely necessary for us to seize the provinces closest to us before the Russians could take them. The empress has decided to prepare an army of fifty thousand for these two eventualities and has ordered a loan of four million to be negotiated."[98]

Frederick II carried out the commission he had assumed. On September 14 (New Style) he wrote the Russian empress a letter exhorting her to conclude peace and suggesting his mediation, something the Porte had requested: "If I may share my thoughts with you as a good and true ally, then it seems to me that at present peace is necessary to avoid the general war which France is trying to ignite in Europe. I know about French actions in Vienna, which aim to stir up bitterness and envy in the hearts of all. Your imperial majesty, put a stop to these pernicious efforts and end the war which has brought such glory to your arms, to your far-reaching plans, and to the splendor of your reign. Be moderate in concluding peace."

Expanding on the significance of moderation and mercy for great nations, Frederick directed Catherine's attention to the Polish disturbances. They had to be stopped soon and with more than temporary measures. He referred to the need for the dissidents to moderate their demands. They themselves should petition the empress on the matter. He expressed confidence that the Austrians would join him and force the confederates to sign new conditions.

On September 16 this letter of Frederick's was presented to the council, after which Panin proposed a reply to the Prussian king: (1) That before beginning any negotiations with the Turks, Obrezkov's release should be attempted. Once freed, in no way was he to be detained in Constantinople. There might be a parallel with 1714, when the Turks put a Russian minister in prison and released him when circumstances changed.[99]. (2) We would welcome very much the mediation of the Prussian king as our true ally, should the Turks choose him as a mediator. But we must realize that we were concerned about our delicate relations with the English court, which from the start of the war did everything to maintain calm and extended every possible assistance during the voyage of our squadrons. Therefore we promised to designate England as a mediator when necessary. The mediation of the Viennese court disturbs us greatly. There is the danger that France, following the English example, may become involved in mediation, something that hitherto we have not intended to allow. Based on all of this we request that the king, together with the Viennese court, decline to mediate. On our part we will conduct negotiations with complete openness and will accept all representations from the courts of Berlin and Vienna. If we have no choice but to accept mediation, Panin continued, we must call upon England to participate, but not allow France to do so.

Panin presented his opinion of the conditions for concluding peace with the Turks. These conditions were: (1) Keep Azov and Taganrog and demand free passage for our merchant ships from the Sea of Azov to the Black Sea. (2) Obtain a general amnesty for all who took up arms to defend themselves against the Porte. If in the meantime our fleet captured some islands in the archipelago, this would have to be a subject for negotiation. (3) If the Tatars have broken away from Turkish rule, they should remain independent. (4) Justice requires that the principalities of Moldavia and Wallachia be kept as compensation for war expenses, which have reached twenty-five million. Her imperial majesty's policy since her accession to the throne impels her to demonstrate to all foreign courts that she does not seek to extend her empire by acquiring territory. Thus we should demand that we keep these principalities for as many years as necessary as compensation until the military expenditures can be recouped from their yearly income. The empress will sacrifice this compensation, however, if the independence of Moldavia and Wallachia is proclaimed and the Danube established as the Turkish frontier.

Panin's opinion how to reply to the Prussian king was accepted, and a letter from the empress to Frederick II was written accordingly, in which mediation was declined and the good offices of a faithful ally were received with gratitude. These good offices could commence only when an answer was received from the vizier to Count Rumiantsev's proposal. In her letter to Frederick, Catherine, referring to the need to decline French mediation, described the duke of Choiseul as "the cursed enemy of my state and my person."

VISIT OF PRINCE HENRY TO RUSSIA

Mediation was declined but on October 1 a special kind of mediator arrived in St. Petersburg. In the summer, when Frederick met with Emperor Joseph, his brother Prince Henry travelled to Stockholm to see his sister the Swedish queen. Naturally the rapprochement between Prussia and Austria, expressed in the second meeting of their sovereigns, could not produce a favorable impression in St. Petersburg. This was because such a rapprochement could cause various countries especially hostile to Russia to rejoice at the prospect of a corresponding weakening of the Russo-Prussian alliance. It was natural that Catherine would want Prince Henry to travel from Stockholm to St. Petersburg to counteract this opinion. Because of the prince's importance and his friendship with and influence on his brother, a meeting with him would be as good as a meeting with Frederick himself. A meeting with Prince Henry was especially desirable because he was returning from Sweden, where

The Winter Palace, St. Petersburg

affairs were particularly unsettled. One could learn from the brother of the hostile Swedish queen what Ostermann[100] and Stakhiev[101] could not provide. He could make suggestions which could influence the future conduct of the queen. Catherine wrote Frederick a letter in which she expressed her desire to see Prince Henry in St. Petersburg. Frederick quickly informed his brother that he should accede to the wish of the Russian empress. The king set two goals for Henry's stay in Russia. He should establish favorable relations between Empress Catherine and their sister the Swedish queen, and should try to hasten the conclusion of peace.

In order to understand Prince Henry's conduct in St. Petersburg and the sense of his correspondence with Frederick II, we should recall the foundations of the latter's policy as reflected in his actions and his words. Above all he needed peace, which would put a halt to Russia's successes in Turkey and the strengthening of Russian influence in Poland. If Russia, frightened by him at the prospect of an armed Austria and a general war, would agree to a peace with Turkey with insignificant gains and would agree to settle Polish matters by concessions on the dissident question, Frederick could be reassured. He would be freed from the disagreeable payment of subsidies required by the treaty of alliance, he would have put a halt to the increase in Russian power and he would have given Turkey an advantageous peace. Moreover he would have reassured Austria and all of Europe, and reduced Russian influence in Poland to secondary status, forcing Russia to accede to his demands. In a word he would acquire a major and decisive influence in European affairs. He would have assumed the leading role, since hitherto he had been irritated by the thought that he was regarded as a satellite of Russia, the submissive tool of its sovereign.

In June, before meeting with Joseph, Frederick had written his brother, Henry: "My little journey to Moravia will make the Russian empress more disposed towards peace than all the armies and public displays in the world. The Austrians are constructing supply depots on the Hungarian frontiers. Truthfully speaking I do not consider them significant, but I am exaggerating the matter in St. Petersburg to the utmost. I hope that peace will be concluded next winter, or the year after that the war could become a general one." Then events in Denmark gave him even more hope that the Russian empress

Rokotov

Count Grigory Grigorevich Orlov

would be disposed towards peace. "In Denmark the French have managed to depose Bernstorff;"[102] he wrote to Prince Henry, "this event certainly will detach Denmark from the Russian alliance, which will be of considerable advantage to us, because we will remain Russia's only ally. The changes in Denmark should force the empress to desire peace."

Russia certainly would not agree to conclude peace with the Porte on moderate terms, as understood by the other powers, and Frederick decided to take advantage of the resulting complications to make certain territorial acquisitions. Frederick considered it most important that these acquisitions be achieved through peaceful negotiations, lest he be drawn into war because of them. Besides it was critical for Frederick not to allow a rapprochement between Russia and Turkey over Turkish affairs, which would lead to a revival of the Elizabethan policy and leave him isolated.[103]

We noted that Frederick in his memoirs agreed to sending the so-called Lynar project to St. Petersburg to test the waters,[104] although he concealed some very important and vital circumstances. According to Frederick no attention was paid to the project in St. Petersburg because the Russians were carried away with their military successes. Panin took the project very seriously and quickly proposed what might be called his own counterproject, inviting Prussia and Austria to cooperate with Russia to drive the Turks out of Europe. This accomplished, Austria would receive compensation from Turkish territory and Prussia from Polish territory. Frederick could not be pleased with this Russian project, because he wanted Russia and Austria to be his partners in the partition of Poland, and Prince Henry could insist on this project to the exclusion of the other one in St. Petersburg.

Prince Henry made a most disagreeable initial impression on the empress and her court. He was not at all like his brother the king. To the same degree that the latter was amiable, apt to converse endlessly on every subject and to talk unusually animatedly and intelligently, Prince Henry was serious, reticent and ponderous in society. In his letters and conversation Frederick was able to get the better of his partner and tire him out by racing from topic to topic (something that so displeased Kaunitz). He would attack unexpectedly and find out what he needed. Since he himself was extraordinarily cautious, he never permitted himself to reveal his hand, but rather hid and concealed his most intimate desires, leaving it to others or to circumstances to bring them to fruition. In the same measure Henry was lacking in this so-called diplomatic finesse. He either kept a stubborn silence or spoke only about what he wanted, and spoke plainly without evasions. He was a valuable man for Frederick at the end of 1770 when a decision had to be reached at whatever cost and with whatever means at hand.

Prince Henry's outward appearance also did not counteract the unfavorable impression created by his cold manner. There was nothing to indicate a man distinguished by his talents and by his heritage. He was of less than average height and very dessicated, in striking contrast to his unusually thick and curly hair, which was combed back into an enormous toupee. He had a high forehead and large eyes. He had a penetrating and observant gaze, but there was nothing pleasing about his appearance, and when he walked he strutted.

Catherine described her first impressions to Alexis Orlov: "Yesterday (October 2) the Prussian Prince Henry was at court for the first time. At the first meeting he was as light on his feet as a lead bird, but so intelligent, yes, very intelligent. They say that when you get to know him he will be courteous and gentle. But the first time he was so stiff that I got very tired of him. To do him justice this stiffness is only his manner, and he did everything that was required of him with great attentiveness in all things. It is only that his appearance is so cold that it is like a hard frost." The courtiers, however, were interested primarily in his unattractive appearance, and they took special delight in the prince's large toupee. Jokes and witticisms began. They said that Henry resembled Samson, and that all his strength was in his hair. The prince, aware of this and of the fate of the Israelite champion, would not allow any Delilah to come near him. They said he resembled a comet which had appeared in the previous year, frightening the northern and eastern rulers with the threat of great changes. It had a small core and an enormous tail.[105]

The comet certainly portended great changes. Frederick II was angered that the Russian court had rejected his mediation in concluding peace with the Porte. He had lost the major role of peacemaker, and he was afraid that at direct negotiations with the Turks Russia would persuade them to give Russia more than what in his opinion Russia needed to acquire. Having received Catherine's letter turning down mediation, Frederick wrote to Henry: "I have decided not to become involved either in the peace negotiations with Turkey or in Polish affairs. I will remain a simple observer of events. They can accept our mediation in St. Petersburg or not, but they cannot be permitted to laugh at us openly."[106]

FREDERICK, CATHERINE AND THE PEACE NEGOTIATIONS

Five days after Prince Henry's arrival the empress stated that she wanted peace, and that she would rely happily on the king's mediation in Constantinople. It was necessary to await the vizier's answer to Rumiantsev's letter and the freeing of Obrezkov. Later Henry mentioned to Panin that dual negotiations, through Rumiantsev and through Prussia, only would harm matters. Panin answered that Russia merely wanted assurance through Rumiantsev whether in principle the Porte intended to negotiate. The allies parted ways. It was important for Prussia to get control of the peace negotiations and to proceed to a peace corresponding to its interests. For Russia it was important to know, in case peace negotiations failed, how reliable the Prussian alliance was, and to what extent Prussia's rapprochement with Austria would change Russo-Prussian relations.

In the middle of October the empress called Prince Henry aside and asked him whether in the event peace was not concluded he advised her to lead the army across the Rubicon (that is what she called the Danube).[107] The prince's brother had insisted to him in his letters that the Rubicon not be crossed under any circumstances. The prince replied that this would disturb the Austrians greatly, that the French would push them forward and that a general war would be precipitated. Although the Prussian king would not allow Russia's undertakings to be halted, Prussia would have to deal with the French. "Thus we should conclude peace," said Catherine, *laughing*. "I want peace," she continued, "but the sultan is a savage, and French perfume will not make him sensible." "The king, my brother, will bring him to reason if your majesty will entrust her interests to him," said the prince. "The matter will not be clarified before January," answered the empress.

Prince Henry also strongly urged drafting a plan to bring peace to Poland, and enlisting the Austrians in this matter. He encountered great mistrust of the Austrians. The prince informed his brother of a disagreement between [Grigory] Orlov and Panin. The former wanted peace to be concluded without any mediation. Panin wanted to pursue the matter together with Prussia and Austria. But we have observed how Panin did not share Frederick II's wishes on this matter.[108] He demanded that Austria and Prussia declare war on the Porte, for which Austria would receive compensation from Turkey, and Prussia in Poland. In conversation with the prince Panin recalled the advantages the Viennese court would receive from waging war against the Porte in alliance with Russia. The prince, in his words, replied laconically. To continue the conversation, which had been cut short by this laconic answer, Saldern[109] turned to the prince. He began by asking whether Panin had mentioned benefits which Austria could demand next: "Yes," answered the prince, "he said if they would like to engage in *political dreams* then, if it is impossible to conclude peace with the Turks, it is possible to contemplate concluding a triple alliance between Prussia, Russia and Austria mutually beneficial for the three states, and then the Turks quickly would be forced to conclude peace."

Here the expression "political dreams" should not confuse us because in his correspondence with Solms Frederick II had described the Lynar plan as a dream. Saldern also did not regard Henry's proposal as a dream and asked if he could inform Count Panin of these ideas. The prince answered that he did not want to be implicated in the matter for fear of new censures on him from the king. In a letter to the king Henry wrote: "In no way have you been compromised by this conversation, and if peace with the Turks does not happen this year, I will be able to render you service by proposals for you to persuade the Viennese court to act on behalf of the same interests and to cooperate with your interests. That is what I want."

FREDERICK'S REACTION

Frederick answered that Panin's and Saldern's suggestion for a triple alliance was senseless because the Turks urgently wanted peace. If the Russians were opposed to peace, then they were rushing wantonly into a new war. In that case he, the Prussian king, could refuse to pay subsidies. The Viennese court never would dissociate itself from France. Kaunitz told him clearly enough that his court would support a balance of power in the east, not allowing Russia to cross the Danube and establish itself there next to Austria. Therefore all hope in St. Petersburg of enlisting Austria in a division of the Turkish conquests should be abandoned.

"I," wrote the king, "will not sacrifice the welfare and benefits of my country to the aggressive intentions of another power without reason. What kind of convention do they want to conclude with me there? What territory are they promising me? Should I bring all the armed forces of Austria and France down on my neck to acquire this territory? I do not have a single ally to support me! This corresponds neither to our forces, exhausted in the last war, nor to the present European situation. Thus they may not cross the Rubicon there, nor do I need any kind of convention. We shall try to compel them to conclude peace as soon as possible, or we shall let some of them wage war with whomever they want. I made an alliance with Russia for my own advantage, just as Austria made an alliance with France, but not to wage a pernicious war under Russian colors, from which I derive nothing.[110] I am waiting for information whether the Russians want to continue the war. Remind them that my obligations do not extend that far. I cannot be enlisted in an undertaking where I assume all the risk, because I risk losing all my possessions on the Rhine."[111]

These letters are very interesting, but it goes without saying that the historian should use them carefully. Thus Frederick writes as if Kaunitz told him that Austria would not allow the Russian forces to cross the Danube. Yet the Austrian chancellor clearly said, that a crossing of the Danube would not be sufficient cause for a clear break between Austria and Russia.

In Russia a triple alliance was wanted for action against Turkey, but in Prussia a partition of Poland was desired. Panin told Prince Henry that he wanted to disclose to him secretly that a triple alliance between Prussia, Russia and Austria was an excellent and fortunate idea. The other European powers would not dare to oppose the measures and plans of such a powerful alliance. Prince Henry informed his brother that in case a triple alliance were unsuccessful, people were wondering in St. Petersburg what benefits to offer to induce Prussia to take part in the war. There was more agreement on compensation in Germany than in Poland. As previously, Frederick did not want to hear about Prussia's participation in the war and repeated that because of France, Austria never wanted to take up arms against the Turks to divide the pie with Russia, and did not want to think about it at all!

"Peace, peace as soon as possible, not requiring conditions too intolerable or too humiliating for the Turks. If general war breaks out, the entire burden falls on me. Presupposing a happy conclusion, when peace is concluded I will keep my present domains, but the lands and the army will have been devastated, and the state revenues will go to the benefit of Russia. For this they will give me empty compliments and a sable coat. I fear lest they milk me like a cow."[112] The purpose of all these insistences was clear to everyone. It was only by forcing Russia to state definitively and exactly what the conditions for peace were, that Frederick would set to work on one side or the other. Only when Russia announced conditions could Austria's intentions be determined. Prolonging the matter made Frederick weary, and he hastened to settle it, and to do so peacefully without the "excellent and fortunate ideas" talked about in St. Petersburg.

An answer finally came from Constantinople to Rumiantsev's letter to the vizier. The answer was that the sultan already had informed Austria and Prussia of his desire for peace, and he was waiting for the first communication from these powers. Then on December 9 the empress sent Frederick a letter which began as follows: "I put no limits on my devotion to your majesty as my best friend and most faithful ally, with whom I am sharing my plan and my most secret thoughts concerning peace with the Porte. Having made your majesty guardian of all my intentions, I am fully confident that you will put them to best use. This I can expect from your friendship and your modesty at the time and under the circumstances you consider most favorable for safeguarding the foundations of my just undertaking, for vindicating the rightness of my intentions and revealing my genuine impartiality and, finally, for hastening the conclusion of peace. In all of this I rely completely on your majesty's wisdom, knowledge and great insight. Here I should direct your majesty's special attention to the fact that the return of my minister Obrezkov should be accomplished before the negotiations are opened, and even before any overture is made.

"Having given me this satisfaction, necessary for my personal honor and the good of my country, if the Turks want to send their plenipotentiaries somewhere in Moldavia or Poland, I will send my own there and will expect the good offices of your majesty if you order your minister in Constantinople to persuade the Porte to comply. Concerning the suggestions your majesty considers necessary to make to the Porte, your good sense will tell you that my plan, as I have formulated it, has been drafted only out of trust and friendship, not to be communicated to a foe. It would be premature, and when the time for it comes, it would need to be reworked in a different form and with different expressions."

Since she relied completely on Frederick concerning Austria, the empress wrote that in her opinion a copy of her plan should not be communicated to the Viennese court unless there were firm assurance that this court would develop better views regarding Russia and would no longer be guided by previous biases. The empress remarked that, on the other hand, she did not want to counteract the benefit for the Russo-Prussian alliance which could come from such a rapprochement by being too reserved and frigid towards the Viennese court. "If such a rapprochement could wean Austria away from its present absurd system and could bring it to our views, Germany would be restored to its natural state, and the house of Austria would be diverted, by means of another perspective, from its designs against your majesty's domains. These intentions are supported by current ties."[113]

The conditions for peace with the Turks were appended to this letter. These were the conditions we have already seen, which Panin had proposed to the council at the session of September 16,[114] with the additional condition that both Kabarda districts should go to Russia.

FREDERICK OPPOSES RUSSIAN PROPOSALS

These conditions, in Frederick's words, made a most unpleasant impression on him and removed any hope of peace. "My hair stood on end when I received the Russian peace proposals;" he wrote to his brother Henry in St. Petersburg. "I would never bring myself to propose them to the Turks or to the Austrians because they truly are unacceptable. The condition about Wallachia in no way can be reconciled with the Austrian system. First, Austria never will abandon the French alliance. Second, it never will tolerate the Russians as neighbors. You can regard these conditions as a declaration of war. They would laugh at us. I cannot compromise myself for Russia's benefit. I will make comments about the consequences of their proposals, and if they do not change them, I will ask them to entrust the matter to some other state. I will leave the game.

"You can count on the Austrians to declare war, and that would be too much, and it would be unbearable for all the European states! States are guided by their own interests. We can do what we can to oblige our allies, but there are limits to everything. I will not communicate this project to Vienna or Constantinople, because that would be tantamount to sending a declaration of war. Thus if the Russians do not moderate this project considerably I will renounce any mediation and leave these gentlemen to their fate. There is nothing more for you to do except leave in decent fashion, because there is nothing more to do and nothing more to be expected from these people."[115]

We can assume that the peace conditions might have seemed very harsh to Frederick, but all the same that was not by itself reason enough to become so irritated and have his hair stand on end. First, why repeat that he could not communicate the conditions either to Vienna or to Constantinople when Catherine herself had asked him specifically not to communicate them either to the Austrians or to the Turks? She still was keeping them a secret which she was revealing to him alone. Consequently it was not at all an ultimatum. Secondly, Frederick had learned about these peace conditions much earlier, and his hair had not stood on end. We saw that he spoke about these conditions to Kaunitz at Neustadt.[116] He had said that in all probability the Russians would insist on retaining Azov and the Crimea, but that he hoped they would renounce their pretensions on Moldavia and Wallachia, and *perhaps also* renounce demanding the independence of those principalities from the Porte.

Moreover in a letter to Prince Henry on October 1 (New Style) Frederick wrote: "The empress has moderated her demands, which makes me hope for an end to this unhappy war." "The empress communicated the conditions to me," he wrote in a letter on October 8, "on the basis of which she expects to conclude peace. I find them so moderate that I do not doubt they will be accepted." Finally, in a letter dated November 12, Frederick wrote: "The moderation with which this sovereign has set conditions for peace with the Turks is the crowning touch to the picture of her grand deeds, adding the final glory to it. It is a fine thing to pardon one's enemies, and an even finer thing not to crush them when they could be crushed."

The conversations between Frederick and Kaunitz proved that in the main the conditions communicated in September were the same as those communicated in December. There he had proposed Azov, the Crimea and the Danubian principalities, the latter of which either would remain temporarily under Russia or be declared independent. Interestingly, Frederick did not speak to Kaunitz about independence for the Tatars, but did speak directly about annexing the Crimea to Russia. Thus although the opening demands were broader in scope than the later, Frederick characterized the former as moderate.

Finally we know about the conversations which proceeded at the end of the year between Frederick and the new Austrian ambassador to his court, van Swieten.[117]

King: Peace must be concluded! Believe me, peace must be concluded!

van Swieten: We want nothing more than the conclusion of peace, but on reasonable conditions.

King: What do you call reasonable conditions?

van Swieten: Those which do not cause an increase in Russian power, now or in the future, and do not weaken Turkey to the point where its continued existence is questionable. Here the ambassador mentioned that, because of its consequences, the annexation of the Crimea to Russia could not be one of those reasonable conditions.

King: Oh, yes, the Crimea! I forgot about it. They (the Russians) wanted it to become independent. They can be granted that.

van Swieten: This independence for the Crimea is an empty phrase. Sooner or later that country, which is inhabited by a warlike people and controls harbors on the Black Sea, will become a Russian

province and will strengthen Russia's might to a significant degree.
King: No, it is only a question of the Budjak Tatars, whose capital
is Bakhchisaray.
van Swieten: This city, sire, is the capital of the Crimea. The
Budjak Tatars, as far as I know, live between Bender and the
Danube.
King: Pardon me, I realize that I am not very familiar with the
country. I know the other countries of Europe better. In any event
it is possible to do that about which Prince Kaunitz spoke to me
in Neustadt. Permit the Tatars, whatever kind they are, to become
independent, then induce them by intrigue to submit to the Porte
again.
van Swieten: This method is not reliable and does not deal at all
with the obvious danger of allowing the Russians to establish
themselves firmly in the Crimea and on the Black Sea. This position
will give them the means to expand trade and construct fleets. They
will be able to plan the most daring kind of enterprise.
King: Trade is slow. Believe me, the Russians have better methods.
The Russian empress has improved her state significantly. She has
set herself Peter I as a model, and she is following that sovereign's
plans. They have assured me that a project for a naval expedition
to the Levant is among his papers. [118]

This conversation occurred before Catherine's letter containing
conditions for peace with the Turks had been received. After they
had been received Frederick's response to van Swieten concerning
the conditions contained the same expressions he had used in writing
to Prince Henry. He called them excessive and intolerable. Austria
could only respond with a declaration of war. He did not reveal
these terrible conditions, and van Swieten could not possibly guess
that for his court there was nothing new in them, except perhaps
an island in the archipelago.[119]

Thus we are right to see Frederick's irritation as a pretext
intended to threaten the Russian court and force it to take other
measures sooner to settle the matter, measures more compatible with
the interests of the Prussian king. It was also intended to threaten
the Austrians with Russia's might and excessive demands, but not
saying whether Prussia would agree to act jointly with Austria to
curtail these demands. All of this was so that Joseph and Kaunitz

would persuade Maria Theresa sooner to enter into an agreement concerning Poland. If we grant that the Prussian king's irritation was genuine, there are no grounds for it in the peace conditions. Frederick could have been irritated greatly by the passage in Catherine's letter where she spoke of opening up other prospects for Austria to make it forget about Silesia. Again we see something which Frederick found intolerable, Russia's striving for rapprochement with Austria by opening up prospects in the Turkish domains. All that Prussia gained would be that Austria forgot about Silesia, while there was no mention of compensation for Prussia at Poland's expense!

In addition Prince Henry informed his brother about his conversation with Panin concerning the peace conditions. When the prince said that Austria considered the cession of the Danubian principalities harmful to its interests, Panin replied: "Then these lands can become independent." "But in that case to whom will they belong?" asked the prince again. "It is all the same to the empress," answered Panin, "only not the Turks." "But what if Austria demands them for itself?" asked Henry. "Why not," answered Panin, "if Austria begins to act straightforwardly and wants to be friendly with you and with us?" Then Henry wrote to his brother: "If the Viennese court were not restrained by France so forcefully, it would be in a position to conduct its affairs to advantage. General Bibikov,[120] a friend of Panin who enjoys empress's good graces, told me about the advantages which the Viennese court could receive at the conclusion of these negotiations. He added that it then would be fair if Prussia also gained an advantage. Vienna does not understand the thinking here. Here everything would be agreeable. If the compensation is only at Turkey's expense, a lesser part of the spoils would be satisfactory here."[121]

AUSTRIA SEIZES POLISH TERRITORY

Luckily for Frederick, Austria already had taken a step which would lead to a resolution in accord with Prussia's interests. It had taken Polish territory and ruled it as its own. Before describing the impact this information produced in St. Petersburg, we shall see the impression it produced in Poland. As early as June strong rumors were circulating about partition, rumors which were attributed to the Polish king himself. The French resident in Danzig, Gérard, wrote to his court: "I am assured that Stanislaw Augustus has offered Polish Prussia to the court of Berlin and the palatinate of Cracow to the Viennese court, with the condition that both courts not only support him on the throne, but also guarantee it for his posterity. A letter of the elector of Saxony[122] is cited as the basis for the information." In November, when it became known that the Austrians had taken Polish districts, the same Gérard wrote: "The conclusion has been drawn from the Austrian occupation of certain Polish lands that partition already has been decided. Some of the landlords from the occupied districts are in Danzig, and I consoled them, saying that if there is partition it will be based upon some of the original and recognized laws, and in that case the Austrian government will not despoil the present landlords." Finally in December Gérard wrote, "Two Prussian regiments entered Great Poland and took up positions on the Warta. It would be hard for the Poles not to regard this as a prelude to the partition of the Commonwealth." Thus the idea of partition was planted everywhere, and thus it was expected hourly. There was a general conviction that there was an agreement between the two courts on this issue.

At the very end of December the empress held a soirée in St. Petersburg, and Prince Henry was there. Jokingly *(en badinant)*, Catherine told him that the Austrians had taken possession of two districts in Poland and had erected the imperial eagles on their frontiers. She added: "But why doesn't everyone seize in this manner?" Henry answered that, although his brother the king had cordoned off the Polish frontiers, he still had not occupied districts. The empress continued to laugh and said: "But why not occupy them?" We cannot fail to pay attention to Catherine's laughter. We saw that she also responded with laughter to the Austrian threat of general war: "So, we must conclude peace."[123] With this laughter she announced that she understood very well her faithful ally's intentions, and that the Austrians by themselves were not very dangerous. She also understood that before the meeting of Joseph and Kaunitz with Frederick they never would have dared to exercise authority in the Polish domains the way they were now.

After the conversation with the empress Count Zakhar Chernyshev came up to Prince Henry and began to talk to him about the same topic. "Why," he asked, "do you not secure the bishopric of Warmia? Everyone should receive something." Chernyshev's words should not surprise us. He remembered that thanks to the Austrian move his project, which had been shelved, could be revived. Henry wrote to inform his brother of these talks: "Although all of this was said in jest, it is apparent still that these conversations are significant. I do not doubt that the situation offers great possibilities. Count Panin is dissatisfied with the Austrian takeover of Polish lands. He said nothing to me about the bishopric of Warmia. All of this is caused by disagreements among council members. Those who want to expand Russia's domains want Russia and everyone else to take, while Count Panin stands for peace and tranquility. I still am trying to explain this matter, and I stand by the opinion that you risk nothing if you seize the bishopric of Warmia on some pretext or other, if it really is true that the Austrians have taken over the two districts."[124]

THE POLISH CONFEDERATES

Thus at the end of 1770 the Polish question again came to the forefront with great urgency. But what happened this year in Poland? The war of the confederates continued as before. Suvorov[125] began to achieve prominence in this war, first with the rank of brigadier general, and since 1770 as major general. Suvorov had been worn out by this war and longed for a transfer to the army fighting against the Turks. He wrote: "Weakened in health: a sea of almost insurmountable troubles. The difficulties will multiply in the future. On all sides the prospect is of almost measureless distances. Progress from one place to another is difficult. Reinforcements for essential needs not expected. Forces weak. Mountains, the Vistula, Warsaw. What a favor it would be for me if there were even a month's rest, that is, let out to pasture. With the help of God, I won't miss any advantage."[126]

The confederates could field only disorganized bands, their operations were not unified enough and they lacked gifted leaders. Since for a long time the people had not been accustomed to war, they could not take advantage of the small size of the Russian forces. They expected help from abroad from the Catholic powers, from Austria and especially from France. Austria's words were very kind, but in fact they did no more than allow the confederates to have their headquarters in the Hungarian city of Eperjes. In May Emperor Joseph received the confederate leaders in the course of a journey in Hungary. He spoke with them very kindly and promised to use his good offices on their behalf at the Russian and Prussian courts. He added: "Look where the French promises and suggestions have brought you, look at the fruits of your trust!"

Not long before this Louis XV wrote concerning Poland: "Assistance for the people is impossible. It is very difficult to give monetary aid, and their use of it is somewhat doubtful."[127] Nevertheless Choiseul found it possible to help the confederates monetarily. He also sent Dumouriez,[128] who later became famous, but who then was just a captain, to bring order and unity in their efforts. Dumouriez described his impressions of the confederates in his memoirs. He regarded the morals of the confederate leaders as Asiatic. Amazing luxury, senseless expenditures, lengthy dinners and dancing were what occupied them! They thought that Dumouriez was bringing them treasure and despaired when he told them that he had come without money and that, judging from their manner of life, they did not need anything.

The confederate army numbered between sixteen and seventeen thousand, but was under the command of eight or nine independent leaders who disagreed among themselves. They were suspicious of each other, sometimes quarreled among themselves and enticed soldiers from each other. The only cavalry was made up of gentry, equal in rank, undisciplined, poorly armed and on poor horses. These gentry were unable to stand up not only against regular Russian forces, but even against cossacks. They had not a single fortress, a single cannon or a single foot soldier. The confederates robbed their own Poles, tyrannized prominent landlords and beat the peasants recruited into the army. Instead of entrusting the supervision of the salt mines to two members of the finance council, the leaders divided the salt among themselves and sold it at low price to Silesian Jews so they could get the money more quickly. *The comrades* (the gentry) refused to stand watch. They sent the peasants to do this, while they played and drank in quarters. At the same time the officers played and danced in neighboring castles.

As far as the character of the individual leaders was concerned, Marshal General Pac,[129] according to Dumouriez, was a man given to pleasure, very courteous and very fickle. He was more ambitious than capable, and more daring than courageous. He was a good orator, a common Polish quality thanks to the diets. The only man with a head on his shoulders was the Lithuanian Bogusz, the general secretary of the confederation, who directed its affairs in despotic fashion. Prince Radziwill[130] was a complete brute, but he was the most prominent noble in Poland. Pulaski[131] was very brave and enterprising but was fickle and loved independence. He could not settle on anything, he was ignorant in military matters and proud of his small successes, which the Poles, because of their tendency to exaggerate, ranked above Sobieski's exploits.[132]

The Poles were brave, magnanimous, courteous and sociable. They loved liberty passionately and eagerly sacrificed their possessions and their lives to this passion, but their social system and their constitution worked against their efforts. The Polish constitution was purely aristocractic, but there were no people for the nobility to govern because it was not possible to call a people the eight or ten million slaves whom they bought, sold and exchanged like domestic animals. The body of Polish society, that miracle, consisted of heads and stomachs, lacking hands and feet. The Polish government was similar to the government of sugar plantations, incapable of independence. Intellectual capabilities, talents and energy in Poland had passed from the men to the women. The women managed affairs while the men enjoyed sensual pleasures. Dumouriez also spoke about the Russians in his memoirs. "They are superior soldiers," he wrote, "but except for the leaders they have few good officers. They do not send the best against the Poles, whom they hold in contempt."

CATHERINE AND PONIATOWSKI

It was hard for Choiseul to have some precisely specified plan for Poland. He wanted one thing, to harm Russia by all means possible. Therefore he supported the confederates in their struggle with the Russian forces. He was ready to support King Stanislaw in his spasmodic efforts to oppose Russia. Thus Choiseul assured the Polish king's emissary in France, Count Chreptowicz, that Louis

XV, pleased with Stanislaw's steadfastness, would help the confederates only on the condition that they support Stanislaw on the throne. Armed with this Stanislaw took a harder line towards Russia. In his letter on February 21 he stated his wishes to Empress Catherine: "I want Poland to be pacified quickly and permanently. That cannot occur if the nation is not satisfied, and the nation will not be satisfied if it does not act on its own, as a whole and in a legal manner. For this the diet is needed, which should be preceded by the provincial diets, which cannot meet unless the majority of the nation is favorably disposed. This disposition can come only from the hope of receiving what the nation desires above all else. It can base its hopes only on a frank declaration from your majesty. Your ambassador's words must not be repeated to the nation, which has learned by experience that it cannot rely on them, and does not wish to trust anyone except the person of your majesty.

"For me or someone else to be successful with the proposed confederation, the following must be said to the invited participants: Here specifically is where I am leading you, here is why I have confidence in it and here is how you can be satisfied. I would not press your majesty if our extreme poverty did not force me to implore your compassion. Hunger threatens to make an end of us. A third of our fields in the most fertile districts have not been planted because all of the grain has been seized. The draught animals have been eaten by the armies or have perished because of the constant transport of supplies. I do not mention the decline in population, some of whom have perished by the sword while others, fleeing poverty, have abandoned the fatherland.

"Perhaps you are told that all this should hasten the submission of the Poles, that it will force them to abandon their obstinacy and that it will do them good. I ought to inform your imperial majesty about the general opinion here. They sooner would agree to suffer and to die than to obligate themselves in some form or other before your majesty vouchsafes to proclaim directly and personally how it pleases you to condescend to the wishes of the Poles. Your majesty, remember the time when so many prominent people with the help of their friends took action everywhere on behalf of the Confederation of 1767. Remember how large an army was needed to force the inhabitants to subscribe to it and how many did not sign because they did not know the goals of the confederation. How large an army would be needed today for a cause which has no leaders and no partisans of the nation anywhere? This is not to mention the most extreme measures, which of course do not correspond to your majesty's views. If force can compel the Poles to take part in this confederation, this merely will give them new grounds for future protest on the basis that everything was done against their will.

"I am a friend of your majesty, and I will glory in this title my whole life. The law of sincerity compels me, however, to tell you that, regardless of all other conditions, the nation always will view the peace as something forced upon it if granted without the participation of the Catholic powers. It always will hope to receive something more with their help as soon as your forces leave the country. The nation will take vengeance on me first for the coercion by which it was subjugated. I am assured on this matter from every quarter, and that gives me a new right to beg you most urgently to agree to the involvement of the Catholic powers in our pacification."

"From your letter," Catherine replied, "I see with regret that you still continue to put your trust in perfidious people who conceal ambitious intentions. I cannot imagine that your majesty himself found the mediation of the Catholic powers in the present affairs of Poland possible and beneficial. As far as I am concerned I am so firm in my principles and so farsighted in regard to consequences that never will I yield to a suggestion where cunning and malice are so clearly evident. I have the habit of speaking openly and telling you the truth. I beg your majesty to rely exclusively on your own reasoning. Which powers are to be summoned to mediation and who will summon them? My views are so different from theirs that there can be no agreement over the means to be employed.

"I want to bring peace to Poland, to maintain the nation with its laws and to keep the king securely on his throne. And I want all of this with no desire for personal gain, and I am not guided by the interests of any religion of any kind. I will not change according to circumstances, I will not grasp at favorable events to support my demands, I have no pretensions and my first words are my sacred obligations. To your concern about peace, which no one can desire more than I do, I bring the same zeal and impartiality, and I would blush with shame if my efforts required foreign aid. But what do

those people want who need this so much and who have convinced
your majesty so forcefully of its necessity? They want to exacerbate
the present troubles by a clash of interests with their fatherland as
the arena and to destroy everything which has been accomplished
thus far in a final time of troubles. A favorable occasion to realize
their plans for arbitrary domination will arise only in the disorders
and desperate situations which are the inevitable consequences."

A rescript was sent to Volkonsky:"[133] "The Polish king's
stubbornness and thoughtlessness poses great obstacles to our
success. Apparently he has forgotten our good deeds and his own
safety. He not only has weakened completely in his devotion to
Russian interests but also has worked openly against them under
the direction of his perfidious uncles. They are using him simply
as a tool in their own lust for power. They have instilled in him the
dream of enjoying once more the love and trust of the people, and
of great freedom henceforth to be useful to his fatherland. On the
other hand it is incontrovertible that this kind of trickery by the old
Czartoryskis has led the king to disagree with us and to reach some
kind of agreement with the mutinous Poles. This can be of no use
either for him or for them, except to plunge both sides into even
greater bewilderment. It is our opinion that a temporary and
unnatural convergence of various opinions provided the means, and
that gradually the crisis developed where the final resolution had
to come.

"Is it possible to imagine that the views of the Polish king, of
his uncles, of the Saxon court and of the Polish rebels, all of whom
are devoted to this court, and of a hostile France, each pursuing
totally different goals, suddenly could rally around the person of
the king, who is hated equally by the latter three? However much
the king, following the crafty counsels of his uncles, might try to
be reconciled with unstable popular elements, such a reconciliation
never can be achieved. That is why, while waiting for a turn of
events these futile efforts soon will bring about, we must be careful
to observe a certain moderation in regard to the king, lest he be
deprived of all hope for the future. Bringing all possible power to
bear on the rebels and striking them wherever possible would deny
them the chance to gain a firm foothold anywhere or to be unified
and noticed. If the Commonwealth presented this image it would

not be possible to declare the throne vacant at the instigation of France and Saxony.

"To overthrow the presently reigning king, whose character has been very trustworthy in regard to our empire, in no way can serve our glory or our interests. To permit this overthrow for the benefit of the elector of Saxony or someone else would give a false impression of us to the world. Either our Northern System is bankrupt, or our influence in Poland cannot stand up to the French, because Russian power is inherently inadequate. Consequently it would be impossible, while war with Turkey continues, to spare enough of a force to protect the first structure which Russia alone has erected from collapse.

"Assuming that we are displeased enough with the Polish king that we decided to deprive him of his crown, who could be chosen to satisfy the nation as a whole, not contravene our interests and help bring peace to Poland? The elector of Saxony is ruled out by our Northern System, and every other Piast would be as inconvenient as the present king, or even more so." Panin added on his own: "In my opinion we will lose nothing by leaving Polish affairs to follow their present disastrous course for the time being. They will play themselves out on their own and reach the critical point at which your majesty can act to the greatest advantage."

VOLKONSKY AND PONIATOWSKI

Meanwhile at the beginning of January Count Gurowski,[134] Master of the Kitchen Poninski,[134] the Mazovian castellan Szydlowski[136] and Goltz,[137] who were friends, came one after another to Prince Volkonsky, all saying the same thing. Stanislaw Augustus had received a letter either from the French king himself or from the Poles Makranowski and Rzewuski who were there [in Paris]. The letter stated that the French king approved of the conduct of the Polish king, and that the senatorial council considered his actions heroic. He was in the hands of Russia but was resisting bravely. The letter also contained promises of help. When he received this letter, the king became very cheerful and said publicly that he considered this the happiest day of his life.

Volkonsky went to the king and asked him directly if it were true that he had received such letters. The king replied coldly that he had not. Volkonsky remarked that if such letters existed there was deception in them, because Prince Karl of Saxony was in the pay of the French court. The king responded coldly, "I know what Prince Karl is looking for there," and changed the subject. He asked what was being done with the stone that was supposed to be the base for the statue of Peter the Great.[138] Volkonsky wrote Panin that the king really was very cheerful, and apparently he was totally beholden to France. Stanislaw Augustus possessed completely that well-known Polish character trait of being unusually impressionable, altering his behavior rapidly, something which raised him up or cast him down depending on circumstances.

He complained to the bishop of Kujawy[139] that Volkonsky did not want to communicate with his ministry. "Volkonsky is acting just the way Repnin did," the king said, "with the difference that Repnin deceived me defiantly while Volkonsky deceives me underhandedly and secretly." The king did not explain the nature of this deceit. Volkonsky said that Russia had raised Poniatowski to the throne. This was the truth and not a deception. Volkonsky said that Russia wanted to keep him on the throne. This was the truth, and the king could believe it and take advantage of it! Stanislaw Augustus forgot that Repnin and Volkonsky were not needed to betray the Poniatowskis. The Mlodziejowskis[140] had deceived the Poniatowskis. Crown Chancellor Mlodziejowski had taken a thousand ducats from Volkonsky and had told him what had happened in secret conferences in which the king took part.

Volkonsky heard in May that the king had sent letters to the senators concerning the diet to be convoked this year. Volkonsky went to the king and expressed his surprise that a diet was being planned which he felt should not open without Russian agreement nor conclude without Russian participation. "I did not think," added Volkonsky, "that your majesty's advisors would force you to conceal this from us." "I did this," replied the king, "not because my advisors coerced me but to ascertain senatorial opinion concerning a diet. Each master is free in his own house, even if soldiers are quartered in it. Doing everything with your agreement means being subject to you." "There is no subjection of any kind here;" said Volkonsky, "her imperial majesty intends to maintain you on the throne and to bring tranquillity to Poland. That is why her forces are here. Consequently measures to attain this goal should be arranged with us. If soldiers are stationed to protect the master, then prudence dictates that he give them advance notice about his orders for the house lest some harm occur because the soldiers are not informed. Such relations between the master and the soldiers in no way should be described as his subjection to them." "I am supposed to communicate with you," said the king, "but you do not communicate with me when orders are given for the movement of your forces!" "This is very natural," replied Volkonsky, "because your majesty has complete trust in his advisors, while some of them are in communication with the rebels." Here Volkonsky was thinking of Lubomirski[141] (who was indeed in correspondence with the rebels). "Why," asked the king, "don't you point out these rebellious accomplices?" "If they are pointed out, they would have to be punished, and the time for that has not yet come."

Prince Volkonsky spent the summer taking the waters at Karlsbad. When he returned in September he had to take measures against the Lithuanian chancellor Prince Czartoryski,[142] the crown marshal Prince Lubomirski; the royal vice chancellor Borch;[143] and the Lithuanian Przediecki.[144] The army was to seize provisions and forage from their villages without compensation. The village stewards were forbidden to make any payments to their lords. Weapons, military supplies and horses were to be collected. Rumors circulated that Pulaski, Zaremba[145] and other leaders of the confederates intended to join forces to make an attempt against Warsaw.

Volkonsky used this opportunity to speak with the king and asked him what precautions he would take in case such an attack was made. The answer, according to Volkonsky, was meaningless and indecisive, after which the conversation turned to the Polish disturbances. "These disturbances cannot be calmed down," said the king, "unless you annul everything that was done at the last diet. Will you dissociate yourself from the dissidents and the guarantee?" "You have to put that out of your head once and for all, and never again be tempted by such a chimerical idea!" replied Volkonsky. "Unless you follow this policy," the king objected, "you never will establish order in Poland." "That is not true," said Volkonsky, "we will establish order if you are not corrupted by your advisors." The king began to sing an old song, "My counsellors are men of virtue, men of reason, patriots," and so on. Volkonsky wrote Panin that the Czartoryskis were suggesting to their friends that never had they found such favor at the Russian court, and that everything that the ambassador had divulged or had done in opposition to them was just a facade.

At the end of September those loyal to Russia met with the primate to consult how Poland could be saved. When he learned about this meeting the king angrily asked the military governor of Kalisz, who had taken part in the meeting, what opinions had been expressed. He had heard that the first condition agreed upon was to remove him from the throne. The military governor answered that this was not true. Rather, seeing the fatherland perishing and the king in danger, their intention was to seek ways to restore order to Poland under Russian protection and to maintain the king on his throne. "I already have taken measures for my own safety," Stanislaw Augustus responded contemptuously, "and you should think about yourselves." The king posed the same question to another magnate, Count Flemming,[146] who had participated in the meeting with the primate. He made a different reply: "Since you neglect the fatherland and are deluded by your counsellors, we thought of looking for ways to save Poland with Russia's help."

RUSSIA, PRUSSIA AND POLAND

Volkonsky and his friends consulted how to establish a general confederation to put an end to the Polish troubles. At the same time that the Russian ambassador was busy with ways to restore order to Poland, the Prussian ambassador, Benoît,[147] was trying to persuade him that it would be more advantageous to leave Poland as it was until the next Turkish campaign or until peace, if peace were concluded beforehand.

Volkonsky was disturbed by letters from Panin. The latter reported that he had discussed Poland with Prince Henry of Prussia. Based on letters from his brother, the prince told Panin that the participation of the Viennese court could be used to advantage. Since Austria was Catholic, the superstitious Poles could not suspect it. Moreover the Prussian king, given his present relations to the Viennese court, and especially to the emperor himself, hoped to induce him to adopt a proper policy and to comply in a way her imperial majesty would welcome. As an ally he had the confidence to ask the sovereign empress whether she would allow the Viennese court to participate directly in the quickest and safest settlement of the Polish question, although this was to be done in concert with her. On his own initiative Prince Henry added a question to this opinion. Suppose the Viennese court took part in negotiations for reconciliation. Suppose that with Prussia's assistance these negotiations were brought to the desired conclusion by both imperial courts. Suppose that together with Russia Vienna agreed to guarantee the agreement for the future so that Poland and the entire Polish public henceforth would be completely tranquil. Would her majesty find that offensive?

A second letter from Panin followed stating that the empress was not in favor of achieving reconciliation through a general confederation. In Catherine's note to Panin on this matter we read the following: "Having read your letter to Prince Volkonsky about Polish reconciliation, the following points occur to me: (1) Undoubtedly it is true that a new confederation either will confuse matters hopelessly or will set them straight. But in either event it will cost us dearly. I would not begrudge the money if I really could be sure that good would come of it. (2) If the present fire can be put out with money, is it not possible that it also can detach the main incendiaries *(boute-feux)* from the present confederation or, (3) Announcing that to preserve the human race, I order a proclamation be made to them that I decree they not be prosecuted if they disperse to their homes and live peacefully. An amnesty will be extended for an entire year, but only on condition that there be no gatherings anywhere, and that in the meantime they be sent to negotiate with the ambassador concerning pacification. It would be easiest to use Mniszech[148] or one of the other powerful figures and employ him as a mediator in negotiations. Surely everyone now is exhausted by epidemics, hunger, destruction and brigandage, and reconciliation is possible. Sometimes the devil is not as terrible as he seems. If a confederation is unavoidable, I expect that we will have to reach an agreement concerning it with the Prussian king."

At the same time news was received in Warsaw from the Hungarian frontier. A cordon of Austrian troops had been stationed there because of a plague epidemic in Poland. The Austrian commanders there recommended that the Polish inhabitants inform the cordoning troops at once if they knew about the approach either of Russian forces or of confederates to within two miles of this cordon. Still more interesting was the news that a commissioner had been appointed by the Austrian government for the occupied Polish territory within the cordon. This commissioner called himself the Commissioner for the Returned Province *(Commissarius Provinciae Reintegratae)*. Under the pretext of a plague epidemic the Prussian king set up a cordon along the Netze river. Stanislaw Augustus was very alarmed by this order, suspecting that the Prussians would remain permanently in the places they had occupied.

Despite all these fears and despite the fact that the confederates announced that they would depose him and proclaim an interregnum, the king did not think to change his behavior towards Russia. Volkonsky felt obliged to speak with the king again. In order to give greater weight to his representations and to heighten the king's fear, he invited Benoît to go with him. The ambassador began the conversation with a question whether the king would participate with the Russian and Prussian courts in the pacification of Poland.

King: I have to know in advance on what conditions this pacification will begin.

Volkonsky: These conditions: (1) Maintenance of the fundamental laws. (2) A guarantee which the Prussian king also will give. Russia will not be opposed if the Viennese court wants to do the same when everything is completed. (3) If the dissidents, after their negotiations with the Commonwealth, freely wish to cede some of their privileges, Russia will not prevent them.

King: That is unsatisfactory. First, I need to go into greater detail.

Volkonsky: It is strange that when it is a question of maintaining and strengthening your majesty on the throne and of tranquillity for the entire realm, you still want to dictate conditions. All that is required is that you dismiss your advisors before we begin.

King: I would be ashamed to stop trusting those people on whom I have ample reason to rely totally.

Volkonsky: If your majesty does not dissociate himself from them, we will act unilaterally, though you could join us later.

King (angrily): No matter how oppressed and unfortunate I am, I would do better to fall than to allow myself to be ordered whom I should trust.

Volkonsky: These people are responsible for all of your misfortunes. They drew you into taking measures incompatible with friendship with her imperial majesty, and that last senatorial council became their instrument.

King: What harm was there in the senatorial council when we wanted to petition the empress to abolish what Repnin had done by force?

Volkonsky: Even if it seemed so to you, there was no force of any kind, since everything was done with proper form and with a sizable majority, and a delegation was sent to the empress with a formal petition.

King: This delegation was sent against my will. Meanwhile the nation hated me, believing that I had agreed to everything, especially the seizure of Soltyk[149] and his comrades.

Volkonsky: You would not be king had we not agreed to it. When Prince Repnin was here there were no complaints against him, and talk began only after he left. Thereafter if they did not like the agreements, they could say about all of them that they had been concluded under duress. Your majesty's advisors say that now because they do not like what was done at the last diet. If they do not change their ways quickly, it will go harder with them than with Soltyk.

King (angrily): My turn will be next!

Volkonsky: Your majesty is becoming embroiled with us to no avail. You have sufficient proof of the friendship of the most gracious sovereign. She raised you to the throne and maintains you on it. Had she taken away her helping hand, there would have been dire consequences long ago. The latest circulars about an interregnum are proof of this.

Benoît: The Czartoryskis would have done well had they resigned their positions and removed themselves, thereby rendering service to your majesty and acting for the benefit of the fatherland.

King: If they wanted to do that, others should not be named to fill their places without a diet. I do not know of what they are guilty.

Volkonsky: All their actions against us are proof of their guilt.

King (angrily, in German): If they wanted to avenge themselves, they already have avenged themselves.

Volkonsky: That is not vengeance, but punishment.

King (in a fit of temper): How can foreign subjects be punished?

Volkonsky (rising from his chair): I never thought that your majesty could utter such words. I will report everything to my court.

King (also rising): I cannot abandon my ministers.

Volkonsky: They are not your ministers but ministers of the Commonwealth.

Having said that he took his leave of the king and Benoît did the same. The next day Count Flemming came to a soirée at Volkonsky's with a declaration from the king that he, the king, would adhere to the Russian confederation when it came into existence, but that he would not dissociate himself from his advisors. Volkonsky directed that the reply be: "I will write about everything to the court."

Since the empress did not agree to revive the confederation, Volkonsky began to attempt to strengthen his party, which he called the *patriotic* party. He announced the main points leading to the pacification of Poland to the members of the party. When Volkonsky showed these points to Benoît, the latter said that he would like to make certain changes in them. The change consisted of striking out the passage which said that Russia and Prussia guaranteed the territory of the Polish Commonwealth. "We," said Benoît, "cannot assume such a guarantee, because then we would have to go to war on Poland's behalf at the slightest pretext."

"This action of Benoît's seemed fairly important to me," Volkonsky wrote to Panin. "I do not know the secrets of the inner workings of government. I will take the liberty of expressing my doubts, doubts which are based only on appearances and have no other foundation than the above mentioned action and the Prussian cordon which runs along the Netze river and which recently has been extended through Zhmud to Courland. Is it not the intention of his Prussian majesty to take advantage of circumstances to gain complete control of this part of Poland which has been occupied?" Before the end of March Benoît reported to his sovereign: "Volkonsky is of the opinion that Russian forces should be withdrawn from Poland and the Poles be left to their own devices.

If they violate the Treaty of Oliva,[150] that is, prohibit the dissidents from exercising their religion freely, Russia and Prussia should take the neighboring provinces away from them and permit the Austrians to do the same." Benoît, informing Frederick II about the Austrian occupation of Polish territory, reported that Volkonsky persistently advised following Vienna's example.[151]

OSTERMANN IN SWEDEN

The brilliant victories over Turkey were celebrated. Turkey's defeat went hand in hand with France's. Meanwhile in a neighboring power it became taken for granted that France and Turkey were its most natural allies. France gained a preponderant influence in Sweden, but recent experience showed what direction preponderant influence took in Russia's neighbors. On January 20 Ostermann informed his court that on the previous day the *careful* diet had ended in a certain *confusion*. Compared with previous diets, if the number of those dissatisfied had not tripled, at least it had doubled. Ostermann boasted that the opposition party's most harmful schemes had not succeeded. That party's first effort was to have their adherents who had been in the French service and those who would enter it be promoted to higher rank than those remaining in Sweden. This would have given the French court a free hand to increase the number of its creatures and a dominant role in the promotion of officers, but this effort was unsuccessful.

An attempt then was made to postpone the forthcoming diet for six years and to order that the diet not be summoned before then, even in the case of an enemy attack. "We," wrote Ostermann, "have bent every effort to prevent this, because otherwise the opposing party would use the hollow pretext of danger from our side to mobilize the entire army. This party was just as sensitive to the failure of a proposal to send forces into Finland to work on the fortresses. This failure meant that their plans to carry out maneuvers on our borders were blocked. This would have caused boasting in Constantinople. The plan was to obtain benefits from France and to force our court to demand explanations, which explanations would have been turned into threats. Count Fersen's[152] malice went so far that he told two of his supporters: 'Your demand not to send forces into Finland comes from Russia.' They answered: 'But your stubbornness in supporting the proposal is French. Thanks to France the state has been involved twice in wars, and it is intolerable that this should happen a third time.' The loyalists were able to keep one of their former deputies on the bench and thus at least were able to learn how matters were proceeding.

"In a word the strength of our opponents declined considerably during that month, and they were forced to yield on many issues, as demonstrated by decreeing a pension for all former senators and forbidding further persecution of the loyalists. Our party would have been destroyed completely had I not succeeded in bringing back the loyalists after the holidays and supporting them. I borrowed money from a banker in daily expectation of the fifty thousand rubles I had been promised. Deliver me from my great distress and send me the promised sum. I would not despair of carrying out your other instructions to restore the loyalist senators to the senate if I did not lack money, and I could participate in the continuation of the diet. The £18,000 requested from the English court have not been sent at all, and nothing has been received from the Danish court. Also if the court obtained payment for its debts, that occurred because it was impossible to prolong the diet. Since they lacked money the king and the queen distributed sizable gifts, not to mention the part played by the crown prince. He invited Mayor Schantz to his private table and summoned the spokesman for the peasant estate, with whom he conversed for more than two hours."

Ostermann was delivered from his great distress. Fifty thousand rubles were sent to him. Thereafter he communicated to his court the program, or testament, of a secret commission, which was supposed to act until the next diet. Maintaining peace was prescribed as the first point, because entering into defensive alliances with other powers was prohibited. Equally prohibited was joining the Northern System, because such a step not only was contrary to Swedish interests but also was strange and absurd. Naturally France and Turkey were designated as the powers most friendly to Sweden, and after them Spain and Austria. A closer union with England should be rejected because that power was the one which most envied Swedish trade and industry. The Russian court was Sweden's most dangerous neighbor, and therefore a closer union with it was unnatural and impossible. Everything that could lead to a breach of good relations should be avoided, however. "No matter what the state officials may say in their testament," the empress wrote on this report of Ostermann's, "every Swede who loves his liberty should recognize that Russia is the most solid basis for this liberty and that Count Ostermann is obligated to support what the freedom-loving Swedes have begun."

In February Cocceji, the Prussian envoy at the Swedish court, announced in the name of his sovereign to Ostermann that the king's brother, Prince Henry, intended to visit his sister the queen of Sweden in the summer, and that Frederick had given him instructions to convert the queen to "a better way of thinking, contrary to the current one." Meanwhile Sinclair and his accomplices asserted that affairs would remain unsettled until the queen was given complete power. It would be easier then for these gentlemen to act because the majority of the town governors belonged to their party. The English envoy told Ostermann that before the diet was concluded he had received information on two occasions from his ministry about a French scheme to execute a sudden and drastic change in the Swedish constitution. The matter would be settled definitively when the Swedish crown prince arrived in France, something that Choiseul was demanding impatiently. The opposition already had put together a plan in strict secrecy for a new government structure and was trying to convert the loyalists to their views. They were agitated, but Ostermann wrote ominously to Panin: "Your excellency knows the timidity of the loyalists, since you have been here." Finally Ostermann asked for money to support them.

PRINCE HENRY IN SWEDEN

Prince Henry arrived in Sweden. It was clear that the journey's real purpose was to convert the Swedish queen to "a better way of thinking, contrary to the present one." The following letter from Prince Henry to his brother the king makes this clear. "It seems that Choiseul's intrigues have managed to succeed only in Sweden. France has maintained its own party in this kingdom constantly since the time of Gustavus Adolphus.[153] Now it has complete control. Fortunately our sister has not yet become accustomed to this. I share your fear, dearest brother, lest they succeed in enticing her to do so. It is hard to block a matter so favored by fortune." This had been written as early as the summer of 1769. When Henry already was in Sweden Frederick wrote to him: "I am delighted that our sister has such good ideas. She can keep to her Frenchmen as much as she wants, except that she should exercise the necessary moderation in her relations with the Russians lest hostility between Russia and Sweden be intensified."[154]

In a letter of September 14 to Panin, Ostermann described his conversation with Prince Henry. The prince began by saying that, following his brother's instructions, he would not cease to persuade his sister the queen of the necessity of maintaining friendship with the Russian empress and of refraining from any actions that might cause cooler relations. The king and the queen answered that never would they abandon their friendship with the empress, that they had no reason for dissatisfaction and that they would strive in every way to maintain this friendship in the future. Their estrangement from those formerly loyal to them resulted from their intention to cut off their opponents' heads in revenge for the events of 1756.[155] The king and the queen could not allow them to do that. Rather they wanted to reconcile both parties, something the loyalist leaders themselves were glad to do. Ostermann answered that he knew the loyalists' desires better than anyone, and that he could assure the prince on his honor that it never had entered their minds to take revenge on the opposing party. Moreover it could not enter their minds because of the empress's specific order to him, Ostermann, to dissuade the loyalists from carrying out any kind of persecution.

The prince replied that the king and queen had confidence in the empress's order and that, contrary to him, Ostermann, they personally were not at all dissatisfied. Some of the loyalists were using personal influence at the Russian court, however, to embroil the empress with the king and the queen. Ostermann answered that all this was made up, and that as far as the protection the king and the queen had extended to those hostile to Russia was concerned, the prince himself easily could understand that this was incompatible with Russian interests as opposed to French interests. "I spoke about this with the king and the queen," answered the prince, "and they assured me that they never had heard that the people in question intended to start a war with Russia. Moreover the king and the queen are only taking a rest, since they have obtained a senate which agrees with them." "Their majesties," said Ostermann, "could obtain the same kind of peace and quiet if they showed the same favor to the former senate." The prince concluded the conversation by saying that his sister the queen had promised to conduct herself with greater composure.

Ostermann wrote to Panin: "I know for certain that he (the prince) really wanted to attempt every means to change his sister's behavior. He might have had some success if secret agreements with the French court, concealed from him, had not been a great hindrance. The Swedish crown prince also swore a solemn oath to the leading French creatures that he would not abandon them as long as he lived. Doubtless this is the reason that these French creatures for a long time, particularly since the arrival of the Prussian prince, have been defaming the queen publicly. On the other hand they have been praising her aforementioned son's special qualities in every way."

St. Petersburg was very disturbed by the results of events in Sweden. This is apparent from the empress's rescript to Ostermann on July 19. "We are more convinced with every passing day that the opposition party of courtiers and creatures of the French in Sweden has not abandoned in any way its intention of shaking and ultimately overthrowing the lawful form of government. Moreover they are trying to hasten this event with all their might and with all means. The time for the definitive realization of their plan and the adoption of extreme measures at the last minute at the first diet has been set to coincide with the presence of the crown prince in France." In the rescript the empress announced that she had ordered thirty thousand rubles sent to Ostermann to counteract the opposition, and also that Denmark and England had agreed to help Russia with these expenditures.

DANISH AFFAIRS

Thanks to Bernstorff relations with Denmark at the beginning of the year could not have been better. Thus when Filosofov[156] stated that Gleichen, the Danish ambassador to France,[157] was harming the interests both of Russia and of Denmark, Gleichen was transferred from France to Naples. Choiseul was incensed and took the liberty of writing to Bernstorff accusing him of acting on the orders of the Russian court and that, in blindly satisfying its interests, he was forgetting the interests of his own sovereign. In May the king agreed to devote a third of his expenditures to Swedish matters. At the same time Filosofov reported that there was great unrest at the Danish court. The king was strongly influenced by his wife (Caroline Matilda, the sister of the English king)[158] and by favorites, while the queen clearly displayed her aversion to Count Bernstorff. She dominated the king with the help of two of their close associates, Struensee, personal physician [to the king],[159] who now was the conference councillor, a man "totally impertinent in his ideas and totally arbitrary in his conduct," and the very youthful chamberlain, Warnstedt.

The ministers of the Bourbon courts and the Swedish minister tried to approach the queen's party and to bring people loyal to French interests into her good graces. The queen, a hot-tempered woman who followed a voluptuous way of life, took advice only from those who indulged her passions. Unfortunately Filosofov's health broke down, forcing him to leave during the summer to take the waters at Pyrmont, depriving Bernstorff of his counsel and assistance. When he returned from Pyrmont in August, Filosofov wrote to Panin that the confused state of affairs soon would end, and that matters would clear up. There was general indignation among the populace and dissatisfaction among those of prudent views. The king's behavior was extremely deranged, and his health, apparently weakened by a terribly disordered life, was very poor. "The present decay of the court which rests on rotten foundations" could not be withstood for long.

On September 5 Filosofov informed the empress that Bernstorff had been removed from his position the previous day, and that a certain Count Rantzau[160] who was hostile to Russia had been named minister. Christian VII felt obligated to inform the empress in a handwritten letter about Bernstorff's retirement. "There are occasions," the king wrote on September 16, "when sovereigns lighten the burden of affairs by sharing their feelings directly with each other. Now is such an occasion. Motives related solely to the domestic administration of the state have compelled me to remove Count Bernstorff from the conduct of affairs. Since he played the major part in negotiations between us, I hasten to assure your majesty that this change will not cause any alteration of course in our affairs, and I hope above all to maintain the good mutual understanding that has been established between us."

The empress answered him on October 18: "I am already more than forty years old and have, I hope, a certain amount of experience. I have great constancy and great respect for the truth. As your ally, as your relative and as your friend, I considered it my duty to tell your majesty everything on my mind. I do not expect great results from my action. I have no doubt that there are those that are disloyal, who will explain it in their own fashion. They will say that I want to control your majesty's will, and that I act as your teacher. They foster mistrust in you and thereby promote their own cause and attain their own goal; namely, to destroy the mutual trust which fortunately has existed between us.

"Your majesty will exercise your authority to your own advantage. I do what duty calls me to do. Here is what I say to you. To dismiss old servants who are zealous, skillful and intelligent is always a great evil for a state because in my opinion every change is in itself an evil if the common good does not require it absolutely. On this occasion our common enemies (do they need to be named?), the French, will be able to profit from the fall of a minister who loved the Northern System. This alliance took shape in his hands, an alliance which in so many matters, not just in Denmark but everywhere, set the proper course for the future. Your majesty unwillingly has opened the way for a countless multitude of intrigues, disturbances and subterfuges. My prophecy will be fulfilled first of all in Sweden. There the French party already is celebrating merely on the basis of rumors of this event. My frankness compels me to tell your majesty that those who have advised you to take such hasty action have paid no attention whatever to your personal glory. The glory of a sovereign requires great constancy in his plans; but how can there be constancy when the people who execute these plans, who are familiar with matters and who have been responsible for initiating them are replaced by others with less experience? Time alone can bring experience, and no qualities and no intelligence can take its place.

"The trust that peoples have for sovereigns is not forced by an exercise of authority, but rather is the reward for ruling wisely. This is the same basis for mutual trust among courts. It also depends in large measure on those to whom the sovereign entrusts his affairs. I confess that I had complete confidence in Count Bernstorff with regard to our system. I am familiar with his great merits and great talent. For twenty years I studied and followed him when I took action. I regard him as another example of Count Panin, whom I long have trusted because of the important services he has rendered and because of my immutable friendship with him."

The king replied, thanking her for her friendship, proof of which he saw in Catherine's letter. He continued to affirm that Bernstorff's retirement was not caused by intrigues, but by the king's own decision. Meanwhile on September 14 Filosofov sent the king a letter in which he said that naming Rantzau minister was completely contrary to the close alliance existing between Russia and Denmark, because Rantzau was known for his hostility to Russia. At the conclusion of the letter Filosofov expressed the hope that Rantzau would be removed from the conduct of affairs and from the court.

The king ordered a reply be sent that he was very pleased to receive the empress's assurances of trust and friendship contained in the first portion of the letter. For his part he would use every opportunity to show how sincerely he was trying to maintain the existing agreement between Denmark and Russia. As far as the further content of the letter was concerned, his majesty did not consider it necessary to reply. He could not imagine that the empress would instruct her ambassador to make such suggestions. Filosofov's general conduct also was too inconsistent with the forms ordinarily observed between friendly and allied courts. The empress then ordered Filosofov to leave Copenhagen for St. Petersburg under the pretext of poor health. Mestmacher, the secretary of the embassy, [161] was named chargé d'affaires. He was a man capable of "keeping an eye on the mischief there," to use Panin's expression.

The king informed the empress in a handwritten letter that he had named Osten[162] minister of foreign affairs precisely because he had been ambassador to St. Petersburg and was known personally to her majesty. Mestmacher told Panin what the dismissed loyalist ministers had communicated to him. Had Osten told the king directly that he would not accept the ministerial position unless the king instructed him to try to extend and to strengthen the friendship with the Russian court in every way possible, then the king gladly would have agreed.

At the end of the year Mestmacher wrote Panin that Osten, "as a shrewd intriguer," was keeping in close contact with the "debauched gang" which had the dominant position at court. He was doing everything possible to win the confidence of intelligent and influential elements. He expressed his regret at the current state of court affairs and swore that he wanted to maintain Denmark's close friendship with Russia. Osten sent a trusted man to Mestmacher to declare his unshakable loyalty to the Russian court. When Mestmacher first visited him Osten greeted him by saying "I accepted the present office solely to devote myself to strengthening the ties between Russia and Denmark, since I personally have been totally loyal to her majesty. It is true that I have been unfortunate in that my enemies have been able to incur for me the disfavor of your great and most wise sovereign and her enlightened minister. But I swear on my honor that this circumstance in no way diminished my veneration for her imperial majesty and my boundless esteem for Count Panin. I feel and always have felt that the close ties between Russia and Denmark have been most advantageous to the entire North. Even if I did not endure such constant persecution from the French court, my conviction of the usefulness of the Russian alliance is sufficient in itself for me to avoid any dealings with proud and perfidious France."

"While leaving everything to the empress's personal decision," Mestmacher replied, "I, for my part, cannot conceal how distressed I am by the recent behavior here, the more so because it seems to be dictated by the French court. Given your loyalty I expect that you will not fail to set matters aright." Osten shrugged his shoulders and said: "The opportune time has not yet come, but I will make every effort and charge you to ask Count Panin most humbly for the time being not to act too harshly in this matter." Conference Councillor Schumacher, with whom Mestmacher had met secretly, made the same request, saying that the present state of affairs at court could not continue because Osten was trying to rid himself of the intolerable burden of young and foolhardy favorites, something impossible to do without overthrowing them. If the Russian court demanded strict and equitable satisfaction now, the king might follow the advice of the dissolute favorites and put himself blindly in French hands.

We have Catherine's comments on these Danish events in her letters to Frau Bielcke.[163] "Count Rantzau," the empress wrote, "has driven away the deserving people and the talented ministers, among whom, it goes without saying, is the talented Count Bernstorff. Others make every effort to find such people, but this boy king shies away from them. But that is so much the worse for him. If, as you write, Count Rantzau brings about a change in the system, that will be a master stroke of stupidity, and we shall see who will regret it more. I have the greatest respect for Count Bernstorff, and I am flattered by his respect for me. I was genuinely distressed by his fall. His service and his talent always deserved the greatest recognition. I think that Mr. Osten is intelligent enough not to allow himself to join in Count Rantzau's nonsense. He has been able to get to know me, and if he really knows me, he should be certain that my confidence cannot be won by intriguing against those who have received their positions from me. Only lunatics, greenhorns and children can pass judgment on their own, and they are terribly mistaken.

"That is in the nature of things, but had not Mr. Osten lost his good sense in Naples I have to suppose he would not decide on such a strange course of action. If he does so decide, I give you my word that he will be making a mistake, and the only thing he will achieve is the reputation of an intriguer who has dissipated his energy in vain. In view of the constant hustle and bustle in Denmark it can be said that that country is swarming with people capable of filling important positions. Changes occur there every minute. People are replaced as easily as the queen changes her skirts, provided she still wears them.[164] If Rantzau is the root of all evil, I would like him to become the grand vizier of Denmark quickly because he would suffer the same fate as ordinarily happens to viziers in time. Viziers are just like him. They invent all the ridiculous titles employed by the sultan. Rantzau tells his sovereign that all Europe is amazed at him. The more the queen helps Struensee, the greater the hope that he will become repulsive to her. All this and the queen's orgies as well will come to a horrible end. These are children who should be beaten. God alone can save this unhappy country."

CATHCART PROMOTES AN ENGLISH ALLIANCE

Sweden decided not to join Russia's Northern System since events at the court of Copenhagen made the Swedes fearful of taking such a step. This created a very unpleasant impression in St. Petersburg. England as before attempted to promote the alliance, and as before the question was not resolved. The English ambassador Lord Cathcart[165] attributed this failure to disagreement between the two most influential personages at the Russian court, Counts Panin and [Grigory] Orlov, and he decided to reconcile them. "When Count Panin and Count Orlov agreed, matters proceeded smoothly," Cathcart wrote to his ministry, "but when Count Orlov could be influenced by other ideas, then Count [Zakhar] Chernyshev and his friends the Golitsyns became agitated, particularly the former. This meant, besides all the other inconveniences caused by the disagreement, that time was wasted until the empress was able to reconcile the two counts."

Cathcart now took it upon himself instead of the empress to achieve this reconciliation. He praised Count Orlov to Saldern, saying that Count Orlov was a fine man, but saying nothing about Count Panin. Was it really difficult to reconcile such talented men? If there was any problem it should be overcome, because not only their personal interests but also the interests of the imperial family and of the state required it. "That is totally correct," replied Saldern, "and I have spoken about it often to Count Panin. It is an extraordinarily difficult and delicate matter. Both of them are very shy. I have brought them together more than once and left them alone, but I am sure that neither will be the first to make an explanation." When Cathcart proposed his mediation Saldern replied that this would be to his great honor and benefit. There was the danger, however, that the same answer would be received from both sides: "We are on the best possible terms."

Nevertheless Cathcart set to work at the first opportunity. Panin praised Orlov and Orlov praised Panin. Orlov was more talkative and expressed regret that he was not more closely acquainted with

Panin, and that they were of different ages, engaged in different duties and enjoyed different amusements. They rarely encountered each other except at meetings on specific issues, where Orlov's animation usually led him to interrupt Panin's methodical presentation as soon as he saw the point of the speech. Panin would frown and fall silent, and so things would come to a standstill and interfere with other business. Thus he, Orlov, would like to meet

Count Zakhar Gregorevich Chernyshev

with Panin frequently without a fixed agenda, and so they would be able to accomplish much more in an open and general discussion. He put all the blame on his own impatience and his unmethodical ways, giving full credit to Panin's knowledge and capability.

Cathcart told Panin about this conversation with Orlov, and Panin was very grateful to him. Although afterwards neither side said anything about the matter, Cathcart nevertheless informed London that there had been a noticeable change. The empress began to treat the grand duke [Paul] with much greater courtesy and paid much greater attention to him in public. Count Orlov began to pay special respect to him and to be more friendly to Panin. Orlov and Panin began to discuss matters between themselves before going to the council. Everyone was satisfied with this except Zakhar Chernyshev.

TURKEY AND THE PROPOSED ENGLISH ALLIANCE

Thus England could think that its minister at the court of St. Petersburg had gained greater stature by the eminent service he had rendered. Thereby he might be more successful in concluding an alliance between Russia and England than his predecessors had been. In August Lord Rochford[166] sent a royal command to Lord Cathcart to take advantage of the first opportunity to propose an alliance to Count Panin, evidently removing the stumbling block which earlier had prevented its conclusion. Apparently England had agreed to include Turkey should there be an alliance (casus foederis). A certain number of warships would be stationed in all European seas, not just in the Baltic. England in fact was removing the possibility of a clash between itself and the Porte, proposing mediation for the conclusion of peace between Russia and Turkey, which the king of England moreover would guarantee. As mediator at the conclusion of peace the king would insist that Turkey cede to Russia Azov, the Tatar districts of the Kuban and all territory Russia had conquered on that coast. Russia also would obtain freedom of navigation on the Black Sea.

This guarantee could not be included as an article in the treaty of alliance between Russia and England lest the suspicions of the Porte be aroused regarding the king's favorable views towards Russia. Therefore Russia should rely upon the honor of the British sovereign until a suitable time. There was another important change from earlier projects for a treaty of alliance. This was that in the event of an attack on England, Russia was obliged, if an alliance existed, to assist, not with land forces, but with fourteen warships. In the event of an alliance such an attack might be by any European power on England, in America or the East Indies.

Even before receiving these documents Cathcart had to inform Rochford that the reconciliation between Orlov and Panin must fail because the empress was living in her country place, whereas Count Panin was in the city. Cunning people (that is, Zakhar Chernyshev) convinced Orlov to assume control of Turkish and Polish affairs. This led to a great clash between him and Panin, so that the latter requested that the empress relieve him of the direction of foreign affairs. Catherine naturally kept him on.

Meanwhile alarming news was received in England that the Porte had requested the joint mediation of Austria and Prussia contingent upon their agreement with England. Rochford wrote Cathcart that if the treaty of alliance between Russia and England were signed, and Russia made the mediation of England in peace negotiations between itself and the Porte a necessary condition (*sine qua non*), the king would undertake such mediation. If the alliance were declined as in the past, the mediation of Austria accepted and the English king invited to mediate in this spirit, that would be like an empty compliment. Cathcart then should convey to the Russian ministry England's apprehension that this kind of mediation could be considered unbefitting the title of the English king. Panin explained to Cathcart the progress of peace negotiations with total frankness and communicated in their entirety the content of the empress's letters to the Prussian king responding to the offer of mediation. He communicated moreover what the council and Count Solms knew "to demonstrate the empress's boundless trust and thoughtfulness."

There was no end of courtesy, but the project for a treaty of alliance proposed by Cathcart met the same fate as those preceding it. Upon conclusion of peace with the Turks there was no foreseeable war in which England's naval help would be needed. Meanwhile clashes between England and Spain in South America easily could lead to war, into which Russia could be drawn if it concluded a treaty of alliance with England. Understandably there were very strong objections to such a treaty in St. Petersburg. It was said that Russia had waged war alone brilliantly without allies and should not make new efforts and assume new expenditures before having a chance to rest. It would be another matter if the proposed treaty contained all the desired advantages, but that was not the case. The English guarantee of a peace treaty with the Porte was conditional upon mediation, but Russia did not want mediation, the more so because the conditions for the Turkish peace proposed by England could not be considered satisfactory.

Obviously it was Count Orlov who spoke loudest of all against the treaty. He was acting at Chernyshev's instigation, as Cathcart attested. He wrote that Count Orlov was an honorable man and an ardent friend of England, but that he considered himself a Russian patriot. On this question he was the spokesman in the council for the opposition to Count Panin. He was encouraged and approved by a silent majority and also by the senior member of the council, Count [Kirill] Razumovsky.[167]

Cathcart further attributed the failure of his project to the suggestions of the empress's guest, Prince Henry. In November Cathcart held a lengthy conversation with the prince, and regretted very much that the empress could not hear it. In Henry's opinion much could be said to justify the Turkish role in Obrezkov's detention, and his release would be a great sacrifice for the Porte. In case peace was not concluded, the obvious and irrefutable interest of England required taking the side of the Porte against Russia to prevent the final ruin of the Ottoman empire. Moreover attention must be paid to Russia's growing naval power, lest it arouse the envy of the maritime powers. Cathcart expressed doubt whether the prince had stated his real convictions, or if he had spoken in order to ascertain the opinions of the English ambassador.

CATHCART'S VIEW OF RUSSIA

A year passed without a definite response from the Russian court to the proposal for an alliance. Thus Cathcart, according to diplomatic custom, depicted the situation in Russia in the gloomiest light. Apparently the empress was not aware of the true situation and the dangerous state of her affairs. Success had made her proud and self-reliant. Her ministers did not help her enough, she took too many matters on herself and for various reasons she frequently intervened in their business. Count Panin was by nature lazy and at present exasperated. He gave the appearance of indifference towards everything, something which coincided with his natural disposition, intensified by force of habit and by a feeling of hatred. Perhaps his despair at the possibility of restoring the past, no matter what he did, also played a part. The result of all this was that matters were in a state of complete stagnation.

Three years earlier Panin had enjoyed the empress's complete confidence. This influence gradually had weakened and, in particular, recently had fallen because what he was doing was inadequate. "I [Cathcart] am afraid that he [Panin] no longer commands respect. Count Grigory Orlov is lazy and sincere, but cunning and enterprising people have access to him. His time is spent in dissipation, and although he lacks driving ambition, his importance grows in proportion as the importance of the ministers declines. Since he intercedes with the empress on behalf of his friends he has acquired the reputation of a powerful patron. Zakhar and Ivan Chernyshev (Ivan returned from England and took the post of vice president of the Admiralty College) are active, cunning, enterprising and capable of complicating a matter, but not of managing it. They are trying to rise as the ministry falls. The other members of the council are unimportant. Because of these relationships nothing is brought to conclusion.

"The empress is dissatisfied, but circumstances offer no way to improve the situation. Both foreign and domestic affairs are neglected, and no precautions are taken for events which in time might occur and be disastrous or favorable depending on the degree they are anticipated. The empress is aging and the grand duke is approaching his majority. No provision has been made for the moment he ceases to be a boy and becomes the heir to the throne, although at one time it was announced she would keep the crown only until his majority. He is almost old enough now to wear the crown, he is intelligent enough to judge and has the character to sense and to understand what is happening now. Nothing has been done with regard to the disorderly Danish court or the pitiful Polish

Commonwealth, little with regard to Sweden, and no definite response has been made to England's clear question, a question proposed at the beginning of September.

"Peace negotiations with the Porte have come to a standstill, and a third campaign is expected. Who will direct it so as to make a fourth campaign unnecessary? No one has any confidence in the commander-in-chief of the First Army [Rumiantsev]. Quartermaster General Bauer opposes him openly, and Bauer enjoys the confidence and favor of the empress. Count Orlov is hated by the generals and defied by the soldiers. Both armies are in a state of exasperation. Officers of all ranks are going into retirement. The men are exhausted by illnesses, fatigue and poor leadership, which is more destructive than enemy arms. The conscription levies are having a pernicious effect on this vast but thinly settled country. The fleet in the archipelago is poorly constructed, poorly led and poorly paid. There is dissension among the officers and sickness among the sailors. The Dardanelles are inaccessible, and the blockade of Constantinople is useless. There are endless expenditures and acts of violence in Poland. Not one real step has been taken towards the establishment of peace.

"There are greater expenditures and losses from the outflow of money into Poland and for the fleet. There is no way to obtain money abroad or at home through new taxes. The treasury is not yet exhausted, but almost. The resources of the bank are overextended, and things are getting still worse, since all taxes soon will be paid in assignats.[168] Coinage is disappearing and has become very scarce. Importing money from abroad is prohibited completely so as to avoid using the mints of the Prussian king and other sovereigns who would take advantage of the debasement of Russian money. In Poland it is accepted at face value, and that is why it is exported there at a half again greater rate.

"Russia suffers from a lack of people who are capable, knowledgeable or honorable. The Russians show their envy and hatred of foreigners and their own incompetence in all their affairs, both civilian and military. Among the Russians there is neither agreement, love nor trust. Lassitude and lack of animation are the order of the day among them, things which in other countries would induce the dissatisfied to proclaim their dissatisfaction, to oppose the measures imposed upon them and to shun those they consider to be enemies of the fatherland."

Catherine wrote to Voltaire what might be considered an answer to Cathcart's dispatch: "It is amusing that the Turks believe that we are not capable of waging a prolonged war. If these people were not ruled by passion, how could they be so forgetful? Peter the Great waged war for thirty years, now with the same Turks, now with the Swedes, now with the Poles, now with the Persians, but the empire was not reduced to extremity. On the contrary, Russia emerged from each war more flourishing than before. The wars inspired industry, and each war gave birth to some new source which revived trade and created new movement. If the so-called Christian sovereigns who took the side of the Muslims envied the successes of this war they should blame themselves. Who ordered them to incite the Muslims to oppose me without foreseeing the consequences? Everything takes its course in Russia. There are districts where they are almost unaware that we have had two years of war. There are no shortages of any kind anywhere. People sing songs of thanksgiving, dance and make merry."

The situation in Austria in Catherine's opinion was much more dangerous. This is apparent from the secret note to the chamberlain Alexis Naryshkin[169] which was sent to Turin: "The Viennese court apparently is displaying more goodwill towards the Turks and is observing the success of our arms. It is afraid that Russia will keep Moldavia and Wallachia for itself and thereby become Austria's immediate neighbor. In time that could cause many problems with its nearby subjects, who are of the same faith as the Wallachians, because the Viennese court has reason to be more afraid of us as neighbors and of our influence in European affairs than of the Turks."

NOTES

CHAPTER I

1. Frederick II the Great (1712-1786) became king of Prussia in 1740. He naturally figures prominently in the matters covered in this volume, particularly his ambitions on Poland. His conquest of Silesia in the War of the Austrian Succession (1740-1748) and his success against the Austrians, the French and the Russians in the Seven Years War (1756-1763) gave Prussia a dominant role in central Europe. In addition to respecting him as a statesman and a military leader, Catherine shared his cultural and intellectual interests and considered him a personal friend.

2. Thomas Dimsdale (1712-1800) was an English physician who achieved an international reputation for research into and promotion of smallpox vaccination in England. He returned to Russia in 1781 to vaccinate Catherine's grandsons, Alexander and Constantine. See "Dimsdale, Thomas (1712-1800)" *Modern Encyclopedia of Russian and Soviet History* (hereafter MERSH), Vol. 9, p. 125.

3. Grigory Grigorevich Orlov (1734-1783) was a longtime favorite of and advisor to Catherine and one of five brothers who played a leading role in her successful bid for power in 1762. He held various military positions, served at court, promoted cultural projects and supervised the Plague Commission of 1771. See John T. Alexander, "Orlov, Grigory Grigorevich (1734-1783)," MERSH, Vol. 26, pp. 107-109.

4. The Legislative Commission of 1767 (Commission on the Law Code) met from 1767 to 1769 to consider legal reforms. Although two hundred and four meetings were held and considerable preparatory work was done, the Commission disbanded without reaching any specific conclusions. See Soloviev, *History of Russia*, Vol. 45, Chapter II, and Paul Dukes, *Catherine the Great and the Russian Nobility* (Cambridge, 1967).

5. Kirill Grigorevich Razumovsky (1728-1803) was the son of a Ukrainian cossack who with his brother Alexis first rose to power under Elizabeth. He served as last hetman of the Ukraine and was rewarded by Catherine for his support in her accession to power in 1762 with various state posts, including membership on the State Council from 1768 to 1771. See R.V. Ovchinnikov, "Razumovskii, Kirill Grigor'evich," MERSH, Vol. 30, p. 214.

6. Gavriil (P.P. Petrov) (1730-1801) was born into a clerical family and graduated from the Slavonic-Greek-Latin Academy in Moscow in 1757. He was a teacher at the seminary in the Holy Trinity-St. Sergius monastery, then served as rector there and subsequently at the Moscow Theological Academy. In 1768 he became bishop of Tver and was named to the Legislative Commission representing the clergy for all of Russia. Gavriil became a member of the Holy Synod in 1769 and archbishop of St. Petersburg in 1770. He was raised to the rank of metropolitan in 1783 and was elected to Academy of Sciences. He retired to Novgorod, whose diocese also had been under his jurisdiction, where he died in 1801.

7. Catherine wrote to I.G. Chernyshev about the boy Ospenny: "This same boy from whom I received the smallpox toxin is the source of amusement now. Everyone recognized that he really is not a scamp, like Alexander the son of Ospin Danilov. He is very playful, intelligent and resourceful beyond his years, and bold to the point of audacity. He is never too familiar either in his answers or in his speech. He is just a six-year-old kid. Your brother, Count Zakhar G. Chernyshev, Count Grigory Grigorevich (Orlov) and Kirill G. Razumovsky himself, like all of us, got down and played with him for three hours and laughed until we were tired. If you want to know to whom he belongs, your brother says that for the time being he is taking Betskoy's place, and don't ask me anything more." (Soloviev's note) Ivan Grigorevich Chernyshev (1726-1797) was a courtier and statesman who held important positions under Elizabeth and Catherine, including diplomatic and naval posts. He promoted economic development and cultural affairs. See Robert E. Jones, "Chernyshev, Ivan Grigor'evich," MERSH, Vol. 7, pp. 18-20. Zakhar Grigorevich Chernyshev (1722-1784) was a member of a prominent family who held important civil, diplomatic and military posts under Elizabeth and Catherine. He had a leading part in the Turkish war of 1768-1774. See Victor Kamendrowsky and David M. Griffiths, "Chernyshev, Zakharii Grigor'evich," MERSH, Vol. 7, pp. 21-22. Ivan Ivanovich Betskoy (1704?-1795) was a courtier and educator who served under Elizabeth and Catherine. He patronized the arts in Catherine's time and was prominent in the various educational initiatives of her reign, particularly the foundling homes. See Mary West Case, "Betskoi, Ivan Ivanovich," MERSH, Vol. 4, pp. 102-106.

8. Peter Semenovich Saltykov (1698?-1772) was born into a family which had achieved prominence under Peter I. He held various military posts in the mid-eighteenth century. He then served as governor general of Moscow after 1763, but lost Catherine's confidence when he failed to control the plague that broke out there in 1770 and 1771. See John T. Alexander, "Saltykov, Petr Semenovich," MERSH, Vol. 33, pp. 49-53 and his *Bubonic Plague in Early Modern Russia* (Baltimore, 1980).

9. Alexis Mikhailovich Obreskov (or Obrezkov) (1718-1787) was a diplomat who spent most of his career on Turkish affairs. His arrest in 1768 was an important issue leading to the outbreak of war. He later played a key role in preparing for the Treaty of Kuchuk-Kainardji. See "Obreskov, Aleksei Mikhailovich," MERSH, Vol. 25, pp. 169-170.

10. Alexander Mikhailovich Golitsyn (1718-1783) was a military officer who held important commands in the Seven Years War and the war with Turkey which began in 1768. He eventually attained the rank of general field marshal. He served in 1783 as governor general of St. Petersburg. See "Golitsyn, Aleksandr Mikhailovich," MERSH, Vol. 12, p. 237.

11. Peter Alexandrovich Rumiantsev (1725-1796) was a military commander who administered Catherine's reforms in the Ukraine in the 1760s, served in the war against Turkey and helped prepare the annexation of the Crimea in 1783. See John T. Alexander, "Rumiantsev, Petr Aleksandrovich," MERSH, Vol. 32, pp. 15-19.

12. Elizabeth (1709-1762) had come to the throne in a coup in 1741 which ousted Ernst Biron, Empress Anna's favorite, who hoped to exercise power as regent for the infant Ivan VI. Initially she restored power to the Senate, which Peter I established in 1711 as the supreme organ of state but which later lost power to the colleges Peter created for various areas of government and then, after 1730, to new bodies formed by Anna. Later in Elizabeth's reign the Senate was overshadowed by the conference she established in 1756. See George E. Munro, "Elizabeth Petrovna (Elizaveth Petrovna) 1709-1762," MERSH, Vol. 10, pp. 178-185; N. P. Eroshkin, "Senate in Russia," MERSH, Vol. 34, pp. 6-8; and George L. Yaney, *The Systemization of Russian Government. Social Evolution in the Domestic Administration of Imperial Russia, 1711-1905* (Urbana, 1973).

13. Nikita Ivanovich Panin (1718-1783) played a leading role both under Elizabeth and Catherine. He proposed plans for an imperial council to coordinate government policy and was the architect of the "Northern System." This envisioned cooperation among Russia, Prussia, England and Denmark as "active" powers, and the participation of Sweden, Poland and Saxony as "passive" powers. It was directed primarily against Austria and France. As Soloviev notes in these chapters the grand design was unpopular at home and ran into serious difficulties abroad. See David L. Ransel, "Panin, Nikita Ivanovich," MERSH, Vol. 26, pp. 215-216 and his *The Politics of Catherinian Russia. The Panin party* (New Haven, 1975).

14. Alexander Alexeevich Viazemsky (1727-1793) enjoyed Catherine's confidence and held a number of important positions during her reign. As procurator general he controlled the Senate and the internal affairs of the empire more effectively than his predecessors. He had a major role in the Legislative Commission, gradually brought greater order in imperial finances and was able to exercise greater control over provincial authorities.

His success was due in large part to his hard work, attention to detail and avoidance of factions. See Robert E. Jones, "Viazemskii, Aleksandr Alekseevich," MERSH, Vol. 42, pp. 76-79.

15. Alexander Mikhailovich Golitsyn (1723-1807) was a diplomat who served in Germany (1749-1754) and as minister plenipotentiary in Great Britain (1755-1762), before becoming vice chancellor (1762-1775) of the College of Foreign Affairs. Although nominally he was second only to Nikita Panin in foreign affairs, in practice others close to Catherine often played a greater role.

16. Peter Ivanovich Panin (1721-1789) was the younger brother of Nikita Panin who after a successful military career held a number of important government positions under Catherine. His distinguished military and administrative record, plus his brother's influence, won him a place on the newly established government council in 1768. From here he assumed command of the Second Army where he succeeded in conquering the fortress of Bender and containing the Crimean Tatars. Disillusioned at what he regarded as inadequate recognition of his accomplishments, he retired for a time from public life and leveled criticism at Catherine and her favorites. Catherine recalled him in 1774 to put down the Pugachev rising, after which he retired permanently from public life. He kept in contact with his brother and his brother's circle and had some influence on Paul I's plans for government reform. See David L. Ransel, "Panin, Petr Ivanovich (1721-1789)," MERSH, Vol. 26, pp. 218-221, and the same author's *Politics of Catherinian Russia.*

17. Mikhail Nikitich Volkonsky (1713-1788) was a soldier, diplomat and statesman who earned Catherine's favor for his support in 1762. He took a key part over the years in promoting Russian interests in Poland and was a member of the Legislative Commission. He later served as governor general of Moscow, where he helped in defense efforts against Pugachev. See John T. Alexander, "Volkonskii, Mikhail Nikitich (1713-1788)," MERSH, Vol. 43, pp. 1-4.

18. Charles Schaw, ninth Baron Cathcart (1721-1776), served as England's ambassador to Russia after a distinguished military career which included a serious wound at Fontenoy. His dispatches are a valuable source, not just for diplomatic, but also for court and domestic Russian affairs.

19. The conscription of churchmen had been government policy since the beginning of the century. Succeeding rulers echoed Peter the Greats' belief that there was a surplus of members in the clerical estate and routinely sought ways to use clerical manpower and church possessions for secular state purposes. See Gregory L. Freeze, *The Russian Levites. Parish Clergy in the Eighteenth Century* (Cambridge, 1977).

20. Despite this solemn promise, the value of the assignats soon declined sharply in comparison with the metal money of Russia and other countries.

21. The Russian term is *katorzhnik.*

22. Catherine's admiration for Montesquieu, whom she had read extensively since her days as grand duchess, is well known. His influence can be seen, not just in such minor issues as this, but in the plans she drafted for Russia on assuming the throne and especially in her 1766 Instruction to the Legislative Commission as well.

23. Khan Kirim Girey ruled as khan of the Crimea from 1758 to 1769. He eagerly answered the Ottoman call to arms in 1768, but died shortly after the campaign described above. He was the last truly independent ruler of the Crimea. See Alan W. Fisher's, *The Russian Annexation of the Crimea 1772-1783* (Cambridge, 1970) and *The Crimean Tatars* (Stanford, 1978).

24. Concerning the particulars of the military actions throughout the war see *Geschichte des gegenwertigen Krieges zwischen Russland, Polen und Ottomanischen Pforte, 1771-1774* (History of the Present War between Russia, Poland and the Ottoman Porte), Vols. 1-36 (Frankfurt and Leipzig, 1771-1775); *Histoire de la Guerre entre la Russie et la Turquie, 1773* (History of the War between Russia and Turkey) (St. Petersburg, 1773); A.N. Petrov, *Voina Rossii s Turtsieii i polskimi konfederatami* (Russia's War with Turkey and the Polish Confederates), Vols. 1-5 (St. Petersburg, 1866-1874). (Soviet editor's note.) Also see R.C. Anderson, *Naval Wars in the Levant,* 1559-1853 (Princeton, 1952) and Donald W. Mitchell, *A History of Russian and Soviet Sea Power.* (New York, 1974), pp. 54-69.

25. Almost certainly a relative of the famous field marshal.

26. Alexander Aleksandrovich Prozorovsky (1732-1809) was a general who served with distinction under Elizabeth and Catherine. After participating in the 1768 war with Turkey, he promoted Russian interests in the Crimea. He later served as governor general of Moscow, where he suppressed actual or suspected dissidents, including Nikolai Novikov. See Daniel L. Schlafly, Jr., "Prozorovskii, Aleksandr Aleksandrovich (1732-1809)," MERSH, Vol. 30, pp. 43-46.

27. Dissatisfaction with Golitsyn's failure found expression in a political satire which circulated in society: "Prince Galitzin having been obliged to retreat from Chotzim, found himself much embarrassed. One night he was so anxious he could not sleep. He rose, dressed himself, and heard two persons speaking at the door of his tent. An old soldier was telling his dream to the sentinel. I dreamed, said he, that I was in a battle; that my head was cut off; consequently that I died; and consequently went to heaven. I knocked at the door. Peter came with a bunch of keys, and made so much noise, that he wakened God, who came in great haste and enquired what was the matter? Why, says Peter, there is a great war upon earth, between the Russians and the Turks. And who, said the Supreme Being, commands the Russians? Count Munich, replied the Saint. Then, said God, I may go and sleep. I awakened, said the old Soldier; but fell asleep and dreamed again. The circumstances of the second dream were precisely the

same with those of the first, excepting that the war in which I fancied myself engaged, was not that of Count Munich, but that which we are now waging. Accordingly, when God asked Peter, who commanded the Russians? the Saint told him, It was Prince Galitzin. Then, said God, get me my boots, for now they need me. — In a short time after, the Turkish bridge over the Neister was swept away by a flood." William Richardson, *Anecdotes of the Russian Empire* (London, 1784), pp. 110-111. (Soloviev's note)

28. Ivan Karlovich Elmpt (1725-1802) was a lieutenant general in 1768 who later attained the rank of general field marshal. In 1790 with Catherine's approval he was named a count of the Holy Roman Empire.

29. Alexander Ilyich Bibikov (1729-1774) was a general and public figure whom Catherine entrusted with several positions, including the post of marshal of the Legislative Commission. He later helped advance Russian interests in Poland and saved Kazan from the Pugachev rebels. See Victor Kamendrowsky, "Bibikov, Aleksandr Il'ich (1729-1774)," MERSH, Vol. 4, pp. 126-128.

30. Yury Vladimirovich Dolgorukov (Dolgoruky) (1740-1830) was a career soldier who served in the Seven Years War and later commanded Russian troops in Poland at the time of Poniatowski's accession to the throne. By 1767 he was a major general. He was unsuccessful in inciting the Montenegrins to revolt in his two years there. Later he served under Rumiantsev, fought in the battle of Kagul and led the defense of Ochakov in the second Turkish war. See "Dolgorukov, Yuri Vladimirovich (1740-1830)," MERSH, Vol. 9, p. 209.

31. Alexis Grigorievich Orlov (1737-1808) was the third of the five Orlov brothers who achieved prominence under Catherine. He directed naval operations in the 1768 war with Turkey and led the Russian fleet at the victory at Chesme in 1770. See George E. Munro, "Orlov, Aleksei Grigor'evich (1737-1808)," MERSH, Vol. 26, pp. 103-106.

32. Alexis Naumovich Siniavin (or Seniavin) (1716-1797) was an admiral who built and commanded the fleet which operated on the Don and in the Sea of Azov in the 1768 war with Turkey. He later helped form the Black Sea Fleet. See J. Dane Hartgrove, "Seniavin, Aleksei Naumovich (1716-1797)," MERSH, Vol. 34, pp. 9-10.

33. In 1762 Heraclius (1716-1798) had united Kartlian and Kakhetian Georgia in a state which embraced a sizable part of the eastern Caucasus including Armenians and Kurds and other Muslim peoples. To the west Solomon I (1730-1784) exercised a more tenuous authority in the territory of the Imereti. As Soloviev describes in these pages, Solomon had asked for Russian help against the Turks in 1766. The outbreak of war with Turkey in 1768 spurred Russian interest in an area where hitherto St. Petersburg had been reluctant to provoke the Turks. Soloviev in these pages describes General Todtleben's expedition, his efforts to coordinate join action with

Heraclius and Solomon against the Turks and the inconclusive results of the campaign. Todtleben was replaced by General A. N. Sukhotin in 1771, but the latter was no more successful than his predecessor and Russian forces were withdrawn in 1772.

Under the Treaty of Kuchuk-Kainardji (1774) Russia renounced all conquests in Georgia and Mingrelia, but in the Treaty of Georgievsk (1783) Heraclius acknowledged Russian sovereignty and gave it the right to control the foreign affairs of his kingdom. In 1801 Heraclius's grandson David proclaimed the union of Georgia and Russia. See W.E.D. Allen, *A History of the Georgian People from the Beginning down to the Russian Conquest in the Nineteenth Century* (New York, 1972), pp. 196-215; and David Marshall Lang, *The Last Years of the Georgian Monarchy*, 1658-1832 (New York, 1957) pp. 154-252.

34. Nazary Alexandrovich Karazin came from a family of Greek or Serbian origin. His son, Vasily Nazarevich, later worked on eductional reforms under Alexander I.

35. Prince Rodion Cantacuzene (or Cantacuzin) (1725-1774) came from a leading Wallachian family. He and some volunteers had clashed with the Turks even before formally joining the Russians in 1770. He continued to play an active role in the struggle thereafter.

36. Hospodar was the title of the governor of Moldavia or Wallachia. The hospodar was chosen by the Porte from the Greek elite of the empire (Phanariots) in return for a large cash payment. The hospodars lived well from the revenues of the principalities and presided over lavish courts. For the history of the principalities in their period see R.W. Seton-Watson, *A History of the Roumanians from Roman Times to the Completion of Unity* (Cambridge, 1934) and Barbara Jelavich, *History of the Balkans* (Cambridge, 1983), Vol. 1, pp. 99-112.

37. Gottlieb Heinrich Todtleben (1710-1773) was born in Saxony. He entered Russian service under Empress Elizabeth and fought in the Seven Years War. He was courtmartialed for retreating as Frederick II approached his forces at Berlin, stripped of his rank and exiled. His distinguished service in this war, however, earned him a pardon.

38. Denis Ivanovich Chicherin was governor of Siberia with residence in Tobolsk from 1764 to 1781.

39. The reference is to Peter the Great and his half-brother Ivan, who ruled jointly from 1682 until 1696, when Peter assumed full power on his own. See Volume 25 of this series.

40. The Zaporozhian Cossacks were one of the oldest and most important of the cossack groups. They lived along the lower course of the Dnieper river where they played an important part in the complicated political struggles of the region among the Russians, the Turks and the Poles. Catherine abolished the Zaporozhian Host in 1775. See Edward D. Sokol,

"Zaporozh'e Cossacks," MERSH, Vol. 45, pp. 164-170. Also see Philip Longworth, *The Cossacks* (New York, 1969).

41. The Russian term is *koshevoi ataman*.

42. Fedor Matveich Voeikov was governor general of Kiev from 1767 to 1775.

43. Grigory Andreevich Spiridov (1713-1790) was a career naval officer who at the outbreak of the war with Turkey was the commander of the Kronstadt naval base. As the highest ranking Russian naval officer with recent experience on active duty, he was the obvious choice to command the expedition, although in the campaign he had difficulty controlling subordinates such as Orlov, Grieg and Elphinstone who eclipsed him in public recognition. See Norman Saul, "Spiridov, Grigorii Andreevich (1713-1790)" MERSH, Vol. 37, pp. 52-54.

44. A common Russian dish made of cooked grain, often buckwheat.

45. An Italian phrase, meaning in secret.

46. Semen Ivanovich Mordvinov (1701-1777) was a career naval officer who saw combat in the Seven Years War and who in 1763 was appointed chairman of a commission established at the admiralty college to improve the Russian fleet. See "Mordvinov, Semen Ivanovich (1701-1777)," MERSH, Vol. 23, p. 62.

47. John Elphinstone (1720-1775) was an Englishman who entered the Russian service in 1769 with the rank of rear admiral. He commanded the ship *Ne tron' menia* ("Don't tangle with me!") in the Mediteranean expedition described here, but was recalled to St. Petersburg and put on trial in 1771.

48. General Mikhail Mikhailovich Filosofov (1731-1811) was Russia's ambassador to Denmark from 1766 to 1770. He later served under Paul I as governor general of Smolensk.

49. Stepan Fedorovich Apraksin (1702-1758) was a career military officer who was promoted to the rank of general field marshal and given command of the Russian army at the outbreak of the Seven Years War in 1756. For logistical and political reasons he procrastinated in marching his army against Prussia. Later he did not follow up the victory at Gross-Jägersdorf but instead withdrew to winter quarters. For this he was relieved of command and charged with treason but died before the case was resolved. See Victor Kamendrowsky, "Apraksin, Stepan Fedorovich (1702-1758)," MERSH, Vol. 2, pp. 68-69.

50. See Soloviev, *History of Russia*, Vol. 45, pp. 156-57.

51. Fedor Grigorevich Orlov (1741-1796) was the fourth of the five Orlov brothers who played such a major role under Catherine, first in her coup of 1762, then in various positions during her reign. Fedor served in the Seven Years War, and after Catherine's accession was named high

procurator of the Senate. He served in Spiridov's squadron and won several naval victories over the Turks. Catherine erected a column ornamented with ships' prows in his honor at Tsarskoe Selo. He retired in 1775.

52. New Serbia was a colony established by Catherine in the territory she acquired on the north shore of the Black sea.

53. Stepan Maly was a Montenegrin impostor who, as Soloviev describes in the following pages, claimed to be Emperor Peter III, and who succeeded for a time in winning great support in Montenegro, thus seriously harming Russian plans there. See M.B. Petrovich, "Catherine II and a Fake Peter III in Montenegro," *Slavic Review*, Vol. 14, No. 2 (1955), pp. 169-194.

54. The bishop of the monastery of Cetinje served as *de facto* head of state in eighteenth-century Montenegro, since the Orthodox church was the major force holding together the often fractious tribes of the region. See Jelavich, *"A History of the Balkans*, Vol. 1, pp. 84-86.

55. Ragusa is present-day Dubrovnik.

56. Peter III (1728-1762) briefly was emperor of Russia (December 1761-June 1762) until he was murdered during Catherine's seizure of power. He was born in Holstein to Peter the Great's daughter Anna and her husband, the duke of Holstein-Gottorp. In 1742 he was brought to Russia by Empress Elizabeth as her designated successor and married to Catherine in 1745. The marriage was a most unhappy one, and Peter almost certainly was not the father of the future Paul I. He already had alienated Russian opinion by his preference for German ways and contempt for the Orthodox church before Elizabeth's death in 1761 put him on the throne. While he was responsible for ending compulsory noble service and for some measures on behalf of the peasants, his immature and obnoxious personality, coupled with his anti-Russian behavior, eroded what support he had. The final straw was his abrupt withdrawal from the coalition which nearly had defeated Frederick II in the Seven Years War. Catherine then saw her chance and took it. It has never been proven whether she ordered his murder after seizing power, but she went to great lengths to tarnish his memory therafter. Yemilian Pugachev was the most famous of the many pretenders who claimed to be the dead Peter III. See Lindsey A.J. Hughes, "Peter III (1728-1762)," MERSH, Vol. 27, pp. 238-244 and R. Nisbet Bain, *Peter III, Emperor of Russia* (London, 1902).

57. Ivan Antonovich, or Ivan VI (1740-1764), was the nominal emperor of Russia from October 17, 1740 to November 25, 1741. He was named emperor as a newborn infant by Anna shortly before her death but was imprisoned after Elizabeth's coup in 1741. His life was spent in confinement, and he was executed by his guards after an abortive attempt to free him in 1764. See Karl W. Schweizer, "Ivan VI (Ivan Antonovich) (1740-1764)," MERSH, Vol. 15, pp. 61-63.

58. The Russian term is *yurodivyi*.

59. Joseph II (1741-1790) had been Holy Roman emperor since his father Francis of Lorraine had died in 1765 but as is evident from this section his mother Maria Theresa still held political power and was willing to exercise it. He chafed at the constraints imposed by her Catholic piety, innate caution and antipathy to Frederick II and to Prussia. Such victories as he won while she was alive, for example obtaining permission to meet with the Prussian king, were won only with effort.

60. Present day Klodzko in Polish Silesia.

61. Paolo N. Maruzzi (1720-1799) came from an old Greek family which had settled in Venice in the fifteenth century. He received the title of marquis from Maria Theresa. He served as Russian representative for the Italian states from 1768 to 1783 with residence in Venice.

62. Prince Wenzel Anton von Kaunitz-Reitberg (1711-1794) was a Moravian nobleman who for over forty years (1753-1794) was minister of foreign affairs under Maria Theresa and Joseph II and one of the most astute diplomats of his age. He became alarmed at Russian successes in the war against Turkey that began in 1768 and increasingly looked for ways to check its influence. See Karl A. Roider, Jr., *Austria's Eastern Question, 1700-1790* (Princeton, 1982).

63. Leopold, duke of Tuscany (1747-1792), was the third son of Maria Theresa and Francis I. He succeeded his father as duke of Tuscany in 1765, where in his twenty-five-year reign he sought to modernize the state administration in the spirit of the Enlightenment. Upon the death of Joseph II, he was elected Holy Roman emperor (1790-1792).

64. Pasquale Paoli (1725-1807) was a Corsican patriot who, after returning to the island from exile in 1755, ended Genoese rule and carried out enlightened reforms. After France bought Corsica from its old enemy, Genoa, he fled to England. He played a leading role in Corsica again in 1790-1795, first siding with revolutionary France, then with England. After the English passed him over in favor of Pozzo di Borgo he retired permanently to England in 1795.

65. Étienne-François, duc de Choiseul (1719-1785), was the foreign minister who played a dominant role under Louis XV. He built up French military power after the reverses of the Seven Years War and actively promoted a strong French role in the Mediterranean. He also served as minister for the marine from 1761 to 1776 and minister of war from 1766 to 1770.

66. There is a handwritten letter in French in Catherine's papers addressed "To the brave Corsicans, defenders of the fatherland and of liberty, and especially to Pasquale Paoli." The letter is signed "Your true friends, the inhabitants of the North Pole." It is obvious that money was sent with the letter. (Soloviev's note)

67. Johanna Dorothea Bielcke was an old Hamburg friend of Catherine's mother with whom Catherine carried on an extensive correspondence.

68. The razing of the Azov and Taganrog fortresses was stipulated in the Treaty of Belgrade which ended Russia's unsuccessful war with Turkey from 1735 to 1739. Despite Austrian support and some initial successes in the Dniester area, the Crimea and around the Sea of Azov, Russian forces were blocked by Turkish resistance and weakened by disease. Although the Russians captured the fortress of Khotin in August, 1739, whose recapture by another Russian force thirty years later Soloviev describes in this volume, they decided to accept the unfavorable provisions of the Treaty of Belgrade in September 1739 when their Austrian allies concluded a separate peace with Turkey. France encouraged Turkey to oppose Russia in this war just as it had in the conflict which began in 1768. See G.P. Mescheriakov, "Russian-Turkish War of 1735-1739," MERSH, Vol. 32, pp. 185-186.

69. The newspapers sometimes made Catherine lose her patience completely, as the following note to [Nikita] Panin shows: "You would do well to order Gross or Simolin to promise the editor of the *Cologne Gazette* a hundred blows with a stick if he continues to use the tone he has assumed, because he persists in writing nothing but impertinences about us, and does this more and more." (Soloviev's note) Friedrich Ulrich Gross (1729-1796) recently had been Russian *chargé d'affaires* in Great Britain and at the time was the Russian resident in lower Saxony and the Hanseatic cities. Johann Matthias von Simolin (1720-1799) was a career diplomat who had served in Copenhagen and Vienna and now was the Russian resident at the German diet in Regensburg. Later he was successively Russian ambassador to Denmark, Sweden, Great Britain and France.

70. The Treaty of Carlowitz (1699) ended hostilities between the Ottoman empire and the Holy League (the Habsburg monarchy, Poland, Venice and Russia) after the victories of Prince Eugene of Savoy. The Habsburgs gained all of Hungary except the Banat of Temsevar, with the addition of Transylvania, Croatia and Slavonia. Venice acquired the Peloponnese and most of Dalmatia. Poland returned its conquests in Moldavia, but regained Podolia and part of Ukraine west of the Dnieper. See G.A. Kleinman, "Karlowitz Congress of 1698-1699," MERSH, Vol. 16, pp. 32-33.

71. The Commonwealth, in Polish *Rzeczpospolita*, was the official designation for the state created by the merger of the kingdom of Poland and the grand duchy of Lithuania by the Union of Lublin in 1569.

72. Joachim Potocki (?-1791) was a leader of the Polish Confederation in 1769. The Potockis for centuries had been one of the leading noble families in Poland. More recently they had enjoyed French backing and

had attempted to put a French-backed candidate on the throne in 1764, only to be outmaneuvered by the Russians and Stanislaw Augustus. No wonder then that the Potockis participated in the anti-Russian Confederation of Bar in 1768. The election of Stanislaw Augustus Poniatowski to succeed Augustus III as king of Poland came after a disorderly interregnum lasting from October 1763 to September 1764. This represented a victory for Catherine, who now had her former lover on the throne after heavy-handed tactics by her ambassador Repnin and a show of force by Russian troops. She already had concluded an alliance with Frederick II of Prussia giving both powers the right to intervene in Polish affairs, using the rights of the Protestant and Orthodox dissidents as a pretext. She also had made common cause with the Czartoryskis, known simply as "the Family," two of whom, August and Michal, were uncles of the new king. Stanislaw Augustus soon showed his eagerness to reform Polish political life and promote national development, something that Russia and Prussia found most unwelcome. Many in Poland also opposed greater rights for the dissidents, which also offended Prussia and Russia. In response Russia formed confederations of Protestants in Thorn and Orthodox in Sluck to block the efforts of the diet to maintain Catholic primacy, and then a general confederation in Radom. The latter, which called upon Catherine to uphold traditional noble rights, attracted the support of some who opposed Poniatowski's reforms. The Russians exerted still more pressure at the diet of 1767-1768, arresting two bishops and two other opponents of dissident rights and forcing Polish acceptance of a treaty guaranteeing these rights. This intensified opposition to Russian pressure and led to the formation of the Confederation of Bar in March 1768 to unite the nation in defense of Poland and of Catholicism. The right to form such an armed league to obtain justice was an ancient and respected Polish tradition, frequently used by individuals and groups of various classes. A formal oath was taken to fight to the death until the grievance which had occasioned the confederation was satisfied. Regular meetings of the confederates were held to pursue the goals of the group. Other confederations were formed to support the Confederation of Bar, and France gave major assistance. Russia's opponents could not achieve unity of command and strategy. The king and the Czartoryskis followed what best could be described as a policy of neutrality towards the confederates, avoiding an open break with Russia, but incurring the wrath of both Russia and the confederates. Meanwhile Russian forces and the royal army under Branicki gained military supremacy over the confederates, although the nation continued to be torn by conflict, as Soloviev describes in this volume. See Herbert H. Kaplan, *The First Partition of Poland* (New York, 1962).

73. Seraskir was a Turkish rank meaning commander-in-chief or minister of war.

74. The agreement between the confederates and the Porte was sent to France by Gérard from Danzig. (Soloviev's note)

75. Stanislaw Augustus Poniatowski (1732-1798) was the last king of Poland, reigning from 1764 to 1795. The scion of a prominent noble family, he received an excellent education, then went to St. Petersburg in 1757 as secretary to the British ambassador. Here he became a lover of the then Grand Duchess Catherine. With her support and that of the Czartoryski family, he succeeded Augustus III as king in 1764. He soon disappointed his Russian patrons by supporting reforms in what would be a vain attempt to maintain Polish independence. He was forced to acquiesce in the three partitions which dismembered his country and culminated in his abdication in 1795. While his talent and intelligence are unquestioned, he has been criticized, as Soloviev does here, for his procrastination and for his failure to resist outside, particularly Russian, pressure forcibly enough. On Stanislaw Augustus in particular and on Polish affairs in general for this period, see Norman Davies, *God's Playground. A History of Poland* (2 vols., Oxford, 1981). Vol. I. *The Origins to 1795*.

76. A. Beer, *Die erste Theilung Polens* (The First Partition of Poland), Vol. I, p. 243. (Soviet editor's note)

77. Count Victor Friedrich Solms (1730-1783) entered Prussian service after university studies. He represented Prussia in Stockholm before replacing Baron von Goltz as Prussian ambassador in St. Petersburg in 1762 upon Catherine's accession to the throne, a post he held for the next seventeen years. He won the trust of Catherine and Nikita Panin and contributed to the general cooperation between Russia and Prussia which characterized this period, for example, in the first partition of Poland.

78. Nicholas Vasilevich Repnin (1734-1801) was the son of an old princely family who had distinguished himself in the Seven Years War, earning the rank of major general in 1762. Despite lack of success as minister plenipoteniary in Prussia (1762-1763), he was appointed ambassador to Poland in 1764, thanks to the influence of his wife's uncle, Nikita Panin. During his tenure in Poland (1764-1769) Repnin forcefully promoted Russian interests, even to the point of using bribery and armed force. As Soloviev describes here, he was recalled in 1769 because of widespread Polish resistance to his methods. He then returned to active military service against the Turks. Following a trip abroad he took part in negotiations for the Treaty of Kuchuk-Kainardji (1774) and served as extraordinary envoy to Turkey (1774-1776). As a result of Panin's eclipse and his connections with the Freemasons, he was shunted off to governor generalships in the western provinces from 1778 through 1791. He saw military service again in the second Turkish war but clashed with Potemkin. From 1792 to 1798 he was governor general of Livonia and Estonia. He

then commanded Russian forces in Poland, imposing harsh rule on the territories acquired in the Third Partition. Initially favored by Paul, who gave him the long-desired rank of field marshal and entrusted him with special assignments, he was forced to retire for good in 1798 when the emperor turned against him. See David L. Ransel, "Repnin, Nikolai Vasil'evich (1734-1801)," MERSH, Vol. 31, pp. 26-28.

79. See Soloviev, *History of Russia*, Vol. 45, pp. 172-174.

80. The Zamoyskis for centuries were one of Poland's most powerful families. Andrzej Zamoyski (1716-1792) served as crown chancellor from 1764 to 1767. He worked closely with the Czartoryskis. As chancellor he tried to limit the *liberum veto* and promoted local reform, but resigned in protest against Repnin's seizure of the opposition leaders in 1767. During the Confederation of Bar he advised the king to resist the Russians and not to antagonize the confederates. He withdrew from public life in 1780.

81. Kazimierz Poniatowski (1721-1800) was the older brother of Stanislaw Augustus. From 1742 to 1773 he was lord high chamberlain. He played a key part in the effort to create a royal party independent of the Czartoryskis in the first years of his brother's reign. He withdrew from politics at the time of the First Partition.

82. Andrzej Stanislaw Mlodziejowski (1717-1780) was a canon of Cracow who became bishop of Przemysl and deputy chancellor in 1766. In 1768 he became bishop of Poznan. When Andrzej Zamoyski stepped down as crown chancellor in 1768, Mlodziejowski replaced him with Repnin's backing. He kept this position until 1775. During the partition diet he supported Russia, insisting, for example, on the maintenance of the Russian guarantee.

83. August Czartoryski (1697-1782) and Michal Czartoryski (1696-1775). These uncles of Stanislaw Augustus played a major role in the political life of Poland in the latter part of the eighteenth century, especially during their nephew's election and reign. Michal was Lithuanian chancellor from 1752 on, and August became general crown hetman in 1764. Also see above, Note 72.

84. Each province in Poland-Lithuania had a dietine (*sejmik*) made up of noble delegates which met at frequent intervals to conduct political and legislative business. Provincial dietines in turn sent delegates to the lower house, which together with the senate constituted the diet (*Sejm*) for the whole Commonwealth. Both the provincial and national diets exercised considerable power in contrast to the weakness of royal institutions.

85. Stanislaw Lubomirski (1719-1783) was an ardent member of the Czartoryski party in the first years of Stanislaw Augustus's reign. He became crown marshal in 1766. During the Confederation of Bar he opposed the king's cooperation with Russia, and he led the opposition of the magnates at the time of the First Partition.

86. Franciszek-Ksavery Branicki (1730-1819) held the rank of hetman (commander) in the last decades of Polish independence. At this time and later he supported Russian interests. Under Russian patronage he took a leading role in the Confederation of Targowica (1792), which opposed the 1791 constitution and led to the Third Partition.

87. The Lithuanian chancellor, Michal Czartoryski, was one of the officers of state appointed by the crown for the grand duchy of Lithuania; a counterpart was appointed for the kingdom of Poland. Both were *ex officio* members of the Senate, or upper house, of the diet.

88. Gédéon de Benoît served as Prussian resident in Warsaw after 1758.

89. Beer, Vol. I, p. 243. (Soloviev's note)

90. A reference to the primate. (Soloviev's note)

91. The archbishop of Gniezno (later Gniezno-Warsaw) historically held the title of primate of Poland and acted as an official spokesman for the Roman Catholic church in Poland. He enjoyed special prerogatives in the governmental structure.

92. Ignacy Massalski (1729-1794) later cooperated with the Russians after the First Partition. He was lynched during the uprising of 1794.

93. Jan Jerzy Flemming (1699-1771) was named Pomeranian military commander in 1766 after a long military career. A supporter of the Czartoryskis, he was married successively to two daughters of Michal Czartoryski, and his own daughter was married to another Czartoryski. Although he supported the confederation summoned by Radziwill in 1764, he took no part in those of Radom or Bar.

94. This was a court office in the grand duchy of Lithuania, in Polish, *kuchmistrz*. Adam Poninski (1732-1798) was later marshal of the diet and played a leading role in the ratification by this diet of the First Partition.

95. See above, p. 57.

96. See above, p. 58.

97. Although the Russians initially had regarded Stanislaw Augustus and the Czartoryskis as their allies, by 1766 Catherine had decided to look elsewhere for allies in Poland. The result was the Russian-inspired confederations in 1767 in Thorn, Sluck and Radom. Polish resentment at the Russian role overshadowed the question of Protestant and Orthodox dissidents' rights which had been the occasion for the formation of the confederations. The diet which met in October 1767 and again in February and March of 1768 saw this feeling erupt with greater force, especially when Repnin arrested four prominent opponents of Russia on October 13, 1767. In the meantime a commission appointed by the diet met with Repnin to negotiate the text of a treaty, which was ratified by the diet in March 1768. Both the negotiations and the ratification were conducted under Russian coercion. The main elements of the treaty were guarantees of greater rights for the dissident Protestants and Orthodox, preservation of

the existing Polish constitution and mutual respect for territorial integrity. With this treaty Russia confirmed its dominant role in Polish affairs. See Kaplan, *The First Partition of Poland.*

98. Jan Jedrzy Józef Borch (1715?-1780) became vice chancellor in 1767. Under Stanislaw Augustus he worked with the Czartoryskis to achieve their plans for reform. He took part in the delegation which met with Russia during the partition diet of 1773. He served as chancellor in the last year of his life.

99. Marie-Thérèse Rodel Geoffrin (1699-1777) presided in Paris over a salon in the Hôtel de Rambouillet which became the most famous meeting place of men of letters, artists and other prominent figures from 1749 to 1777. She particularly encouraged the *philosophes* and subsidized the publication of the *Encyclopedia.* She struck up a lifelong friendship with Stanislaw Augustus during his stay in Paris, sometimes even paying his debts, and visited him in Warsaw in 1766. She also corresponded with Catherine the Great.

100. Jeanroy Charles Saint Pol was the secretary of Andrzej Zamoyski who was sent to Paris by Stanislaw Augustus in 1769.

101. Gabriel Podoski (d. 1793) was a dissolute priest who held the title of crown referendary, or official in one of the royal appeals courts. He was an avid partisan of Russia and later was rewarded by Catherine with the rank of archbishop and then primate. He later fled to France to escape popular wrath, and when he died in exile in Marseille in 1794 his body was disinterred, torn to pieces and thrown into the sea.

102. Ignacy Oginski (c.1698-1774) became castellan of Wilno in 1768 after holding other offices in the grand duchy of Lithuania. He was a member of two delgations to St. Petersburg, including the one in 1769 mentioned here.

103. Jerzy August Mniszech (1715-1778) served as court marshal from 1742 to 1767. He organized the court party and opposed the Czartoryskis. In 1766 he insisted upon denying rights to the dissidents. He was a leader in the Confederation of Radom and organized provincial confederations to support it in Great Poland.

104. It is unclear if the reference is to the election of the first Saxon king, Augustus II, in 1697 and, after a temporary deposition in 1704, again in 1709, or to the election of Augustus III in 1734. In each election the Russians initially supported the Saxon candidate and enjoyed great freedom of action in Poland during their reigns.

105. Antoni Tadeusz Przezdiecki (1718-1772) was a follower of the Czartoryskis who helped organize the Confederation of Wilno in 1764. After the election of Stanislaw Augustus he was named Lithuanian vice chancellor. Like the Czartoryskis he took a neutral stand when the Confederation of Bar was proclaimed in 1768. In 1769 and 1770 he opposed

close ties with Russia and use of the Polish army against the confederates, hence the strong Russian opposition to his political role.

106. Kajetan Soltyk was the bishop of Cracow and a senator in the diet of 1768 who was arrested with three others on Repnin's orders for his opposition to dissident rights. They were imprisoned in Kaluga until 1773. In the diet of 1773 he was one of the few who protested openly against the First Partition.

107. See Soloviev, *History of Russia*, Vol. 45, pp. 91 ff.

108. Letter of Frederick to his brother, Prince Henry. *Oeuvres*, Vol. XXVI, p. 312. (Soloviev's note)

109. A. Beer, *Die erste Theilung Polens*, Vol. I, p. 269. (Soviet editor's note)

110. The Swedish constitution of 1720 restored the hereditary monarchy, which was abolished in 1719, but severely limited the power of the crown. Thus Swedish politics until 1772 were dominated by conflicts between rival aristocratic parties, offering foreign powers ample opportunity to intervene in Swedish affairs by supporting one or the other.

111. M. Duncker, *Aus der Zeit Friedrich's des Grossen und Friedrich Wilhelm's III* (From the Era of Frederick the Great and Frederick William III) (Leipzig, 1876), pp. 167-168. (Soviet editor's note)

112. F. Raumer, *Beiträge zur neueren Geschichte aus dem britischen und französischen Reichsarchive. Th. IV. Europa vom Ende des siebenjährigen bis zum Ende amerikanischen Krieges* (Essays on Recent History out of the British and French State Archives. Part IV. Europe From the End of the Seven Years War to the End of the American War of Independence) (Leipzig, 1839), p. 230. (Soviet editor's note)

113. Maria Theresa (1717-1780) became empress of Austria in 1740 but immediately faced challenges from Bavaria, France, the Spanish Bourbons and Prussia. In the War of the Austrian Succession (1740-1748) she was able to gain control of the lands she had inherited, with the important exception of Silesia, which Frederick II of Prussia seized and held. Efforts to regain the province in an alliance with France and Russia against Prussia and England in the Seven Years War (1756-1763) failed. Her bitterness at this loss was a major, if not the major, force shaping Austrian attitudes described in this volume. Later, however, she was drawn into the First Partition of Poland in 1772. The future Joseph II did not share her antipathy to Prussia and to Frederick II and, as Soloviev describes here, was eager to make common cause with Frederick II and Catherine II.

114. A. Beer, *Die erste Theilung Polens*, Vol. V, p. 293. (Soviet editor's note) For an explanation of the guarantee see Chapter I, note 72.

115. Matteo Boiardo (1441?-1494) was an Italian poet of the Renaissance who wrote chivalrous epics and personal lyrics.

116. *Mémoires de Frédéric II, roi de Prusse, écrits en français par lui-même* (Memoirs of Frederick II, King of Prussia, Written in French by Himself), Vol. II (Paris, 1866), p. 314. (Soviet editor's note)

117. Silesia was lost to Prussia as a result of the War of the Austrian Succession (1740-1748). Empress Elizabeth was a staunch ally of Austria, France and other countries opposing Prussia, England and some smaller German states during the Seven Years War. The recovery of Silesia was a major war aim for Austria. But the death of Elizabeth on January 5, 1762 (New Style) shattered the anti-Prussian coalition at a time when it was on the brink of victory. The new Russian emperor, Peter III, a great admirer of Frederick and of Prussia, returned captured Prussian territory, withdrew Russian forces and even signed an alliance with Prussia. While Catherine, who came to power a few months later, backed away from the alliance, she did not renew the war, and Prussia retained Silesia by the Treaty of Hubertusburg which ended the war in February 1763.

118. A. Beer, *Die erste Theilung Polens*, Vol. V, p. 293. (Soviet editor's note)

119. "Greek" was the usual term at the time for all the Orthodox churches which traced their origin to the patriarchate of Constantinople. While many of the Orthodox in the kingdom of Hungary were Slavs, such as the Ruthenians and Serbs, there were also a large number of Romanian Orthodox and smaller groups of ethnic Greeks.

120. A. R. Arneth, *Maria Theresia und Joseph II* (Maria Theresa and Joseph II), (Vienna, 1867), Vol. I, pp. 300-308. (Soviet editor's note)

121. Italian for "a queen of great intellect."

122. When the Turks fled from Khotin and the Russians took the Danubian principalities, Frederick made the following observation about the campaign in his memoirs. "Catherine's generals had no understanding whatsoever of encampments and tactics. The sultan's generals had even less knowledge. To understand this war correctly, imagine the one-eyed fighting the blind and gaining the upper hand over them." (Soloviev's note)

123. Nikolai Konstantinovich Khotinsky (1727-18??) served in the Russian embassy in Holland in 1760 and in Spain in 1765. He was *chargé d'affaires* in France from 1767 to 1773 and from 1780 to 1782.

124. Count Hermann Karl von Keyserling (1696-1765) served in the Justice College for Livonian and Estonian affairs before embarking on a diplomatic career that took him to Poland (1733-1744), Prussia (1747-1748) and Austria (1752-1761) before his service in France.

125. Count Francis Florimand Claude Mercy-Argenteau served as Austrian ambassador to France from 1766 to 1790.

126. A. Beer, *Die erste Theilung Polens, Documente*, pp. 5-11. (Soviet editor's note)

127. Soloviev refers to a Prince Karl of Saxony. Karl August of Saxony-Weimar-Eisenach (1757-1828), later famous as a patron of Goethe, was only twelve years old at this time and still under the regency of his mother, Anna Amalia. The reference must be to Friedrick Augustus (1750-1827), who succeeded his father, Frederick Augustus II of Saxony, Augustus III of Poland, as elector of Saxony in 1763, but not as king of Poland, whose crown passed instead to Stanislaw Augustus Poniatowski in 1764. The queen mother, Maria Antonia, nevertheless continued to dream of the Polish crown for her son and kept up secret contacts with personages in Poland, some of whom came to Dresden. Friedrich Augustus did not renounce his claims to the Polish crown formally until 1796.

128. Michal Wielhorski (c.1716-1804) was the Lithuanian royal master of the kitchen from 1762. He was a foe of Stanislaw Augustus and the Czartoryskis. He was sent to Paris in 1770 on behalf of the Confederation of Bar.

129. Russian policy towards Denmark was complicated by the chaotic court politics there. Russia's old friend Count Johann Hartwig von Bernstorff (1717-1781), who was foreign minister since 1751, and who loyally supported Panin's Northern System, including restraining Sweden, was under attack, both on personal and policy grounds. The new king, Christian VII (1749-1808), who had come to the throne in 1766, was not only mentally ill but also dissolute, opening the door to court intrigue of all kinds. His unhappy queen, Caroline Matilda (1751-1775), a sister of George III of England, was attracted to the king's German physician Johann Friedrich Struensee (1737-1772), who by 1770 became her lover and virtual dictator of Denmark. With Struensee's rise, Count Adolf Siegfried von der Osten (1726-1797), who had held various diplomatic posts, replaced Bernstorff as foreign minister, causing dismay in Russia. Another figure who came to the fore with Struensee's ascendancy was Count Carl Shack Rantzau (1717-1789), a career military man. Struensee's rule proved brief. The public scandal of his relationship with the queen helped turn opinion against him, and he was overthrown and executed in 1772. The unfortunate queen was forced to surrender a son by the king and a daughter by Struensee and go into exile in Germany, where she died in 1775.

130. The Danish West Indies were acquired in 1754 and, except for brief periods of British rule in the early nineteenth century, remained under Denmark until they were sold to the United States in 1917. They are known now as the United States Virgin Islands.

131. This was a traditional title of the king of France.

132. By this time Sweden had recovered from its losses in the Great Northern War (1700-1721) but was no longer the dominant Baltic power. In fact, like Poland and Denmark, it was subject to the interference of more powerful states in its domestic affairs. As early as the 1730s the French and Russians had begun cultivating factions in the *riksdag*, or parliament, with the help of generous subsidies, a practice which Soloviev describes in this section. In 1751 Adolf Frederick (1710-1771) became king. His wife, the talented and energetic Louisa Ulrika (1720-1784), a sister of Frederick II of Prussia, exercised great influence over him, becoming the center of international attention. The aristocracy was divided into two main parties, the Caps and the Hats. The Caps generally promoted Russian interests and the Hats the French. The aristocratic party strife became more intense after the queen attempted a coup in 1756 to extend royal power and undo the restrictions on the crown dictated by the constitution of 1720, but failed. The now triumphant Hat party, spurred on by the French, entered the Seven Years War on the French side, an action which brought no benefit and great losses to Sweden. By 1765-1766 the Caps were again in power but, as Soloviev describes here, were defeated by the Hats despite political pressure and financial subsidies brought to bear by the Russians, the Prussians and the English against the Hats and their French allies. As in Poland the Russians supported the constitution limiting royal power as a way to preserve their freedom to intervene among aristocratic factions. Meanwhile the French assiduously cultivated the crown prince (1746-1792), who ruled as Gustavus III upon the death of his father in 1771. His dramatic assassination at a masked ball was the inspiration for Verdi's opera *Un Ballo in Maschera*.

133. Ivan Andrevich Ostermann (1725-1811) was the son of Heinrich Johann Friedrich Ostermann who had made his career under Peter I and Anna, only to fall from power under Elizabeth. After travel abroad and service in the Russian embassy in Paris, the son was ambassador to Sweden from 1760 to 1774. He returned to St. Petersburg in 1774, where he enjoyed the favor of Catherine and later of Paul. He served as vice chancellor from 1775 to 1776 and chancellor from 1796 until he retired in 1797.

134. Karlskrona is a port on the southern coast which was the head-quarters of the Swedish fleet.

135. Fredrik Axel Fersen (1719-1794) had a distinguished military career and was a forceful spokesman for the aristocracy in its efforts to restrain the power of the crown. He was also a lifelong friend of France, and as a youth had fought for the French in the War of the Austrian Succession. His son, Hans Axel Fersen, also spent time in French military service and planned the abortive flight of the French royal family to Varennes in 1791.

136. See Soloviev, *History of Russia*, Vol. 45, p. 192.

137. William Henry Zuylestein, fourth earl of Rochford (1717-1781), was a strong Whig supporter who held various government posts, including extraordinary ambassador to Spain (1763-1766) and ambassador to France (1766-1768). In 1768 he became secretary for the northern department, which included Russia. He resigned this position in 1775 because of problems in dealing with the American colonies.

138. John Goodricke represented England in Sweden.

CHAPTER II

1. That is, (Grigory) Orlov. (Soviet editor's note) See Chapter I, Note 3.

2. On Rumiantsev see Chapter I, Note 11.

3. See above, pp. 18-20.

4. Johann Christoph von Stoffeln (1718-1770) followed a military career and served in Russia's principal wars from 1738. He was named general quartermaster in 1757 and saw considerable action in the Seven Years War. He was present with his corps in Poland during the election of Stanislaw Augustus in 1764.

5. Grigory Alexandrovich Potemkin (1739-1791) by this time already had attracted Catherine's attention for his assistance in the coup of 1762 and had held various roles at court thereafter. He volunteered for service against Turkey in 1769 and served as a staff officer under Golitsyn and Rumiantsev. After appealing to Catherine he received a field command and took part in the successful Russian campaign of 1770. Later successes in battle and Grigory Orlov's fall from favor led Catherine to install him in the Winter Palace in 1774, where for a time he was her lover and principal advisor. Although the former role ended by 1776, he continued to play a major part as a governor and military commander in the areas acquired from the Turks in the south until his death in 1791. See George E. Munro, "Potemkin, Grigorii Aleksandrovich (1739-1791)," MERSH, Vol. 29, pp. 123-128 and George Soloveytchik, *Potemkin. Soldier, Statesman, Lover and Consort of Catherine of Russia* (New York, 1947).

6. The reference is obviously to the Seven Years War, in which Russia took an active part from 1757 to 1762. In this war there were several large-scale campaigns by Russian armies on Prussian territory.

7. See Chapter I, Note 14.

8. Catherine appointed a military commission in 1762 which, among other reforms, after a review of the armed forces in 1764-1765, resulted in the establishment of a general staff (1770). Rumiantsev, however, like several other field commanders, felt that serious problems still remained. See John L. H. Keep, *Soldiers of the Tsar* (Oxford, 1985).

9 In the second Punic War Hannibal led a Carthaginian army across the Alps, arriving in northern Italy early in 217 B.C. After the great victories on the Trevia river and at Lake Trasimene, the Roman commander Quintus Fabius Maximus, later surnamed Cunctator, or Delayer, avoided open battle with Hannibal whenever possible. He realized that Hannibal's superior generalship would give him the advantage and sought to wear the enemy down with a defensive strategy. Fabius's strategy proved successful, for Hannibal failed to capture Rome and was forced to abandon Italy in 203 B.C. General Mikhail Kutuzov followed a similar strategy against Napoleon in 1812 and was compared with Fabius frequently then and later.

10. The actions of Polish confederates opposing Russian interests there are discussed extensively in Chapter I, pp. 51-53, 55-78, 84, 88.

11. See Chapter I, Note 78.

12. Friedrich Wilhelm von Bauer (1731-1783) served as quartermaster general for the Second Army from 1769 to 1772. He later held the rank of engineer general from 1778 to 1783 with responsibility for all military engineering.

13. See Chapter I, Note 16.

14. Literally "oaks."

15. The Russian term "rebiata," meaning "children" does not have the patronizing quality of the literal English equivalent. This expression was and is used by a superior to encourage his subordinates.

16. See Chapter I, Note 30.

17. Semen Romanovich Vorontsov (1744-1832) was imprisoned briefly for standing by Peter III in Catherine's coup of 1762. After two years in diplomatic service in Vienna he served with distinction in the Turkish war of 1768 in addition to the commendation mentioned here. He then served two years as minister plenipotentiary in Venice before spending 1784 to 1806 as ambassador to England, except for a brief period, 1800-1801, when he incurred the displeasure of Paul I. He ably represented Russian interests in London and was successful in maintaining close ties with England. He retired in 1806 and remained in England, which for him really was a second fatherland, until his death in 1832. See George F. Jewsbury "Vorontsov, Semen Romanovich (1744-1832)," MERSH, Vol. 43, pp. 58-60.

18. See above, pp. 27-28.

19. Second major was the lowest staff officer rank.

20. For the consequences of this decision, see Alan W. Fisher, *The Russian Annexation of the Crimea, 1773-1784.*

21. See Chapter I, Note 23.

22. A district in Bulgaria.

23. One of the titles of the Ottoman sultan, meaning sovereign.

24. Meaning "the settled ones" in Russian.

25. *Belyi tsar*, or white tsar, was an ancient title of the Russian tsar.

26. See Soloviev, *Istoriia Rossii*, Vol. 3, pp. 455-496. Also see Fisher, *The Crimean Tatars*; Boris S. Ischboldin, *Essays in Tatar History* (New Delhi, 1963); Andreas Kappeler, "Die Moskauer 'Nationalitätenpolitik' unter Ivan IV, (The Muscovite "nationalities policy" under Ivan IV)," *Russian History*, Vol. 14, Nos. 1-4 (1987), pp. 263-282; and William H. McNeill, *Europe's Steppe Frontiers, 1500-1800*, (Chicago, 1964).

27. Bakhchisaray, the capital of the Crimea, is in the southwestern part of the peninsula.

28. See Chapter I, pp. 28-32. On Spiridov, see Chapter I, Note 43.

29. See Chapter I, Note 31.

30. See Chapter I, Note 51.

31. See Chapter I, Note 47.

32. Rear Admiral Ivan Nikolaevich Harf was one of several Danes recruited for the Russian service in 1770. After participating in the Mediterranean campaign described here by Soloviev, he was released from service on his return to St Petersburg in 1772.

33. See also Jelavich, *A History of the Balkans*, Vol. 2, p. 78; and L.S. Stavrianos, *The Balkans since 1453* (New York, 1953) p. 189.

34. See Chapter I, Note 34.

35. When the Athenians consulted the oracle of Delphi during the Persian invasion of 480 B.C. the response was to rely on a "wooden wall" of ships rather than attempt to resist the enemy on land. The decisive victory of the Athenian fleet at Salamis that year effectively blocked the Persian offensive.

36. See above, pp. 43-47.

37. See in addition to Anderson, *Naval Wars in the Levant, 1554-1853*, Patrick J. Rollins, "Chesma, Battle of (1770)," MERSH, Vol. 7, pp. 32-33.

38. See Chapter I, Note 7.

39. Catherine refers here to God's promises to Abraham and Isaac in Genesis that their progeny will be as numerous as the dust on the earth or the stars in heaven in future generations.

40. Samuel Grieg (1735-1788) was born in Scotland and entered Russian service in 1764 after several years in the Royal Navy. After commanding several ships in the Baltic, he led part of the Russian force which sailed to the Mediterranean in 1770. He continued naval operations there until 1773. From 1775 to 1785 he commanded the Kronstadt naval base, working to improve ships and shore facilities. He saw action again in 1788, doing battle with the Swedes. He died at sea off the Swedish fortress of Sveaborg in 1788.

41. François de Tott (1733-1793) was sent by France to the Crimea as consul "extraordinary" in 1767. Here he played a part in inciting the Crimean Tatars to take up arms against Russia, and he accompanied the Tatar army which entered southern Russia in January 1769.

42. The term "Franks" was used in the Ottoman Empire for all western Europeans, not just the French.

43. The letter was not written at this time. The expression "burned again" proves that the letter was written after the news of the events at Chesme. The mention of events in Moscow at the end necessitates ascribing a still later date to it. (Soloviev's note)

44. In the protocols of the council for February 28, 1773 we read: "A note from London was read about the petitions of Rear Admiral Elphinstone and his threats to make public all the orders given to him so he might justify himself. The council recognized the need to satisfy this agitated man as soon as possible." (Soloviev's note)

45. See Chapter I, Note 37.

46. For a description of the earlier stages of this campaign see above, pp. 22-23.

47. Nikolai Naumovich Choglokov (1718-1754) and his wife Maria Simonovna Choglokova, née Gendrikova (1723-1756) served on Empress Elizabeth's orders as models for and supervisors of the future Peter III and his young bride Catherine from 1747 to 1754. This was a thankless job, made worse by the tactless way the Choglokovs carried out their duties. Affairs by both of their young charges discredited them in Elizabeth's eyes, and they were dismissed in 1756. The Naum Nikolaevich Choglokov (1743-1798) discussed here was one of their eight children. After the abortive acts of defiance Soloviev describes here, he was sentenced to exile in Siberia. In 1796 he was pardoned by Paul I to live the remainder of his life under the supervision of the governor of Novgorod.

48. See Chapter I, Note 9.

49. See Chapter I, Note 32.

50. See Chapter I, Note 1.

51. See Chapter I, Note 113.

52. See Chapter I, Note 65.

53. See pp. 82-84. On Joseph II, see Chapter I, Note 59.

54. Moritz Karl, Count Lynar (1702-1768) was born in Saxony. He first represented Saxony in Russia from 1733 to 1736 and again from 1740 to 1741, where he was a special favorite of Empress Anna and became deeply involved in Russian court politics. This aroused great Russian resentment. Although Anna offered to take him into Russian service, he remained with Saxony and later worked against Russian interests in Poland.

55. The Convention of Kloster-Zeven was signed on September 8, 1757 (New Style) by the duke of Cumberland who was commanding Hanoverian forces for Hanover's sovereign, George II of England, with the duke of Richelieu, the commander of the advancing French army. This convention left Hanover at the mercy of the French, dispersed a large part of Cumberland's army and left Prussia open to a French invasion. Frederick

II's victory at Rossbach two months later persuaded the British to repudiate the convention on November 28, 1757 (New Style) and to join Prussia against France, Austria and Russia.

56. This city is mentioned in various forms such as Lemberg (German), Lviv (Ukrainian), Lwów (Polish) and Lvov (Russian).

57. See Chapter I, Note 77.

58. On the Northern System see Chapter I, Note 13.

59. The political testament of 1768, like that of 1752, contained Frederck II's reflections on the duties of a prince as well as analyses of actual and potential political situations, such as the possibility of acquiring Prussian Poland discussed here. See Gerhard Ritter, *Frederick the Great* (Berkeley, 1970).

60. *Mémoires de Frédéric II* (Memoirs of Frederick II) Vol. 2, p. 335. Max Duncker, p. 176. (Soloviev's note)

61. See above, pp. 78-79, 82-84.

62. See above, p. 140.

63. Frederick William I (1688-1740) was king in Prussia who made his realm into a major state in Europe through careful administration, strict economy, and fostering military power. His successes in foreign affairs, particularly the acquisition of new territory, were limited.

64. Augustus II (1670-1733) became elector of Saxony in 1694 and king of Poland in 1697 after an election marked by bribery and threats. Augustus had not only Saxon but also Russian support, and so was able to outmaneuver the Austrian-backed candidate, Jakub Sobieski, son of the previous king, and a French-backed candidate, the Prince de Conti. In 1699 he made an alliance with Russia and Denmark with an eye to conquering Swedish Livonia, but was defeated in 1702 by Charles XII of Sweden and deposed in 1704. He recovered the Polish crown in 1709, but at the cost of submitting to Russian influence thereafter. For Augustus II, as well as for Polish affairs in general, from quite a different point of view of Russian policy than Soloviev's, see Norman Davies, *God's Playground. A History of Poland*, Vol. 1, pp. 492-504.

65. Frederick I (1657-1713) became elector of Brandenburg in 1688 and after gaining the support of Holy Roman Emperor Leopold I crowned himself "King in Prussia" in 1701. While Prussia already had *de facto* control in East Prussia, this act marked the end of any vestigial Polish sovereignty there.

66. Charles XII (1682-1718) was the king of Sweden who, soon after ascending the throne in 1697, succeeded in inflicting early defeats on Russia in the Great Northern War (1700-1721) and in defeating the Saxon king of Poland, Augustus II. Although he later placed his own candidate Stanislaw Lesczynski on the Polish throne in 1706, his ambitious invasion of Russia ended in disaster at the battle of Poltava in the Ukraine in 1709.

After escaping to Turkey he returned to Sweden in 1714 and attempted to renew the struggle. By this time Augustus II had regained the Polish crown, and the tide had turned in Russia's favor. He was killed in action in Norway in 1718.

67. Johann Reinhold von Patkul (1660-1707) was a Livonian adventurer whose hostility to Sweden's rule of his province led him to put together a coalition of Poland, Denmark, and Russia to oppose Sweden in the Northern War. After Charles XII's victory over Poland, Patkul was surrendered to the Swedes and executed. See "Patkul, Johann Reinhold von (1660-1707)," MERSH, Vol. 27, pp. 55-56.

68. See Chapter II, Note 66.

69. Stanislaw Leszczynski (1677-1766) was first elected king of Poland in 1704 under the patronage of Charles XII of Sweden, but was deposed by his predecessor, Augustus II in 1709, thanks to Russian intervention. He briefly recovered the Polish crown in 1733 with French help, only to be removed definitively in 1738 after the War of the Polish Succession. He spent the rest of his life as duke of Lorraine and Bar in France.

70. J. G. Drohsen, *Geschichte der Preussischen Politik*. Th. V, *Friedrich der Grosse* (History of Prussian Foreign Policy. Part V. Frederick the Great), (Leipzig, 1874), Vol. 1, pp. 287-350. (Soviet editor's note) See Soloviev, *Istoriia Rossii*, Vol. 9, pp. 311, 431.

71. The future Augustus III of Poland (1696-1763) succeeded his father as elector of Saxony and king of Poland in 1733, although he was not finally recognized as king until 1736 when, with Russian help, he had driven his rival Stanislaw Leszczynski from the land. His long reign was marked by continuous and powerful Russian influence, combined with growing political stagnation and anarchy. At the end of his life Catherine II was working closely with the Czartoryskis and Poniatowskis against him.

72. See Soloviev, *Istoriia Rossii*, Vol. 10., p. 353.

73. See Soloviev, *Istoriia Rossii*, Vol. 12, p. 270.

74. This was Alexander Mikhailovich Golitsyn (1723-1807). See Chapter I, Note 10.

75. See Chapter I, Note 7.

76. See Soloviev, *Istoriia Rossii*, Vol. 23, pp. 253-255.

77. Arneth, *Maria-Theresia's letzte Regierungszeit* (The Last Years of Maria Theresa's reign), Vol. 2, p. 33. (Soloviev's note)

78. Ibid., p. 37. (Soloviev's note)

79. See Chapter I, Note 75.

80. See Chapter I, Note 62.

81. Prince Henry (Heinrich) of Prussia (1726-1803) was a younger brother of Frederick II. As Soloviev shows in this section, he was a shrewd and effective statesman, although colder and more abrupt than his even more talented brother. He showed great military talent as commander of a

Prussian force in the Seven Years War and later helped represent Prussian interests in the First Partition of Poland. He never reconciled himself to the secondary role dictated by birth, and growing differences between him and his brother meant that after 1778 he played no further major political role.

82. The reference is to the formal agreement concluded in 40 B.C. between the two leading successors to Julius Caesar. Octavian, later Augustus Caesar, took control of the western provinces and Antony of the eastern.

83. Duncker, *Aus der Zeit Friedrich's des Grossen* (From the Time of Frederick the Great), p. 188; *Oeuvres* (Works), Vol. 26, p. 313. (Soloviev's note)

84. See Chapter I, Note 125.

85. Arneth, p. 570. (Soloviev's note)

86. Baron Franz Maria von Thugut (1739-1818) represented Austria in Constantinople from 1769 to 1774, where he promoted Austria's offer to mediate between Russia and Turkey. He later headed the Austrian foreign ministry from 1794 to 1801.

87. Beer, *Die erste Theilung Polens* (The First Partition of Poland), I, p. 311. (Soloviev's note)

88. The reference is to the famous "Diplomatic Revolution" achieved by Kaunitz in 1756. Taking advantage of the blunders of England and Prussia, he won France and then Russia as allies in his quest for revenge against Prussia in the Seven Years War. His success was particularly remarkable given the centuries of hostility between France and the Habsburgs which had preceded it.

89. Jacob (John) Robert Nugent-Westmeath (1720-1794) was born in Ireland and was serving in the Austrian army by the age of fifteen. After a distinguished military career he came to Berlin as Austrian ambassador in 1764.

90. When Maria Theresa appeared before the Hungarian estates in 1741, the nobles swore to sacrifice "*vitam et sanguinem pro rege nostro* (sic) *Maria Theresa.*"

91. As Frederick the Great remarked cynically at the time, "*Elle pleurait, elle prenait toujours*" "(She wept but she still took)."

92. See Chapter I, Note 7.

93. A. Beer, *Die Zusammenkünfte Josefs II und Friedrichs II* (The Meetings between Joseph II and Frederick II), (Vienna, 1871) pp. 114-116. (Soviet editor's note)

94. Ibid. (Soloviev's note)

95. Beer, *Die erste Theilung*, Vol. 2, p. 49. (Soloviev's note)

96. See Chapter I, Note 63.

97. The Treaty of Belgrade (1739) ended the war waged by Austria and Russia against Turkey which began in 1736. Russia and Austria had

underestimated their opponent and agreed in the treaty to the cession of Belgrade, which the Austrians had held since 1718, as well as of Austrian holdings in Serbia and Wallachia. Russia had to abandon the newly-captured fortress of Khotin, keep ships out of the Black Sea and make other concessions.

98. Arneth, *Maria Theresia und Joseph II*, Vol. 1, p. 316. (Soloviev's note)

99. Peter Pavlovich Shafirov (1669-1739) was a trusted diplomatic advisor to Peter the Great who negotiated the Treaty of Pruth with Turkey in 1711 which ended Peter's disastrous campaign that year. He and B.P. Sheremetev were sent to Constantinople as hostages to ensure Russian compliance with the treaty and were put in prison when the Russians refused to carry out some of the terms. Shafirov continued to negotiate effectively while in prison and was released with the other Russian hostages in January 1714. See George E. Munro, "Shafirov, Peter Pavlovich (1669-1739)," MERSH, Vol. 34, pp. 122-126.

100. See Chapter I, Note 133.

101. Alexander Stakhievich Stakhiev (1724-1794) studied at the College of Foreign Affairs, then held various diplomatic posts in Sweden from 1745 to 1775, becoming resident in 1764. From 1775 to 1781 he served as extraordinary ambassador and minister plenipotentiary in Constantinople, where he helped prepare for the annexation of the Crimea by Russia and gain freedom of navigation for Russia on the Black Sea. He also was secretary of the Free Economic Association.

102. See Chapter I, Note 129.

103. The reference is to Russia's participation in the alliance with Austria and France, which led to these powers fighting against Prussia in the Seven Years War, with England as Prussia's only major ally.

104. See above, pp. 139-140.

105. *Anecdotes of the Russian Empire*, pp. 326-327. (Soloviev's note)

106. *Oeuvres de Frédéric le Grand* (Works of Frederick the Great), Vol. 26, pp. 320, 326, 330. (Soloviev's note)

107. In 49 B.C. Julius Caesar led a single legion across the Rubicon river, which was the boundary between Cisalpine Gaul and eastern Italy. This broke a law prohibiting a governor from leaving his province with his troops and was a clear sign of Ceasar's intention to seize power. Since then crossing the Rubicon has signified any decisive action.

108. See above, p. 140.

109. Caspar Saldern (1711-1788) was born in Holstein and served there on behalf of the future Peter III. Recalled to Russia in 1763, he later undertook various diplomatic missions for Nikita Panin in Holstein, Denmark and Prussia in the years 1766-1768. He replaced Volkonsky as Russian ambassador to Poland in 1771, where he was noted for his harsh dealings with the Poles and his perceptive reports to St Petersburg. Excluded

from the negotiations leading to the First Partition, he turned again to Holstein affairs. Catherine, enraged when she discovered he was involved in plots against his former superior Panin, forced him out of both the Russian and the Holstein service.

110. Duncker, pp. 210-214. (Soloviev's note)

111. *Oeuvres*, Vol. 26, p. 337. (Soloviev's note)

112. Duncker, p. 218. (Soloviev's note)

113. Concerning Catherine's last words, which refer to Silesia, the following information is interesting. When rumors arose about the possibility of a rift between Russia and the Porte as early as the spring of 1768, the Saxon minister at the court of St. Petersburg, Sacken, made a report to his government. Apparently Count Chernyshev had suggested to Prince Lobkowitz that the acquisition of Belgrade and the surrounding territory would be of greater benefit than the acquisition of Silesia, which had gone to Prussia. From Lobkowitz's answers it is possible to guess that his court shared almost the same opinion. Sacken's dispatch is found in Herrmann, *Geschichte des russischen Staats* (History of the Russian State), Vol. 5, p. 694. (Soloviev's note) Prince Joseph Maria Lobkowitz (1725-1802) followed a military career, including distinguished service in the Seven Years War. He became Austrian ambassador to Russia in 1764, remaining in that post until 1777, where among other assignments he represented Austria in the negotiations for the First Partition of Poland.

114. See above pp. 155-156.

115. *Oeuvres*, Vol. 26, p. 344. (Soloviev's note)

116. See above pp. 150-152.

117. Gottfried van Swieten (1734-1803), the son of Maria Theresa's personal physician, Gerhard van Swieten, served as Austria's ambassador in Brussels, Paris, Warsaw, and finally Berlin. From 1777 to 1803 he was prefect of the court library in Vienna, a position his father had held before him. He was also a great music lover, and such famous musicians as Mozart and Haydn took part in the gatherings he organized.

118. Throughout the eighteenth century rumors circulated about various plans, projects or testaments of Peter the Great which envisioned a dominant Russian position in Europe, the Mediterranean and the Near East at the expense of the other European powers and Turkey. The anti-Russian party in France naturally gave credence to this material which confirmed their image of a hostile and expansionist Russia, and doubtless Frederick II learned about them through his web of official and unofficial contacts. See Orest Subtelny, "Peter I's Testament. A Reassessment," *Slavic Review*, Vol. 33, No. 4 (1974), pp. 663-677.

119. *Oeuvres*, Vol. 26, pp. 326, 327, 335. Beer, *Friedrich II und van Swieten* (Frederick II and van Swieten), pp. 1-9. (Soloviev's note)

120. See Chapter I, Note 29.

121. Duncker, pp. 220, 228. (Soloviev's note)

122. Frederick Augustus III (1750-1827). See Chapter I, Note 127.

123. See above, p. 163.

124. *Oeuvres*, Vol. 26, pp. 345-346. (Soloviev's note)

125. Alexander Vasilevich Suvorov (1729-1800) was perhaps the greatest military commander Russia has ever known. After service in the Seven Years War against Prussia, he earned victories against the Confederation of Bar, as Soloviev describes in this section. He also won glory in the later stages of the Turkish war of 1768-1774. He helped put down the remnants of the Pugachev rising in 1774 and served successively in the Crimea, the Kuban and in the Turkish war of 1789-1791, earning the title of Count of Rimnic for a victory in 1789 there. He led the Russian forces which took Warsaw and ended Polish resistance to the Third Partition in 1794. Although he fell out of favor with Paul I and retired in 1797, he was recalled to active duty at England's insistence in 1797. At the end of his life he won his greatest victories against the French in Italy and Switzerland in 1799. In addition to his prowess in the field, Suvorov was a great strategist who emphasized offensive action, surprise, maneuver and concentration of Forces. He won the affection of his troops and has remained a hero throughout the tsarist and Soviet eras. See Philip Longworth, *The Art of Victory. The Life and Achievements of Field-Marshal Suvorov (1711-1800)* (New York, 1965).

126. Suvorov's terse phrases are typical of military dispatches and reports the world over. Immediate description often takes precedence over grammar and literary style, as for example in the journal of the Lewis and Clark expedition to the American Northwest.

127. M.E. Boutaric, *Correspondance secrète inédite de Louis XV* (Secret Unedited Correspondence of Louis XV), Paris, 1866, Vol. 1, p. 154. (Soviet editor's note)

128. Charles François Dumouriez (1739-1823) was sent by Choiseul to aid the Confederation of Bar. He agreed to the attempt to depose Stanislaw Augustus in 1770 and fought with the confederation against Suvorov. Recalled to France, he served as foreign minister in 1792, then commanded French revolutionary armies in 1792 and 1793. He defected to Austria and after 1804 lived in England, playing no further political role.

129. Michal Jan Pac (?1728-1787) took part in the Confederation of Radom, then served as marshal in the Confederation of Bar. He was chosen Lithuanian marshal by the general confederation in 1769 and assumed leadership of this confederation. After the collapse of the Confederation of Bar he emigrated.

130. Karol Stanislaw Radziwill (1734-1790) fought against the Czartoryskis during the interregnum after the death of Augustus III. Temporarily forced out of his positions because of the pressure of the Russian forces, he recovered these thanks to Repnin, through whose intercession he became marshal of the Confederation of Radom. Later he

joined the Confederation of Bar, and after its collapse spent until 1777 abroad. Reconciled with the king by Catherine II, he later opposed his reform measures preceding the Third Partition.

131. Józef Pulaski (1704-1769), one of the founders of the Confederation of Bar, was chosen marshal of this confederation. He had been a supporter of the Czartoryskis and had taken part in the Confederation of Radom. He died in Turkish captivity.

132. Jan Sobieski (1629-1696) became king of Poland in 1674. Before becoming king he had shown his military talent in campaigns against the cossacks, the Swedes and the Turks, but is best remembered for lifting the siege of Vienna by the Turks in 1683, where he personally commanded the Polish cavalry.

133. See Chapter I, Note 17.

134. Wladyslaw Roch Gurowski (1715-1790) served in the French army before returning to Poland in 1758. In 1768 he became Lithuanian court marshal. He was won over to the Russian side by Repnin, who gave him money. He supported the Russian guarantee for the Commonwealth.

135. See Chapter I, Note 94.

136. Teodor Szydlowski was castellan of Mazovia and later palatine of Plock.

137. August Stanislaw von Goltz (?-1788) was, with his brother, Jerzy Wilhelm, a dissident leader and took his place as marshal of the Confederation of Thorn in 1767. He sided with Repnin in the diet of 1767-1768.

138. The reference is to the famous equestrian statue of Peter the Great cast by the French sculptor Étienne-Maurice Falconet with the assistance of his apprentice Marie Anne Collot, who molded the head. Falconet came to St. Petersburg in 1766 on Diderot's recommendation and finished a model of the statue in 1770. The finished product was unveiled in 1782.

139. Antony Kazimierz Ostrowski (1713-1784), the bishop of Kujawy, was pro-Russian. He was a signatory of the 1766 treaty with Russia on the dissident question.

140. See Chapter I, Note 82.

141. See Chapter I, Note 85.

142. See Chapter I, Note 83.

143. See Chapter I, Note 98.

144. See Chapter I, Note 105.

145. Józef Zaremba was a major general, the starosta of Sokolnik, and served as delegate from Sieradze.

146. See Chapter I, Note 93.

147. See Chapter I, Note 88.

148. See Chapter I, Note 103.

149. See Chapter I, Note 106.

150. The Treaty of Oliva (1660) ended the long Polish-Swedish War of Succession (1600-1660). Sweden retained its Livonian holdings and

ended Jan Kazimierz's claims on the Swedish crown beyond his own lifetime. It also confirmed the Treaty of Wehlau (1657) by which sovereignty over Ducal Prussia was transferred from the Polish crown to the elector of Brandenburg.

151. Duncker, p. 226. The French agent in Warsaw wrote to Choiseul that Volkonsky complained in person about the Czartoryskis because they had informed him that the Lithuanian chancellor had called him narrow-minded. Volkonsky made no secret of his wish to leave Poland. Panin unwillingly had recalled Repnin, his relative, and had been forced to replace him with Volkonsky, Orlov's friend. He gave imprecise instructions to the new ambassador, which provided no basis for action. This was so the futility of his embassy could demonstrate Repnin's superiority, whom Panin wanted to send back to Poland. It is impossible to deny that this report contained a certain element of truth, and that it sheds a certain amount of light on relations in St. Petersburg. (Soloviev's note)

152. See Chapter I, Note 135.

153. Gustavus Adolphus (1594-1632) transformed Sweden from a weak and divided country into a great European power. He won the co-operation of the estates in his enterprises and extended Sweden's domains in the Baltic and, for a time, deep into Germany in the Thirty Years War. France supported him as a powerful ally against their common Habsburg opponent.

154. *Oeuvres*, Vol. 26, pp. 315, 323. (Soloviev's note)

155. See Chapter I, Note 132.

156. See Chapter I, Note 48.

157. Baron Carl Heinrich Gleichen (1733-1807) was Danish ambassador to France from 1763 to 1770. He was a close associate of Choiseul.

158. See Chapter I, Note 129.

159. See Chapter I, Note 129.

160. See Chapter I, Note 129.

161. Baron Ivan (Johann) Ivanovich Mestmacher (1732-1805) served as Russian ambassador to Denmark from 1770 to 1772, to Holstein from 1774 to 1784, to Courland from 1784 to 1789, and to Saxony from 1789 to 1799.

162. See Chapter I, Note 129.

163. See Chapter I, Note 67.

164. Queen Caroline Matilda had aroused public amazement and scorn by appearing in masculine riding costume.

165. See Chapter I, Note 18.

166. See Chapter I, Note 137.

167. See Chapter I, Note 5.

168. See above, pp. 12-13.

169. Alexis Vasilevich Naryshkin (1742-1800) was an associate of Grigory Orlov who had earned a reputation as a writer by the 1760s. He was a deputy to the Legislative Commission and later served as a provincial governor and senator.

COURT AND MILITARY TERMS

Russian	English	Class in Table of Ranks
admiral	admiral	II
baron	baron	
bey	bey	
brigadir	brigadier	V
burgomistr	burgomaster	
deistvitelny statsky sovetnik	senior state councillor	IV
diuk	duke	
feldmarshal	field marshal	I
general	general	II
general-anshef	general en chef	II
general-feldseigmeister	quartermaster general	II
general-kvarermeister	quartermaster general	II
general-maior	major general	IV
general-poruchik	lieutenant general	III
generalny-marshal	marshal general	I
general-prokuror	procurator general	
gertsog	prince	
glavnokomaduiushchy	commander in chief	
graf	count	
gubernator	governor	
gubernator-general	governor general	
imperator	emperor	
imperatritsa	empress	
kamerger	chamberlain	
kamer-iunker	chamberlain	
kantsler	chancellor	I
kantaliarny sovetnik	chancellery councillor	
kapitan	captain	IX
kapitan-brigadir	brigadier captain	V
kastelian	castellan	

khan	khan	
konferentsy sovetnik	conference councillor	
kniaz	prince	
konsul	consul	
kontr-admiral	rear admiral	IV
kornet	cornet	XIV
korol	king	
koshevoi ataman	commanding hetman	
kukmistr koronny	royal master of the kitchen	
kurfiurst	elector	
kurfiurstina	wife of the elector	
landmarshal	land marshal	
leib-medik	personal physician	
litovsky kantsler	Lithuanian chancellor	
maior	major	VIII
marshal	marshal	
marshal koronny	crown marshal	
murza	member of the Turkish gentry class	
nasledny prints	crown prince	
ober-kamerger	lord high chamberain	
ober-ofitser	commissioned officer	
podpolkovnik	lieutenant colonel	VII
polkovnik	colonel	VI
poruchik	lieutenant	XII, XIII
poslannik	ambassador	
poverenny v delakh	chargé d'affaires	
president	president	
primas	primate	
prints	prince	
proveditor	governor	
reis-Effendi	chancellor	
resident	resident	
sekund-maior	second major	IX
senator	senator	
seraskir	commander in chief, minister of war	
serdar	military commander	
sovetnik	councillor	II-VII, IX

sultan	sultan
tsar	tsar
veliky kantsler koronny	crown chancellor
veliky kniaz	grand duke
vitse-kantsler	vice chancellor
vitse-president	vice president
vizir	vizier
voevoda	military commander
yanichar-aga	master of the janissaries

DIPLOMATS MENTIONED IN THE TEXT
(dates in office when known)

In Russian Service
Foreign Minister:
   Nikita Ivanovich Panin (1763-1780)

To Austria:
   Karl Hermann von Keyserling (1752-1761)

To Denmark:
   Mikhail Mikhailovich Filosofov (1766-1770)
   Ivan Ivanovich Mestmacher (1769, 1770-1772)

To England:
   Ivan Grigorevich Chernyshev (1768-1769)

To France:
   Nikolai Konstantinovich Khotinsky (1767-1773)

To the German Diet in Regensburg:
   Johann Matthias von Simolin (1762-1771)

To Lower Saxony and the Hanseatic Cities:
   Friedrich Ulrich Gross (1767-1796)

To Poland:
   Nikolai Vasilevich Repnin (1764-1769)
   Mikhail Nikitich Volkonsky (1761-1771)
   Caspar von Saldern (1771-1772)

To Prussia:
Nikolai Vasilevich Repnin (1762-1763)

To Sweden:
Ivan Andreevich Ostermann (1760-1774)
Aleksandr Stakhievich Stakhiev (1764-1775)

To Turkey:
Aleksei Mikhailovich Obrezkov (1751-1768)

To Venice and other Italian states:
Paulo Maruzzi (1768-1783)

In Austrian Serivce
Foreign Minister:
Wenzel Anton von Kaunitz-Reitberg (1753-1780)

To France:
Francis Florimund Claude Mercy-Argenteau (1766-1790)

To Prussia:
Jacob (John) Robert Nugent-Westmeath (1751-1770)
Gottfried van Swieten (1768-1776)

To Russia:
Joseph Maria Karl von Lobkowitz (1764-1777)

To Turkey:
Franz Maria von Thugut (1769-1774)

In Danish Service:
Foreign Minister:
Johann Hartwig von Bernstorff (1751-1770)
Adolf Siegfried von der Osten (1770-)

To France:
Carl Heinrich Gleichen (1763-1770)

To Naples:
Carl Heinrich Gleichen (1770-)

In English Service:
Secretary for the Northern Department:
William Henry Zuylestein, Earl of Rochford (1768-1775)

To Russia:
Charles Schaw, Lord Cathcart (1768-1771)

To Sweden:
John Goodricke

In French Service:
Foreign Minister:
Étienne François, Duke of Choiseul (1758-1770)

To Danzig:
Gérard

To England:
Chatelier

To Russia:
Beranger

To Sweden:
Modein

Special Envoy to Turkey:
François de Tott (1767-)
Valcroissant

In Polish Service:
Special Envoy to France:
Jeanroy Charles St. Pol (1769)
Count Chreptowicz

To Russia:
Psarski

In Prussian Service:
Special Envoy to France:
Wilhelm Bernhard von Goltz (1769)

To Poland:
Gédéon de Benoit (1758-)

To Russia:
Victor Friedrich Solms (1762-1779)

To Sweden:
Cocceji

In Saxon Service
To Russia:
Sacken

120, 142, 156-158, 186-190, 190-192, 196, 202-203, 206, 214, 220, 222-224, 226, 228-229, 231, 234-235.
Swedish Livonia, 142, 228.
Swedish Pomerania, 79-80.
Swieten, Gottfried van, Austrian envoy in Berlin, xxix, 168-169, 232.
Switzerland, 233.
Szydlowski, Teodor, Polish noble, 178, 234.

Taganrog, 21, 49, 51, 87, 89, 155, 214.
Taman, 21, 114, 138.
Tamovich, Marko, Montenegrin, 39.
Targowica. See Confederation of Targowica.
Tashkent, 26.
Tatars, xxi, xxvii, 7, 14, 16, 27-28, 49-50, 56, 85, 104, 107, 109, 112-119, 138, 156, 168-169, 198, 207-208, 226. See also Belgorod Tatars, Budjak Tatars, Crimean Tatars, Dzhambuluky Tatars, Kazan Tatars, Nogay Tatars, Osedly Tatars, Yedichkuly Tatars, Yedisan Tatars.
Tefkelev, 24.
Teimuraz, Georgian leader, 22.
Temir Sultan, 118.
Terek river, 23.
Teschen, 83, 88.
Testament of Peter I. See Peter I.
Thirty Years War, 235.
Thorn, 65, 140, 148, 215, 218, 234.
Thugut, Baron Franz Maria von, Austrian envoy to Turkey, 146, 153, 230.
Tiflis, 22-23, 133, 135-136.
Time of Troubles, xxxi.
Tobolsk, 26, 210.
Todtleben, Gottlieb Heinrich, Russian general, 23, 37, 133-136, 209-210.
Tomatis, Italian count, 89.
Tomsk Regiment, 135-136.
Torelli, S., painter, 48.

Tott, François de, French agent, 130, 226, 233.
Trajan, Roman emperor, 109.
Transcaucasia, 133, 136.
Transylvania, 87, 154, 214.
Trasimene, lake, battle, 225.
Treadgold, Donald W., 208.
Trevia, 225.
Tripolis, 121-122.
Troitskoe, 21.
Trupaki, Greek captain, 9.
Tsargrad. See Constantinople.
Tsarskoe Selo, 4, 212.
Turin, 203.
Turkey, Turks, Ottoman Empire, The Porte, xv, xviii-xxx, 4-14, 16, 18-29, 32-39, 41-53, 55-58, 63-66, 69-71, 73, 75, 78-79, 81-85, 87, 89, 92-95, 97-104, 106-109, 111-134, 137-141, 143, 145-151, 153-156, 158, 160, 162-170, 172, 178, 181, 186-187, 198-200, 202-203, 205-206, 208-216, 221, 224-225, 229-234; and the proposed English alliance, 198.
Turkey, European, 133.
Tuscany, 45, 213.
Tver, 3, 205.

Ubashi, 23.
Ukraine, 8, 51, 204, 206, 214, 228.
Un Ballo in Maschera, 223.
United States, 222.
United States Virgin Islands, 222.

Valcroissant, French colonel, 84, 130.
Vandini, Italian, 41.
Varennes, 223.
Varna, 107-108, 138.
Vasily, Montenegrin hierarch. See Petrovich, Vasily.
Venice, Venetians, xix, 19-20, 32, 34, 37, 43-44, 83, 148, 213-214, 225.
Verden, 142.
Verdi, Giuseppi, 223.
Versailles, 73, 85, 87-88, 91.
Veselitsky, chancellery councilor, 118.

THE EDITOR AND TRANSLATOR

Daniel L. Schlafly, Jr. is Associate Professor of History and Director of Russian and East European Studies at Saint Louis University in St. Louis, Missouri. Born in St. Louis, he earned an A.B. at Georgetown University, then studied at the University of Munich. He received an M.A., a Certificate of the Russian Institute, and Ph.D. from Columbia University. He has published articles in the *Cahiers du monde russe et soviétique, Études sur le XVIIIe siècle, Communio,* and *The Modern Encyclopedia of Russian and Soviet History.* He has travelled extensively in Eastern Europe and the former Soviet Union. He lives in St. Louis with his wife and two daughters.

FROM ACADEMIC INTERNATIONAL PRESS*

*Request catalogs   **OP–out of print